The VOLUNTEERS

The VOLUNTEERS

How Halifax Women Won The Second World War

LEZLIE LOWE

NIMBUS
PUBLISHING
— NIMBUS.CA —

Nimbus Publishing Limited
3660 Strawberry Hill Street, Halifax, NS, B3K 5A9
(902) 455-4286 nimbus.ca

Printed and bound in Canada

NB1386

Cover design: John van der Woude
Interior design: Jenn Embree
Editor: Angela Mombourquette

Library and Archives Canada Cataloguing in Publication

Title: The volunteers : how Halifax women won the Second World War /
Lezlie Lowe.
Names: Lowe, Lezlie, 1972- author.
Description: Includes bibliographical references.
Identifiers: Canadiana (print) 20210382007 | Canadiana (ebook) 20210382546
ISBN 9781774710548 (softcover) | ISBN 9781774710555 (EPUB)
Subjects: LCSH: World War, 1939-1945—Women—Nova Scotia—Halifax. |
LCSH: World War, 1939-1945—War work—Nova Scotia—Halifax. | LCSH:
Women—Nova Scotia—Halifax—Social conditions—20th century. | LCSH:
World War, 1939-1945—Nova Scotia—Halifax.
Classification: LCC D810.W7 L69 2022 | DDC 940.53082/09716225—dc23

Nimbus Publishing acknowledges the financial support for its publishing activities from the Government of Canada, the Canada Council for the Arts, and from the Province of Nova Scotia. We are pleased to work in partnership with the Province of Nova Scotia to develop and promote our creative industries for the benefit of all Nova Scotians.

For Marie

TABLE *of* CONTENTS

PREFACE

"Civilization is a stream with banks," historian and author Will Durant told a reporter for *Life* magazine in October 1963. "The stream is sometimes filled with blood from people killing, stealing, shouting and doing the things historians usually record, while on the banks, unnoticed, people build homes, make love, raise children, sing songs, write poetry and even whittle statues. The story of civilization is the story of what happened on the banks."

In *The Volunteers*, I've worked to write the story of the banks. That's because I'm a journalist and a writer of creative non-fiction, not an academic or a historian, whom Durant, though one himself, calls "pessimists," for "they ignore the banks for the river."

I won't set up the same dichotomy between historians and storytellers as one of pessimists versus optimists. To me, historians seek comprehensiveness; storytellers, engagement. And to that end, I've curated here, rather than exhaustively listing. I've worked for narrative. For history that's real.

Where historians and journalists do share common ground is in a cleaving to truth. And here's the bigger truth I found, a provocation, perhaps: Halifax women won the Second World War. Getting to bigger truths is always a matter of working through smaller ones. And getting to truth in the stories of the women whose work I've profiled in this book was challenging. Though the archival material that was available was just sitting there in boxes, waiting to be trawled through, there wasn't a lot. And particularly prickly was the task of getting everything right after the passage of so much time. When sources couldn't remember details, and even when they could, I sought out photos or videos or other accounts to corroborate facts. Where sources were unsure, or I was, I said so.

Then there were the names. Volunteer whirlwinds the Macneill sisters were Edith, Isabel, and Janet. But get this: Edith's full name was Edith Isabel Macneill, Isabel was Isabel Janet MacNeill, and Janet was Ruth Murrene Janet Macneill. Two Isabels, two Janets, and a third name as a first name, all among three sisters. Dizzying. Another notable confusion in any Halifax history project is numeric: in 1958, Halifax Council set about renumbering all peninsular buildings. All of them. The city changed existing building numbers, which were formerly one, two, three, and so on, to four-number civic addresses based on a municipal grid scheme. The phasing in of the program took until 1965. There's a municipal database that allows researchers to cross-reference addresses (can I get a hallelujah on that one?), but this still adds a layer of challenge to finding old build-ings. For example: I read one account featuring a reference to the Knights of Columbus Hall. (I'll hold my commentary here about the frustrating interchangeability of the hall/hut/club/hostel designation.) In 1941, the Knights of Columbus Hall was at 370–372 Barrington Street. But that building was no longer there at the civic address changeover in 1965. Using the database, I determined that 375 Barrington is today's 1533 Barrington, which is the Freemasons' Hall at the northwest corner of Barrington and Salter Streets. That had to mean the Knight of Columbus Hall was across the street. Then I found a photo that placed it one building north of St. Mary's Glebe House. This is how you spend an hour down an archival rabbit hole trying to find a single building that makes up a single sentence in an entire book.

But, you know what? That's the fun, too.

Every time I went to the archives, I found a reference to a new organization engaging in a new activity or forming a new subcommittee. There were groups I only read the names of once, like the Gyrette Club.

That sounds fun, I thought, what did they do…? I had to stop before I became overwhelmed. Other groups are missing entirely, or their stories are incomplete. I've written in these pages about the dearth of material about African Nova Scotian women's volunteer work. And what about Mi'kmaw women? A Mi'kmaw woman, Mrs. Malti, no first name (and in most accounts "Malti" is anglicized to "Martin"), worked as a shipbuilder in Pictou during the war. But what about Mi'kmaw volunteers in Halifax? What about Halifax's Chinese population during the war? I want to know more, too, about the women who worked in brothels during the war, at a time when women's company, even the non-sexual kind, was commodified as a leisure activity—something to be accessed, like a movie ticket, or a meal. I want to know where women terminated pregnancies during the war. I want to know about sexual assault. I read *Chatelaine* magazines from the spring of 1939 through the postwar period, and the subject is left untouched. Yet not one but two women I interviewed disclosed wartime sexual assaults.

All the women—and the one man—I interviewed and spent time with were a delight. But they were part of the problem, too. They clearly didn't value their own contributions during the war. And I found myself struggling: who am I to tell anyone that the way they see their own story is wrong? I worked to convince them that what they did mattered.

The Volunteers started out as a happy book. I researched it, outlined it, pitched it, and sold a story of redemption that would culminate in the unveiling of groundbreaking The Volunteers/Les Bénévoles statues on the Halifax waterfront. My storyline was supposed to be dead simple: these women, once ignored, now have their recognition. But that just wasn't the story. *The Volunteers* as a mere redemption tale is a vast oversimplification—the waterfront monument opens an important door, but The Volunteers/Les Bénévoles doesn't fix the structural devaluing these women faced, and it doesn't solve the problem of women's unpaid labour being unvalued and undervalued still today.

And then there was my grandmother. My sweet Marie. I've chosen to lead the book with her, as a means of getting into the meat of Halifax and the war. But including Marie meant including me. And in that, I uncovered an uncomfortable truth. I was an active participant in the dismissal and forgetting of women's stories, too.

I forged on, finding cold comfort, but also inspiration, in a comment made to me by archivist Susan McClure at the Halifax Municipal Archives as I sat one day working my way through a box of papers from the Halifax Women's Voluntary Services files. "Women," Susan said, off-handedly from her nearby desk, "were running this city during the war."

Indeed they were. And those women, by my wager, won it, too.

INTRODUCTION

As a child I knew nothing about the Second World War in Halifax. Nothing about the clamour and chaos of its population explosion. Nothing about the glamour, the glory, or the grind of the times. My grandparents met during the war, lived through the war, recovered from the war. But the war wasn't part of our home. I find this odd in retrospect. After all, these events weren't mere passing clouds in history. The Second World War rocked populations—and decidedly Halifax's. But that's just the thing: no one got out unaffected. No one in the city at the time avoided the impact of the war. It was, literally, what it was. The ubiquity made it benign. I knew my grandfather saw terrible things, but I only ever caught whispers of the details. My grandmother didn't seem to know much more, though I caught her once telling the story of a stranger showing up at her door one day while my grandfather was at sea. The man had been rescued from the water and over tea he'd reported to Marie that my grandfather had taken the blankets from his berth to cover him, soaked, shivering, and reeking of spilled fuel.

There are battle stories. *So* many battle stories. And there are the stories of those left at home. These parallel stories fall decidedly along gender lines, though it wasn't strictly true during the Second World War that men went to fight and women stayed at home. After all, there were some seven thousand wartime members of the Women's Royal Canadian Naval Service (WRCNS), who provided operational support to the Canadian Forces. The Army and Air Force each had their own women's branches. By mid-war, in June 1943, the WRCNS training centre in Galt, Ontario, became the first female commission in the Canadian Navy when Lieutenant-Commander Isabel Macneill took the reins. Macneill, one of those three formidable and challengingly named sisters, was a Halifax native. We'll get back to Isabel; don't worry.

In our home, the battles went unheralded and the at-home tales unrepeated. Why bother talking up what's universal, I guess...?

This turned out to be a theme that came up time and again with the women I got to know writing this book. None dared declare the volunteer work they'd done was something important. They shared a similar version of the same line: they were only doing what everyone was doing. Some trained in voluntary nursing aid. Some were dedicated amateur musicians. Most gave simply by extending their usual routines and tasks to the many strangers in their midst—making meals, sewing buttons, visiting the wounded, or greeting trains. The so-called soft skills of kitchen and domestic competence, of sociability and small talk, don't particularly rate today against hard skills and trades. And they were likewise devalued in Halifax during the war.

But these women volunteers did a collective job no government could have organized or, frankly, afforded. This army of volunteer women helped win the war. Yet their contributions remain largely invisible in the documentary history of the conflict. The volume of help has been chronicled piecemeal, through scant archival material, personal photos, and oral histories. The small-but-mighty Halifax Women's History Society has done the heavy lifting in daylighting women's war stories since its inception in 2013. The organization also spearheaded the funding, design, and creation of a monument dedicated to women war volunteers. When they were unveiled on the Halifax waterfront in 2017, The Volunteers/Les Bénévoles became Halifax's first statues featuring full-sized figures of women. (Real women, not headless or armless or naked; and not fictional women, like the three exceptional Victorian statues in the Halifax Public Gardens of Roman

When The Volunteers/Les Bénévoles was unveiled on the Halifax waterfront in 2017, the statues became Halifax's first monuments featuring full-sized figures of women. (NIMBUS PUBLISHING)

goddesses Ceres, Flora, and Diana.) The media attention around The Volunteers/Les Bénévoles was the first time many Nova Scotians had ever heard about Halifax women's volunteer contributions during the Second World War.

No wonder. No one tells these women's stories. The federal government only initiated an index of wartime charities by 1941, two years after the war's start, and concerned itself only with registered volunteer work. If you were a woman who curtained off a portion of your kitchen to make space for a cot for a visiting mother and child who'd be otherwise on the street, you didn't count. If you opened your front door to a stranger in uniform who said he'd been sent to the house by your uncle, the meal and company you shared with this service member (and likely a couple of his friends) wasn't recognized. By design, the index of wartime charities failed to capture the scope of women's voluntary work. But it's more than that. The war was intricately tracked by way of battles and deaths, in bomb tonnage and inches gained, not by the sustaining work of women who fed troops, packaged magazines for deploying ships, or concerned themselves, fundamentally, with community and well-being. In the broadest strokes, men engaged in quantitative work; women volunteers in qualitative work. One countable; one not. One tracked; one nodded to and then materially dismissed.

This goes, even, for the splashiest of Halifax's Second World War women volunteers—like Edith Girouard of the Women's Voluntary Services organization, who almost single-handedly recruited and supplied volunteers to the city's official and not-so-official volunteer hotspots, and Dolly McEuen of the Ajax Club, who took it upon herself to right the classist wrong that only officers in the Navy were permitted to drink beer while on shore leave—or, in any case, who *tried* to right this wrong before the sanctimonious powers-that-be shut her down. Edith and Dolly were forces of nature. And even their stories are, by contrast to the cataloging of battles, largely gone—collected by chance donation in boxes at the municipal and provincial archives. I barely found Girouard's and McEuen's names in more than a week spent sifting through files at Library and Archives Canada. Countless others? Those who weren't women of means like Girouard and McEuen? The unnamed working-class women who gave innumerable anonymous hours? Their contributions were silent and have stayed silent. The berg under a barely seen tip. The reality for the stories of African Nova Scotian and other minority volunteers is even more grim. Halifax was a segregated city in the 1940s; partly by law, mostly by custom and discrimination. If a service member was Black, he attended dinner-dances at Gerrish Street Hall. That's simply how it was: segregation was the norm. Were there other venues where Black military members were "allowed" to go? None I was told of. None that I found.

Even when there was a concrete quantitative measure to their toil, women volunteers themselves frequently failed to ascribe value to their work. At many organizations' annual general meetings, reports were tabled detailing pairs of mittens knitted and pounds of potatoes boiled. Some of those numbers survived. But something else was lost. Those women who knitted and boiled could look around the meeting rooms at each other and understand the subtext of those numbers, the hours spent, and, on top of that, the unspoken calculus of what those many hours away from home and friends and family meant. But there was no time, or no means, or no interest in tracing the value of that volunteer work. The numbers are preserved in meeting minutes. The women and their impact? Chiefly forgotten. No surprise—the meagre few Halifax women volunteers still here, those I got to sit with and hear from and gently prod, consistently told me they, and their contributions, were nothing but everyday.

I'm hoping here, to convince you, and them, otherwise.

Chapter One

SENTIMENTAL JOURNEY

My grandmother Marie was an everyday Haligonian who came from a family of everyday Haligonians.

Her mother's name, whenever some sundry official wrote it on some sundry document, was variably "Jeanette" or "Janette." But she signed everything "Nettie." She became a widow with three children, Joe, six; Harold, three; and Dot, four days short of her first birthday, when her first husband, Joseph, died of pleurisy in 1919. Nettie was twenty-six. The following year, she married a labourer, Arthur Henry Crompton. In October 1921, they welcomed Marie.

Arthur and Nettie lived on Stairs Street in Halifax's north end. Marie attended nearby Richmond School. The grade school had been rebuilt in 1919, after the December 6, 1917, Halifax Explosion flattened its former location on nearby Roome Street. The disaster, still the largest non-nuclear explosion in history, killed two thousand and injured nine thousand. It's a false grace that only two students were killed inside Roome Street School, which, on a 1918 map of the area devastated by the explosion, is coded "badly wrecked." Grove Presbyterian Church, next door, was reduced to a literal pile of sticks. Another eighty-six children died from the blast in their homes, or on their way to school that morning, gawking, as the masses in Halifax were on December 6, at the burning benzol-drenched deck of the SS *Mont Blanc* drifting toward Pier 6 at the foot of Richmond Street. Had Nettie seen it? Was she injured? I never got a chance to ask her. I was only seven when she died. My memories of my great-grand-mother are physical—Nettie was a great down pillow of a woman, who enveloped me in squishy hugs against her ample bust. This was all I knew of her when she was alive. To me, she wasn't an explosion survivor, she wasn't twice-widowed (Arthur, my great-grandfather, died on Christmas Eve 1961), she hadn't lived through two world wars in a city of the utmost strategic importance to the battles. She wasn't a valuable repository of Halifax history I dearly wish I had access to now. She was one giant hug.

Nettie died in 1979. I remember as a child coming along with Marie and her older sister, Dot, and others to clear out Nettie's apart-ment at Sunrise Manor, her final home, down Gottingen Street from the Richmond neighbourhood where from she lived from the 1920s on. My great-grandfather Arthur's family had been in their rented Stairs Street house since my great-great-grandfather took up residence in 1900. Cleaning out Nettie's apartment, I remember a mood of pervasive sadness. But what's more sad today is that I simply left it at that. I never, in the decades that followed, asked Marie about her mother; never tried to mine the memories Nettie might have passed down to her. Marie was the most important person in my life. We talked on the phone or saw each other practically daily until she died at ninety-two. The opportunity to ask her about all these things was just sitting there. For my whole life. But I never asked. I'm no historian. But I am a journalist. So, I know better. And I should have done better.

Marie's short academic career at Richmond School ended after she graduated grade nine. She declared herself done. The next year and a half or so, from mid-1936 to 1938, are a black hole for me in Marie's history. I have images from the time, a tattered album of Nettie's with crack-ing Scotch-taped photos and newspaper clippings. But nothing's dated.

This fragile book casts an out-of-order family trajectory from Nettie's childhood in the 1890s though about 1960. In it, I see the Marie I knew already from other family photos—embracing my grandfather in his Navy uniform, holding my mother as a baby. I also see a Marie I never knew until this photo album passed into my hands in 2016—Marie and Dot in bathing suits with their two brothers; Marie as a late teen, sitting side-saddle over the wide fender of a 1934 Auburn; Marie as a child in a class picture in front of Richmond School, front row, light-coloured short-sleeve dress, knee socks. All the pupils around her are white, it seems, despite the school being close to Africville, a Black settlement that had been on the shores of Bedford Basin since the mid-1700s. Africville had its own school, but this grade-school photo of Marie's Richmond School class speaks, nonetheless, to the deep racial divide that existed in Halifax at the time, during the war, and still.

These photos reinforce a socio-economic tale that any Haligonian then or today who knew Nettie and Arthur's home address could spell out: the Crompton brood was solidly working class. (Education wasn't so much prized by Marie as tolerated. She was supportive of me as I advanced through high school and my university degrees, but with obvious, and bluntly shared, bewilderment.) Marie never spoke of deprivation; the Cromptons got by. But she and Dot were not the kind of young women who were mailed invitations to the swanky dress-uniform or black-tie and long-gown parties that lit up Admiralty House, the stone base mansion at Stadacona, just down Gottingen Street from their home. When an Allied destroyer came to port, Marie was not a daughter among the stratum of Halifax daughters whose names were on those invite lists—the young women who would be assigned to an officer, one who would pick them up and be their date for the night. She also wasn't down at the Silver Slipper Dance Club, a near-forgotten dive on Barrington Street south of Cornwallis Street, on the water side. You'd occasionally find Marie at dances at the Nova Scotian Hotel and at the North End Services Canteen.

And that's exactly where my Able Seaman grandfather Ted found her in 1939.

That Ted and Marie met at a dance is by no means a rare story in the saga of Second World War–era Halifax. Ted first "went steady" with my grandmother's older sister, Dot. As a kid I viewed this as an objective scandal. But with the benefit of age and my wartime research I now know it was par for the course. There was a lot of dating during the war. A lot of promises made. Dot was nearer Ted's age—a tender twenty—in 1939 when he was one of the half-million Canadian service members who shipped out from the port en route to war—in his case as a member of the Royal Canadian Navy, sailing into the watery chaos of the Battle of the Atlantic. For a reason lost to time and that no one ever explained during Sunday dinners—overcooked roast, mashed potatoes, a stove-warmed canned-peas-and-carrots combo—Ted wound up with my grandmother, Marie. She turned eighteen near Halloween 1939. I have her middle name.

Ted and Marie, 1939.
(AUTHOR'S COLLECTION)

They didn't just meet at a dance. Dancing had everything to do with Ted and Marie's love.

In later years, when they gave up going regularly to dances—which happened after my grandfather left the Navy in 1968—they could still dance in a way I never understood. I don't mean swing dance itself (though, look—I paid for lessons; they didn't take). I mean Ted and Marie moved together in a way I couldn't comprehend—seeming to know, without words, each other's next move. They pounced upon the floor like smiling fools, lost in impenetrable coordination to each other's faces and bodies.

I've watched videos of many couples from the war and postwar years, and I see the same thing—foxtrot, jive, and jitterbug—a synchronicity of movement that appears to come from hours of practice. Ted and Marie certainly didn't practice. They just…did it. They danced whenever called upon, humbly and quickly taking to the parquet at wedding receptions and anniversaries and big birthdays. Another thing I didn't understand—even into young adulthood when I should have known better—was how two people who I believed were so impossibly old could move so fluidly in this romantic, joyous exercise.

But they did. Someone would ask them to dance and everyone would clear the floor at the church hall or legion or tavern backroom to stand back and marvel at their unspoken physical harmony. They were pleasing the crowd, whose members would marvel and hoot and well up. But they were clearly striking, too, at some pilot light burning in them from decades past. I can see them now. My grandmother, invariably, in a dress and low pumps and some plastic-y matching earrings-and-necklace set. My grandfather, in trousers and Oxfords and a button-down shirt. Always with a tie-your-own bowtie. In the photos I keep around, their dancing bodies are a Rorschach test of stopped-in-time movement—hands connected, bodies apart, opposite arms out, fingers splayed. Such smiles. What were they thinking? What were they remembering?

I wish I had asked.

Dances like the one where Ted and Marie met were common in Halifax during the Second World War.

No, no: it's not what you're thinking. It's way more than you're imagining.

And that statement—*it's way more than you're imagining*—is the underlying flavour of the war in Halifax. Of this book itself. When I tell you something happened "a lot" or that there were "many," and you think you've got it, you can rest assured that unless you were there, you do not. The city was so desperately overwhelmed with service members, war workers, and all their sundry family members, that Wartime Administrator of Canadian Atlantic Ports E. L. Cousins signed an Order-in-Council in November 1943 warning "the citizens of Canada" to avoid travel to Halifax or its sister city, Dartmouth. In the too-little, too-late fashion of the federal approach to Halifax's well-being during the war, the order was non-enforceable. Halifax, by 1943, was already underwater. Cousins's sternly worded statute wasn't going to turn off the taps, let alone drain the bath.

In 1939, the *Halifax–Dartmouth City Directories* published by Might Directories Atlantic Limited listed sixty-one restaurants and lunchrooms in the city; the number shot up by twenty in the next year, and had doubled by 1944. These eating establishments ranged from Barrington Street's beloved Green Lantern, with its lunch counter, vinyl booths, and fifteen-cent marshmallow sundaes, to the honestly named "Hot Dog Stand, 109 Almon." There could have been a hundred hot dog stands, serving day and night. It wouldn't have been enough to feed the influx of visitors. They stayed in hostels, in the handful of hotels, and in curtained-off areas of people's homes. Halifax's population exploded from a little more than sixty-eight thousand at the war's start to seventy-six thousand a year later. That almost 12 percent jump must have felt extreme, but it was nothing compared to what came after. By 1944, there were one hundred and seven thousand people in Halifax, a 61 percent increase. Imagine every four-person household in your apartment or condo building, or on your block, becoming six. But that wasn't the extent of the crush—the official numbers mostly didn't capture the countless transient folks—service members, plus their wives and girl-friends and mothers and children who were staying in the city temporarily while their partners and parents were waiting to be deployed.

There are other numbers that lend perspective to the impact of the war and the response the city mustered, though their sheer scale almost fails sense. The Central Magazine Exchange, a volunteer depot for the collection, packaging, and distribution of reading materials for troops to consume during long hours at sea or on watch, oversaw the doling out of four million magazines within the first three years of the war alone—more than thirty thousand magazines every week from the war's start through June 1942. In two years, the North End Services Canteen served 400,000 hot meals to service members. That's 550 meals a day, every day of the year, without respite. But numbers pale. Sometimes during the war, Haligonians would turn on their water taps and dribbles would come out—that's how many others were calling on the system.

None of the women I interviewed for this book—women I relied on to give me the flavour and texture of wartime Halifax—remembered dry water taps. But I was so glad to have found these women and to hear their stories. The Halifax that existed from 1939 into the postwar years is a Halifax few living residents recall. The volume of people and events, the crowding and homelessness, the ships and service members and booze, and the unbelievable need and strain—it was nothing anyone had seen in the city before and nothing anyone has seen since.

And dances? There were dances every day. Some afternoons, on top of the evenings—dances in church halls, in community centres, in clubs. Dances were the done thing. Dances were where everyone met everyone. The very dry kindling of war-era romances—the war years saw on average a 40 percent increase in marriages compared to the ten years' worth of weddings that preceded the conflict. That is a *lot* of weddings.

The dances most talked about in wartime remembrance were at the Nova Scotian Hotel, on Hollis Street at the base of South, overlooking Pier 19 and the harbour. The Nova Scotian was, and is, a railway hotel—during wartime it was still new, bustling, grand, and admired. Its Atlantic Ballroom hosted weekly supper-dances for all comers. Halifax women put on their best, stashed their dates' flasks in their handbags, and headed through the hotel's elegant portico. No date? No problem. The rest of the country was absolutely drained of young men because all of them were in Halifax. The atmosphere was electric. The booze, circulated on the sly under tables, fuelled the buzz. These were some of the stories the women told me. I might have dropped the ball on asking my grandparents enough about the war—missed the chance to hear from Marie what Halifax felt like during those years and how she coped—but there are women still here whose stories I could learn from. So I asked.

⁓ⱽⱽ⁓

The North End Services Canteen, where my grandparents met, was the city's first civilian-organized provider of comfort, food, and company for the servicemen who, like a swell, began to inundate Halifax once war was declared on September 10, 1939. To put a finer point on it: the opening of the North End Services Canteen on Russell Street at Gottingen in October 1939 was the first moment women stepped up to take on a necessary war effort that the federal government was categorically failing to tend to.

Like I said, Marie was no debutante. She was from the north end of Halifax, not the south. She was from a working-class, not wealthy, clan. After she left Richmond School, she took a job as a dipper at Moirs Chocolate on Argyle Street. It was downtown, and she would hop on the Richmond tram on Gottingen Street, a block from her house, and head south to Argyle. Her sister, Dot, got her the position and it was one hell

The North End Services Canteen on Russell Street, behind St. Mark's Church.
(**NS ARCHIVES**)

of a challenge, not merely because once Marie started that job, she needed to keep it; even by the war's start in 1939, Canada was still dealing with the dregs of the Great Depression and facing a general unemployment rate above 12 percent. Among women who worked outside the home, more than a third were employed as domestic servants.

Marie's problem was that she was left-handed, and so, repeatedly clanging elbows with her dipper line-mates and splashing melted chocolate all over herself. Dot and Marie told and re-told a story decades later—I can see the two of them on a floral sofa, hair set and sprayed into matching Q-tip puffs, talking together and collapsing into a heap of laughter. In the tale, Dot drags Marie, on her first shift, into the employee bathroom at Moirs to try to wipe the chocolate from Marie's clothes and face and arms and hair. Marie would laugh at how livid Dot was, worried her bozo sister would lose both of them their positions. Dot was always the Felix Unger of this sibling odd couple—tidy, tall, slim, perennially put-together. I won't say Marie was the Oscar Madison. She was no slob; she had an eye for a good outfit and never left the house without her lipstick. Only…Marie was a loveable goofball. She was shorter and plumper than her half-sister. Funnier and clumsier. She laughed at herself easily, and that made you love her all the more.

Dot and Marie didn't last in chocolate. The war heated up and jobs became more plentiful. Dot became a filing clerk in 1943, at the Halifax Shipyards, where her and Marie's two brothers, Harold and Joe, worked, and where she met her future husband, Dugald, a Scottish immigrant. Later, Dot would move to the perfume counter at Eaton's. It *so* fit. Marie moved to clothing sales early in the war, in 1940. And that so fit her. She never left the industry. She worked at uptown Halifax Gottingen Street mainstays Heinish's, Klein's, and The New York Dress Shop, before moving in the late 1970s to the House of Bridal Fashions—where she spent the next couple of decades at its various locations, outfitting brides, mothers-of-the-bride, and, as it happens, many a drag queen from The Turret Social Club, a gay and lesbian dance club that operated from 1976 to 1982 out of the third floor of the Khyber Building, across Barrington Street from the House of Bridal Fashions. She loved it.

My grandparents had a big hand in raising me, and I remember driving with my grandfather from north Dartmouth to downtown Halifax every day to pick up Marie after work. If she was running late, I would be allowed to pop in to get a bag of Hickory Sticks at the Zellers department store on the corner of Barrington and Sackville Streets. I didn't know it then, but it had been one of the many downtown businesses ransacked at the end of the war in the VE day riots of May 7 and 8, 1945—display cases smashed and cash registers upended. Signage was pulled from the walls and merchandise was carried away by drunken servicemen, opportunistic locals, and caught-up-in-the-moment men and women.

By war's call, Halifax's ample natural basin was already busily polka-dotted with ships. Halifax knew this feeling; a déjà vu. The port city had been a staging ground for the North Atlantic battles of European settlers for generations. Rudyard Kipling wrote about the city's strategic importance to myriad Western battles in his "The Song of the Cities" poem, published in a collection in 1896.

> *Into the mist my guardian prows put forth,*
> *Behind the mist my virgin ramparts lie,*
> *The Warden of the Honour of the North,*
> *Sleepless and veiled am I!*

Halifax was veiled, indeed, during the Second World War. A sleepy place. But also veiled because its strategic role was kept top secret. Wartime censors only allowed it to be referred to, in correspondence and in the media, as "an East Coast Port." Kipling's equally vague but more poetic "Warden of the North" moniker at least speaks to Halifax's wartime contribution. Thomas H. Raddall used it to title his still-fascinating 1948 history of Halifax. It's a Governor General's Literary Award winner, though it needs to be considered in context—it's a white history, and a male one, which ought not be a surprise, given it was written to commemorate the two-hundredth anniversary of Halifax's founding, an idea itself premised on the concept that it was white settlers who first, and without help, sniffed out this magical, never-before-seen place. *Halifax: Warden of the North* relies on racist stereotypes about Mi'kmaw people, merely skims the surface of the contributions of Black residents, and relegates women to the back shelf. The updated 2010 version with additional chapters covering the mid-1960s through 2009 by Stephen Kimber works assiduously to address these failings of the original. Read that one. But also take away this: Raddall, publishing in 1948, hammered home Halifax's historic role as a military town and held a clear party line through his writing—one that has persisted in the decades since: women barely had a role, African Nova Scotian and Indigenous contributions were segregated and all that much smaller.

Halifax's position as a primary east coast port is felt keenly today, even without the flurry of war pressing against the city and its resources. The impact of the military on the city, and on the north end particularly, is palpable. Canadian Forces Base (CFB) Halifax–Stadacona is the country's largest military installation, hosting some eleven thousand service members and civilian support employees, plus forty-five hundred reserve members and fourteen thousand youth cadets. On the Halifax peninsula alone, it eats up more than two linear kilometres of prime waterfront, creeping up imposingly toward the residential north end, commercial Gottingen Street, and acting as a hard northern stop for Halifax's downtown core. As CFB Halifax–Stadacona today unceremoniously swallows a large portion of the geography and civic psyche of Halifax, from the fall of 1939 through repatriation, the war quickly suffocated the base known then as HMCS *Stadacona* before hungrily advancing on Halifax as a whole.

Halifax proper is a kidney-shaped peninsula. There's only so much room. Eighteen square kilometres, in fact. About the same space taken up by Toronto Pearson International Airport. As Halifax's wartime military establishment grew, every industry that served it, commercial and criminal, from bread-making to bootlegging, grew as well. Service members from all three branches reported to the city from across the country to await deployment. Many, naturally, brought family members to Halifax, squeezing out precious moments before being sent to Europe, or into the bedlam of the North Atlantic. There wasn't even room for military members in Halifax's existing facilities, let alone for their wives and children in the rest of the city—too few flats, too little shared lodging, and a negligible number of hotel rooms. The city was immediately and profoundly overwhelmed.

It's no spoiler to say that these early challenges were never properly acknowledged nor adequately addressed. After all, this is a book about how Halifax's women, seeing a dearth of action, stepped up, took charge, and did what needed to be done, from the beginning of the conflict through repatriation and beyond. Halifax author William D. Naftel spared no scorn for the federal government in his book *Halifax at War: Searchlights, Squadrons and Submarines 1939–1945*. "In many respects," he wrote, "the government of Canada was guilty of neglect because, despite plentiful evidence that the influx was causing serious problems, its response was slow, reluctant and parsimonious." Halifax's women were in place, quick, willing, and generous.

Despite the deterioration of social and sanitary conditions (we'll get to the diphtheria later), and functional abandonment by Ottawa and the defence establishment, there was joy, unquestionably, in early wartime Halifax. A newness and bustle. That exhilaration would wear first into weariness, with long lines for every possible service and good, empty stores, and exorbitant prices. Later, it would devolve into acrimony and riot. But in late 1939, the elation in the city was palpable. And my grandparents, Marie and Ted, typified it—a young serviceman from central Canada and a never-been-kissed Halifax teen, ready to experience the world, even if only through the mass of strangers unendingly landing in her soporific hometown, and even if only by way of travel to St. Mark's Church Hall, half a kilometre from her Stairs Street house, where the North End Services Canteen made its early home.

Marie Jeanette Crompton and Edward Albert Rigby were married on a Friday evening in late May 1940, at the very same St. Mark's Church. Marie wore a white satin dress and a lily-of-the-valley crown with an attached veil that fell into a puddle of tulle surrounding her feet. She carried pink and white carnations. Ted's uniform trousers had perfect horizontal creases. All this was eight months after the start of the war, and only seven months after the earliest date that they could possibly have met. And Ted fit a stint in there going steady with Dot, too. Talk about speed dating.

They wasted no time. Then, I suppose, they hadn't any to waste. My grandmother later told a story about Ted having to take off midway through their wedding reception, held in my great-grandparents' Stairs Street living room, to go back to base and then to sea. She didn't see him again for months. She told the story so often, and so passingly, I never questioned it. It became a gauzy film of wartime narrative laid over the more important things in my life—friends, boyfriends, school, TV, magazines, hairspray. I know from service records that Ted was on the HMCS *Ottawa* from March through June 1940, but I can't confirm the more granular details of his convoy duty departures and arrivals. Was Marie being literal? Did he leave this wedding party in his pressed uniform and go back to the ship? Was he gone a week? A month? Or did it all just feel this way to an eighteen-year-old Halifax girl who had just married a dashing sailor from Ottawa? A man she met at a dance only a few months before. Through a modern-day lens, it's all hard to imagine.

So much of the war is, truly, unimaginable.

—⁓—

Marie continued to live on Stairs after she was married, with her parents and Dot, her brother Harold, who was a helper at the shipyards, and her brother Joe, who was a riveter there. Long after, in fact. There seemed no need to move since Ted was away at sea for such long stretches.

While the north end seemed to hold Marie like a magnet, Ted never returned to live in his own hometown of Ottawa. My grandfather had joined the Navy in the fall of 1936, when he was seventeen and the war was a mere whisper. He was itching to go long before that. J. F. Gorman, the rector of St. John's Church in Ottawa, sat down and wrote a note of recommendation for him on October 17, 1933, attesting to fourteen-year-old Ted's "excellent character" and "promise of becoming a fine man." It was the same month German Chancellor Adolf Hitler withdrew from the League of Nations, taking the first step in realizing the country's ambitions toward the large-scale military buildup that preceded the Second World War. My grandfather used Gorman's letter, along with his certificate of baptism, to apply to the Royal Canadian Navy. He got his answer from the Department of National Defence three weeks plus a day later, on November 8, 1933. "Your name has been entered on the list of candidates for consideration in your turn when a vacancy occurs as a Boy (Seaman Class) after you have attained the required age of 16 1/2 years."

He bided what must have been an excruciatingly long almost-three years studying and working as a part-time delivery boy before he finally arrived at Stadacona as a Boy Seaman on September 23, 1936, for seven months' new entry training. He managed to get home at some point in the new year, before Ottawa's always-epic snow would have departed, and the family arranged for a portrait sitting with society photographer Paul Horsdal, who came to their Lewis Street home for the occasion. Pricey, I'm imagining. My uniformed grandfather is impossibly young in the shots. In one, he stands alone with feet astride and hands behind his back, his black seaman's cap at a jaunty tilt and the lanyard for his bo's'n whistle tucked in a practiced curve at his lower rib cage. His shoes are so shined they seem to emit light, his trousers a paragon of horizontal creasing. He wears a broad, almost embarrassed smile, as if someone has just told him a joke. In another, he stands behind my seated great-grandfather, who wears his First World War Army mess dress uniform; his 1914–1915 Star, British War, and Victory medals; and his Governor General's Foot Guards Efficiency Medal.

Both of them smile, but something about my grandfather's stance makes him look like he's impatient for Horsdal's flash so he can launch himself out the door. This is a boy—decidedly not yet a man—who has been ready to go to sea since he was fourteen. He returned to Halifax soon after and shipped out on the HMCS *St. Laurent* in April 1937, the day after his training finished. It was the same ship on which he crossed the line for the first time on February 17, 1938, in the Pacific Ocean, almost one hundred kilometres north-northwest of Manta, Ecuador. On that day, he dove, shirtless, at a graceful forty-five degree angle, from the HMCS *St. Laurent*'s deck. Two months later, he joined the crew of the HMCS *Skeena*, having risen through the ranks from Boy to Ordinary to Able Seaman by December 1938.

War was coming. In March 1939, Germany invaded Czechoslovakia. (In different terms, the Munich Agreement, created to appease Hitler's territorial ambitions, handed a material share of Czechoslovakia over to the German chancellor on a plate.) With little international political rebuke for swallowing up Czechoslovakia, Germany spent the next six months making bold alliances with Italy and Japan while drawing up its own quiet plans to next take Poland. If events moved at first slowly, they moved soon with incredible speed. Germany invaded Poland on September 1, 1939. Britain and France declared war on September 3. Germany, the same day, sank the British ocean liner SS *Athenia*, which carried eleven hundred passengers, mostly tourists, and three hundred crew. More than one hundred died. And my grandfather, that same day, sailed out of Halifax on the HMCS *Skeena*, headed south to Bermuda to transport Admiral Sir Sidney Meyrick, the commander-in-chief of the America and West Indies Station.

Ted's stints at sea through the tail end of 1939 and into the spring of 1940, on HMCS *Skeena* and HMCS *Ottawa*, were punctuated by training, and presumably leave, at Stadacona. The courtship between he and Marie would have bloomed during these precious months, and his place in Halifax was cemented by their eventual marriage. Ted achieved a status hard won in Nova Scotia, and in all of Atlantic Canada—that of not being considered a "come-from-away." When or how he ascended? Another mystery about which I failed to enquire. He visited Ottawa, and his family, of course. As did Marie. My great-grandmother Nettie's Scotch-taped album includes shots of Marie on the front steps of my grandfather's Lewis Street family home, arms wrapped around Ted's five siblings. My mother, in fact, was born in Ottawa, in 1947, while my grandfather was posted at HMCS *Bytown* (not a ship, but a so-called stone frigate or shore posting) from April 1946 to January 1948. I want to know about this time, about so much, but even the passed-down stories aren't accessible; my mom died only a year after Marie. There's an orphaned feeling to all this for me—I just want a resource and there isn't one. A lesson learned too late—memories go with those who hold them.

My grandfather was reposted to Stadacona in 1948 and Marie, along with my infant mother, moved once again back to Stairs Street. She also went back to work, bucking the expectation of the time that women stopped employment after marriage, even though the social view of such behaviour was that it implied her husband could not provide for his family. She left my mother in Nettie's care and hopped on the familiar Richmond tram to head down to Gottingen Street. Marie needed to be out and doing something. Always. She was social to the nth degree. She curled. She played broomball. She bowled. This was always about the camaraderie, not the workout. She did not like exercise. She played bingo. Into her nineties she rode the Number 53 bus daily with her friend Elsie, just to get out and see people. I gave up trying to get grocery shopping done with her in less than two hours. She stopped to chat with every person who dared make eye contact.

Did she put her natural social skills to use as a wartime volunteer? I am embarrassed to say I only ever asked her about the war once. When I read Stephen Kimber's 2002 book *Sailors, Slackers and Blind Pigs: Halifax at War*, a rich and wonderful account of the war centred on the VE day riots of May 1945, I asked her what she remembered of that end-of-war commotion. Nothing, she told me. She stayed home with her mother to avoid, in her words, "them yahoos." Of course she did, I thought. She hated conflict. And because of it, she foolishly missed the most infamous moment of the war in Halifax. And with that internal eye roll, I failed entirely to mine the importance of the very moment of the war's end, what it meant to Marie, her family, her marriage, or the future trajectory of her life.

I won't torture myself. Women's stories of the war, I learned through cultural osmosis, didn't matter. Only two narratives of women's wartime roles have risen over the nearly eighty years since the war's end. The most common is the old chestnut that women were empowered by taking on "men's" work. (Spoiler: they were not.) The alternative narrative is that women waited. That clichéd catch-all: they kept the home fires burning. But this story doesn't bear out either. Because women didn't wait. They worked. They volunteered. They added onto their existing labour load, contributing to the war effort and to society's effort bit by bit, most by way of simply meeting the moment. Women fed, clothed, entertained, visited, accompanied, lodged, soothed, and more. These stories have made do as footnote to the rest—explored passionately by a few, unexplored in any material way by the rest.

Chapter Two

FOOLS RUSH IN

Jackie Wrixon bounded toward her grandfather's car from her Robie Street front door.
Her Halifax box-style house, with its over-under three-panel bay windows
and otherwise simple style, epitomized her working- and middle-class
north end neighbourhood. Wartime Halifax housing ran from sprawling
estate to shambly hovel. The Wrixons were in the middle, living in what
was, at the time, one of the last houses at the far north end of Robie Street,
right next door to her grandparents. Jackie wore her best dress for the
drive. Girls always wore dresses in Halifax in the 1940s. Women and older
teenagers might have had the relative luxury of choosing a skirt and blouse,
but for Jackie, who was only ten years old by the time the war ended, it was
a dress every single day.

With her grandfather at the wheel, the family bumped and lumped
along the Bedford Highway. The two-lane road—"highway" a misno-
mer then, as now—ran from Halifax north to the suburbs. The Bedford
Highway was then unpaved, making a Sunday trip around the basin no
brief jaunt. There were no traffic lights along the route, either. None, in
fact, anywhere in the city, though at some point during the war, the first
was installed—oddly, in Armdale, a suburban area off the Halifax peninsula. The lack of this modern urban infrastructure is cited in many accounts
of Halifax during the war, presented as a hallmark not only of the city's
size but of its intractable behind-the-times–ness.

Other major eastern Canadian cities, such as Saint John and Moncton, New Brunswick, got their first traffic signals in the 1920s. In Halifax, of the 195 kilometres of roads that existed in 1939, only 55 kilometres were paved, according to the Might city directory; the rest were cobblestones or dirt. Private vehicles were not common; there were 6,074 registered. Trams were the transportation mode of choice, and they abounded. But there also weren't enough. These electric streetcars handled about nine million rides annually before the war. Two years in, that number almost quadrupled to thirty-one million. Milk was delivered to homes by horse-drawn wagon from dairies on Brunswick, Agricola, and Oxford Streets. At the city's few busy intersections, full-time traffic constables kept private and commercial vehicles—whether fuel- or hay-powered—in line. Halifax, you see, at the beginning of the Second World War, was decidedly old school.

"Old habits survived and the inhabitants did not alter," wrote Hugh MacLennan about Haligonians in his novel *Barometer Rising*, a romance set during the Halifax Explosion of 1917. MacLennan's character Neil Macrae is a Halifax native returning to his city after being on the battlefields of the First World War. "All of them still went to church regularly," Macrae observes disdainfully of the city's residents. "He was certain they still drank tea with all their meals." *Barometer Rising* may be set two decades earlier, but MacLennan researched and wrote the novel at the cusp of the Second World War, publishing in 1941. He knew the city well. He was born in Cape Breton and lived in Halifax from age six through the end of his undergraduate degree at Dalhousie University. MacLennan's biting characterization served to show the embittered character of Macrae. But, really, MacLennan wasn't off base about Nova Scotia's capital city, and the book reads a little like a personal indictment by the author.

Tea with every meal seems a likelihood of the time of the Second World War, if my grandmother Marie was any barometer. Schools in Halifax were segregated by religion—Catholics here; Protestants there. Jewish Haligonians, it's noted by William D. Naftel in *Halifax at War*, counted as Protestants. Most Black peninsula-dwellers lived in Africville and attended school there. Places of worship abounded and were overwhelmingly Protestant, of the Anglican or United denominations (for this particular categorization, Jews were *not* honorary Protestants; in 1939 there were two synagogues). Married women, as tradition dictated, stayed home. They also became functionally invisible by the measure of city directories of the day, which listed *unmarried* women by their places of residence, but erased those same women from city directory listings once they wed—an annoyance for researchers today who find women there one year and gone the next. As if, somehow, they never existed.

In her grandfather's car, Jackie pressed her small face to the back window and peered out at Halifax Harbour and the Basin, a large, ice-free deepwater port. She stared at the dozens of vessels specking the wide water: corvettes, merchant ships, frigates, submarines, and even ocean liners repurposed as troop carriers. She scanned for destroyers. Richmond School, which she attended through grade four, would let out early when a new one was being launched and all the children would rush down to the pier to see the ceremony. As the car bounced along, Jackie perhaps dreamed of how she would spend the money from the War Savings Stamps her grandmother bought her once a month. Twenty-five cents each, which she'd get back, plus 3 percent interest.

For Jackie, who became an Eisner after she married, all her earliest memories are from wartime, even though, as a child, she didn't recognize it as a time different from any other. The commotion, the confusion, the interference to daily life was, to children, Halifax's permanent and usual state. She and an older friend used to travel regularly to the Empire Theatre at the corner of Gottingen and North Streets to see films. The military newsreels that screened prior to the features were simply the norm; the messaging that accompanied them (Poor pressure shortens the life of tires! Careless filling wastes fuel! Paper is valuable salvage! EVERY SCRAP COUNTS!) were lessons internalized and practiced, even by children.

The official newsreels Jackie and thousands of other Canadians, young and old, consumed during the war were professionally shot and scored PR masterpieces. Viewed together, they present a simple narrative: this is challenging work, but Canadians are up to the task. Canada is ready.

Readers, Canada was not ready.

It's been argued that Canada was, in fact, in denial about the approach of conflict. By 1937, Hitler was already wantonly violating the Treaty of Versailles, marching German troops into the Rhineland demilitarized zone set up to protect Belgium, the Netherlands, and France from German aggression after the First World War. Also by this time, he was systematically depriving German Jews of property, education, and employment rights. War was in the air. *Again.* Canada had lost sixty-one thousand people to battle two decades earlier in the First World War and seen one hundred and seventy-two thousand return from the front injured. The country, especially Quebec, had little appetite to see a repeat of the country shipping forces toward European conflict, by voluntary signup or, worse, conscription.

Against this backdrop, Canadian Prime Minister William Lyon Mackenzie King paid a visit to Hitler, popping in on the German chancellor in Berlin in June 1937, politely asking after a reprieve from war. With the benefit of hindsight, the world now understands the German leader's aspirations as equal measures insatiable and bloody. But Hitler soothed, and quite entranced, Prime Minister King, who after the meeting called the German leader "eminently wise." The wilfully unaware Canadian leader wrote in his personal diary that Hitler professed "no desire" for conflict. Except, Hitler had already annexed Austria, even before King showed up. Within months, he would be stamping the passports of German Jews with a "J." Germany was arming up, too. Hitler's actions screamed war. But perhaps King was reading the *Toronto Star*, which, even into 1939, was, in Naftel's estimation in *Halifax at War*, ignoring the growing tensions in Europe and feeding readers "an escapist diet of news about babies, local crime, and agricultural fairs."

Haligonians didn't have the luxury of living in denial.

Stadacona, the north-end Halifax base, had been functionally ignored by the federal government during the inter-war years. The federal naval establishment was low priority, and Halifax, specifically, wasn't on Ottawa's radar as a centre of defence or supply. Jay White, in his 1984 thesis, *The Ajax Affair: Citizens and Sailors in Wartime Halifax, 1939–1945*, says Halifax at the war's cusp was seen as "a dingy, anonymous way station noted for its intransigent backwardness." In 1938, federal Liberal cabinet minister C. D. Howe said in a speech that there was "no future for Halifax except as an occasional port of call for tramp freighters." Ouch.

Then something changed.

Between 1938 and early 1939, Halifax was tapped to play a central role—*the* central role—in the impending war, whenever and if ever it arrived. Halifax was volun-told to take on the star part as the most important port in North America. As early as March 1939, Nova Scotia Light and Power was quietly drawing up plans for protecting generating stations and streetcar facilities in the case of attack. The Haligonians who worked for Nova Scotia Light and Power and for the Royal Canadian Mounted Police, the organization in charge of helping with the defence strategy for this essential infrastructure, must have come home and told their families about this work. In August 1939, Halifax established an Air Raid Precautions Committee, a volunteer group in charge of auxiliary firefighting and medical aid, as well as air raid practice and protocol. Basically, these were average citizens who would help protect Halifax from, and respond to, enemy attack. Halifax didn't *know* war was coming, but Halifax knew: war was coming. It was in the undercurrents. And it arrived in the city before any other in Canada.

Survivors of the torpedoed British liner Athenia *arriving in Halifax, as reported in the* Halifax Chronicle, *September 14, 1939.* (NS ARCHIVES)

On September 1, 1939, when Germany invaded Poland, the military in Halifax was ordered to mobilize, forts were staffed, and the dockyard lit up. By September 5, Halifax had already completed its first blackout drill. These would become so routine in the city that by 1942, the Simpson's department store on Mumford Road boasted a small "blackout needs" section, selling light-blocking curtains, its showcase walls decked out with a somewhat terrifying painted image of a bomber plane dropping explosives. Between sunset and sunrise, all exterior light sources in the city had to be extinguished. Cars could use headlights, but street lights had to be hooded.

Halifax's engagement with the war was already full-on when Canada finally, officially, declared war on September 10, 1939. HMCS *Saguenay* was by then completing anti–U-boat patrols at the entrance to the Halifax Harbour and within three days of the parliamentary vote, the American freighter SS *City of Flint* arrived carrying the survivors of the German-sunk British passenger ship SS *Athenia*. It was a portent of the many flocks of strangers—diplomats, refugees, emissaries, war workers, military personnel, merchant sailors, and their family members—who would flow in over the coming half-decade, as from a left-on spigot. By September 16, the first convoy was gone, disappearing out the mouth of the harbour past McNabs Island and into the breach. Long story short: it was a hell of a two-week stretch for Halifax. And as much as the city's secretive months-long gearing up had made this early efficiency and eagerness possible, this launch into the war was merely the beginning of a very long haul, the impact of which residents had no practical ability to predict.

But Halifax would soon find out.

—⁓⁓—

The fall of 1939 and early 1940 is referred to as the period of the "phoney war." As with most narratives about the conflict, this designation focuses on battle, and by virtue, solely on men's contributions. For eight months after war was declared, there was only one offensive, from France into Germany. William D. Naftel, in another of his books, *Wartime Halifax: The Photo History of a Canadian City at War 1939–1945*, notes the limited impact of the war during this period. "Most of Canada would not notice much difference for over a year, and then only when rationing began to make daily life difficult." The idea of the war's phoniness ignores a significant fact: families across Canada were, during this time, shipping their loved ones off to danger and possible death. Fathers and brothers and sons were missing from dinner tables and beds. Missing from family farms.

The idea also ignores Halifax.

The months of the phoney war were, in Halifax, an explosion. In contrast to the rest of the country, "garrisons filtered out to the old forks at the Harbour mouth," Naftel writes. "The first group of soldiers to head overseas, the 1st division, gathered for a December departure. A squadron of Wapiti bombers of the tiny RCAF dropped out of the sky onto the grassy runways of the old Halifax civic airport from their former prairie home. Railway flat cars bearing anti-aircraft guns rolled into the rail yards from Picton, Ontario."

The immediate concern, in all this activity, was bodies.

Just as Halifax's pre-war backwardness was typified by its lack of traffic lights, so its wartime woes are frequently illustrated by its population boom. But the numbers mean nothing except by considering their impact.

As the initial throng of military personnel converged on Halifax, all the usual places to sleep and rest were taken up. Most of this first wave comprised naval "ratings," an old-fashioned term for enlisted personnel, a.k.a. non-officers. Ratings were any members who held the rank of Ordinary Seamen, Able Seaman, Leading Seaman, Petty Officer, or Chief Petty Officer. The city was lousy with them. As Stephen Kimber puts it in *Sailors, Slackers and Blind Pigs*, "Ready or not, fit for human habitation or not, the dockyards barracks were soon spilling over with freshly minted naval ratings. They hung their hammocks in the dockyards gym, in the skating rink, and in other assorted buildings and sheds." When eventually the sheds and skating rinks and gyms were full, the Navy was dispatching hundreds of sailors a night to find their own accommodation. "They spread out across the city, renting every available room or closet." Still, anywhere from four hundred to eight hundred were without beds each night. This isn't counting the hundreds of merchant seamen in the city at any given time, also on the hunt for accommodations.

It gets worse. Many service members brought their loved ones along.

In her book about Navy spouses, *There's No Wife Like It*, Dianne Taylor quotes the reminiscences of one woman arriving in Halifax to see off her husband, who was prepping for convoy. "When we got to the hotel they told us there wasn't a room for us. So I sat on the chesterfield and our son napped while my husband went tearing around, speaking to everyone that he knew till he found us a room on Spring Garden Road." They were lucky. They at least had a bed, though no kitchen: "I lived in that room with my two-year-old son and had to take him out for every meal from February through early April."

The core problem? This was officially no one's problem. The municipal and provincial governments knew military support was a federal government issue. The federal government was of the opinion that it didn't concern itself with the housing and well-being of military families. After all, if you shipped overseas, you left your wife and kids at home. If they happened to follow you as far as Halifax? Well, that was their problem.

There's more. Halifax's strategic role wasn't only as a troop clearinghouse, but as a supply yard for the war and relief efforts. And it took scads of people to move those goods—administrators and office staff, stevedores, and other dock workers. Like service members, many—merchant mariners and war workers, alike—who arrived in Halifax to fill the labour gap brought their families with them. Wouldn't you, if you were moving for a job? All this accounts for Halifax's out-of-all-reason population spikes, which in the highest-count year, 1944, was as if the entire population of Regina, Saskatchewan picked up and moved to the city. That's how many people were crowding in. And as bad as those numbers are, they are also kind of without merit, because they represent only residents—not those in port for the short-term, like merchant marines, or Army or Air Force members waiting to deploy. Particular attention needs to be paid to naval ratings, who deployed from Halifax, just like Air Force and Army members, but who didn't reliably stay away from the city. They returned again and again and again. Halifax wasn't just a short-term staging area for them before they went overseas for months or years. Many were posted to Halifax for the duration of the war. And even if they weren't technically

The shortage of available housing meant families like this one, shown in a 1940 newspaper article, were forced to live in horrific conditions. (**NS ARCHIVES**)

posted to Halifax, they came back to Halifax often, which is why they brought their spouses and families. Merchant sailors might not be back as regularly or predictably, but there was no shortage of them in port, either. Many must have relocated their families to Halifax, too.

The multi-angle pressure on the city's housing stock forced families into horrific conditions. A 1940 photo essay by C. G. Robinson catalogued at the Nova Scotia Archives shows an example of the low-calibre housing Haligonians suffered through. One photo shows a mother and seven children—the oldest, perhaps twelve, the youngest an infant—in a family of ten who share one room, for lack of any other place to rent. In the shot there's one bed, an armchair, and, within feet, a dining table covered in a grimy cloth. Outerwear and laundry litter several surfaces. Groceries clutter the windowsill. The children smile or stare. The baby cries. Everyone needs a bath and a fresh set of clothes. You can practically smell the photo.

Halifax was caught as the war gained momentum. The population was surging, the conditions were untenable, and the rest of the country, at least early on, wasn't actually allowed to know exactly what was happening in this unnamed "East Coast Port." Because of the risk of attack from abroad, Halifax's conditions were hidden. It faced a literally unspeakable burden. As Jay White notes, "The city was besieged from within and without." By 1940, it faced a "blitzkrieg of people."

Some phoney war, eh?

Eventually, ads began appearing in newspapers across Canada. In the words of Thomas H. Raddall in *Halifax: Warden of the North*, they first "suggested, urged, and finally commanded" people with no business in Halifax to stay away. "All this was blithely ignored," Raddall writes. "From 1939 onwards every train arriving in the city decanted women and children eager to join their men in this strange exciting place, none with any idea of conditions in the port, all confident of finding a place in which to live." Administrator of Canadian Atlantic Ports E. L. Cousins signed that unenforceable November 1943 Order-in-Council warning civilians to please, for the love of god, stop arriving, but it took until June 1944 for printed posters to go up in rail and bus stations and airports. Seven months later. And, really, who's going to choose not to make a journey after they've packed their bags, bid their goodbyes, and are standing at the station with a ticket? The YWCA opened temporary beds for mothers visiting sons in hospital and those arriving unawares with young children. The vacancy rate approached zero. New arrivals, instead of scanning the papers for rentals, took to posting their own ads, begging for bed and board, and offering rewards to anyone who provided a lead.

"Nova Scotia," in the words of a January 1941 federal government memo, was "essentially a war zone."

Little Jackie Wrixon didn't see any of this. Not the crowding and home-lessness. Not the jostling, overstuffed trams. Not the frequently empty store shelves. But the war was still all-consuming in her elementary-school–sized world. The overlapping assaulting waves of Halifax's emergency air raid sirens could go off at any time. Halifax's sirens were electronically operated and deafeningly loud. They were also terrifying. There was no way to know until the all-clear was given whether the siren signalled a practice or the actual approach of aerial bombers. "You never knew when it was happening," Jackie says. "When it was something real." And in that way, it was *always* real. Jackie and her mother flicked off all the lights if the sirens screamed at night and ran together to the basement in their nightclothes. They sometimes lit a candle for a glimmer of light, but that was about it. The goal was absolute darkness. Everyone in Halifax during the war knew that sound. And the panic.

Madeline Taylor moved to Halifax from rural Nova Scotia in early 1941, following her husband, Walter, who left farm work for a job at the Canadian National Railway roundhouse near Africville. Walter had arrived in the fall of 1940, but Madeline, sensibly, waited at home with her three-year-old until Walter found the family an apartment. They lived in Fairview, where Madeline could look out her windows and see ships prepping for convoy in Bedford Basin. Some mornings, she'd wake to see the massive bowl drained of vessels and know that a convoy had left silently during the night—which happened on average every eight days—"What a feeling," she wrote in a letter outlining her remembrances of Halifax during the Second World War. Fairview, back then, was a dirt-road enclave west of the Halifax peninsula. But it wasn't out of reach of the emergency air raid sirens, which would routinely go off at night. Madeline was twenty-one, and often alone because Walter was needed for so much overtime at the busy switching yard. She installed blackout curtains and kept a pail

An image taken from the air in 1942 shows a convoy of ships in the Bedford Basin. (NS ARCHIVES)

of sand in case of fire and became, in her words, a "nervous wreck in no time." At the siren's wail, she turned out the lights, not even daring to put a match to a cigarette, and peeked out. "High in the sky," she once wrote, "dozens of searchlights would focus on a plane; scared to death, I would fear it was a German plane, relief when the siren was still." William D. Naftel characterized this kind of noise and confusion as the constant backdrop of wartime for Haligonians, who tried "unsuccessfully to shut out the unending racket."

Jackie Wrixon had reason to mind the sirens a little less than most. Her father, John, was an air raid warden, tasked with maintaining order and instructing civilians during air raid practices. These wartime volunteers were treated as auxiliary police, and his respected position dulled the sting of what Jackie calls her "first embarrassment"—that her father could not serve in the military because he had poor eyesight. "You just had that feeling, 'Oh maybe my dad's not doing what he should.'" In truth, air raid wardens were performing absolutely vital voluntary work at home. There were few other cities in North America where such protection was so essential—and in Canada, none other.

The split between the volunteer roles of Jackie's parents, John Wrixon and Ruth Wrixon, was gendered, as was typical. Women were expected to take their place in the voluntary war effort, but only in the ways the silent and not-so-silent gender norms of the day allowed. And the Wrixons did just that. John took on his air raid warden duties. Ruth would head down to Pier 21 on Saturdays with Jackie's grandmother to make bandages for use overseas. "Old sheets? You never threw sheets away." Jackie only ever saw her mother remove worn spots. The rest would be cut up for use on the battlefield. This was a precision task: bandages needed to be a consistent seven-by-four inches, and rolled to fit their packaging. She also knit socks and mittens for service members, as part of a group of regular knitters who would gather at women's homes to chat and undertake the task.

Madeline Taylor, who lived in her apartment overlooking the basin, also knit for service members, travelling to the Fairview Red Cross once a week. And she, like Ruth and so many others, would roll sheet bandages and make field dressings using cheesecloth, which volunteers would lay out, cut, and fold to specific dimensions. Madeline saw the good work of these bandages. She and her friend Dot would visit wounded service members who were recuperating at the Military Hospital on Cogswell Street, adjacent to Citadel Hill. "So many patients with broken bones," she remembered. "Broken bodies and so ill.... I didn't think I could go back. But when our regular day came, we would go." Once the war ended and eventually the tide of returning wounded stemmed, she and Dot moved their good deeds to Pier 21 to help greet war brides and displaced persons. Many travelled with children, whom Madeline and Dot would entertain or bottle-feed while their mothers cleared customs. Some would have been on the water for six long, bumpy days, "a scary and stressful time." But one that Madeline hoped her help might ease.

This was the everyday volunteer war work of women. A little here, a little there; a move to this spot, then to that; work, like knitting, undertaken in the home, added on top of existing labour. It's easy to fall in love with the big stories of women volunteers, when they surface; to be drawn to their drive and tirelessness and panache, but we can't forget the Ruth Wrixons and the Madeline Taylors, nor the contributions of anonymous thousands of other women who were doers on a small scale, their volunteer labour piecemeal but compounding. This work was mirrored in cities and towns across Canada, where most women were not in the paid workforce. Sharon MacDonald, a researcher and author, in her thesis on women volunteers, *Hidden Costs, Hidden Labours: Women in Nova Scotia During Two World Wars*, neatly lays out the over-and-above nature of women's war work. While they remained in the home, caring for families and some running farms, they involved themselves, she writes:

> *...organizing, fundraising, producing, packing, shipping, and distributing millions of essential supplies, such as clothing, bedding, bandages, and food for overseas comfort and relief.... Women provided countless services to the military in the form of hospitality and recreation; they organized salvage collection; they had a major role in domestic food production; and they mobilized and coordinated children's unpaid volunteer contribution to the war effort.*

They did this all on top of their regular duties and lives. In Halifax, because of the city's unchosen strategic role, the need was, in volume, scope, and importance, magnified.

Another slice of volunteer work that Halifax women routinely added to the pile was taking on boarders. And, when the call went out, Ruth

Red Cross drills, Halifax, 1941 (NS ARCHIVES)

Wrixon rented out a small bedroom in her family's Robie Street house. As it happens, she rented out Jackie's bedroom, shifting Jackie in with her new baby brother. Nearly eight decades later, Jackie raises an eyebrow and laughs. "It wasn't funny," she says. "I had to move in with this baby!" Ruth (in the parlance of the time, as "Mrs. John Wrixon") registered her eight-by-ten-foot room and charged $5.50 per person per week for single occupancy, or $4.50 per person per week for double. No meals. Jackie recalls that these boarders, who floated in and out of her young life without much attention paid, were usually wives of servicemen who were stationed in the city or waiting on convoy deployment. "They came and they went. That was it."

Besides, Jackie, dreaming of a far-off day when she might enjoy such delights as not always having to always wear a dress, had her own war work on the go. She was a member of the Junior Red Cross, which meant that Fridays after school she and the other girls would gather to learn to knit. (Older girls knitted and also participated in Red Cross drills; boys of all ages drilled, though no boys learned to knit. Child and teen volunteering, as with the adult variety, ran clearly along gender lines.) The students would also each bring five cents on Fridays to support English war relief. Jackie knew it was important; she knew everyone did it. But she only had a vague sense of why. "Bombed or starving children in England. I mean, they were far away, right?" Comprehension aside, those nickels made a difference. Junior Red Cross branches mobbed the province. During the 1944–1945 academic year there were 2,276 Nova Scotia branches with 67,696 members. If each member contributed one nickel, that's a one-week haul of nearly $3,400.

It's no wonder there were so many Junior Red Cross students. There were just so many students, period. The accumulation of servicemen and their wives and families, plus war workers and theirs, wasn't the only population surging. Halifax was knee-deep in children. Halifax schools started running classes on double-shift schedules near the beginning of the war due to overcrowding. This extreme measure was instituted so early in the conflict for the same reasons that Halifax was immediately overrun in the fall of 1939: the city was living with inadequate infrastructure and schools were at capacity long before Hitler waltzed over the Rhineland demilitarized zone. Halifax in 1939 was a soaked sponge trying to sop up an ever-creeping puddle. So even the split-class schedules, with half the students attending in the morning and the other half in the afternoon, couldn't satisfy the swelling mass of learners. Principals turned auditoriums into classrooms and moved students out into the basements of nearby churches. Schools—and, let's be clear in meaning, here: long-suffering teachers, themselves mostly women—stepped up in other ways, too. Jackie didn't only knit and bring in her nickels to class. Schools were also recruitment spots for volunteer salvage campaigns. The message to contribute came from all angles. And, so, like her classmates, Jackie did her duty, collecting the foil from her parents' cigarette packaging, as well as other metal, and toting it over to the salvage depot on Kempt Road.

That nine-year-old children were concerning themselves deeply with the business of war is not the modern way of thinking. As I write this, there are several major armed conflicts taking place in Asia and Africa. Children there pay a steep price for the fighting and are, no doubt, decidedly and unfairly consumed with war. But ask yourself: is Canada at war right now? No? Are you sure? What was the last war Canada was a part of? If you can't answer decisively without an internet search, you can understand that there's no comparing the zeitgeist surrounding the Second World War against, for example, the war in Afghanistan. (For the record, that was Canada's most recent combat mission and, in fact, its longest war, with Canada's involvement in the conflict spanning 2001 to 2014.)

The difference between then and now? Total war.

—∿∿—

The idea of total war was both spoken and unspoken during the Second World War.

I associate it most with The Blitz, the period between September 7, 1940, and May 11, 1941, when London and other targets suffered nightly, unimaginable bombing by the German Luftwaffe. The Blitz, (in German, "Blitzkrieg," or "lightning war") was a specific eight-month-and-five-day campaign, though over time it's become a catch-all shorthand for the generalized bombing inflicted on England during the war. During the bombing, attacks were fierce and broad. The German goal was to destroy not merely military targets, but to kill the means of war production in England: factories and ports and industrial installations. Any city with a war industry understood it was a target. Over the campaign's 157 days, almost a million Britons became homeless. More than forty-three thousand civilians were killed. There was no ignoring that. When every day ended with the fresh fear of being killed in your bed, your backyard air raid shelter, or the subway station your family was sheltering in along with tens of thousands of others, you couldn't forget war. It was total.

In Halifax the fear of bombing was real, if never realized. But the fact of total war was more than that. It was a pervasive, clear, consistent messaging: this war is a society-moving effort. All in. No question. (In fact, many did question, and despite their epic support, those questioners were in a material way, women. But the glance-view, and the predominant sentiment, was simple: the war effort was a shared responsibility, involving the very young to the very old, and it was wholly embraced.) Want a picture of this commitment? Take a visit to Library and Archives Canada to pore over its many boxes of crinkled and cracked Second World War documents. There, one quickly gets an understanding of how serious Canadians were about supporting the war and how committed they were to the effort. Among the archived pieces of correspondence is a hand-written letter from a Mrs. A. J. Adams, addressed to the Governor General. Adams notes that she is enclosing $1.00 (that's about the equivalent of $15.00 today), which she would like directed to the benefit of Air Raid Victims, specifically to the Christmas in Shelter Fund. Kind Mrs. Adams is no one-off. A letter from Andrew Dunsmore of Nanaimo, British Colombia, notes an enclosed cheque for $26.59 raised by the students of the Nanaimo Dramatic Academy, the Tucker Violin School, and the Dunsmore Music Studio, where, presumably, Andrew Dunsmore is proprietor. He, unlike Mrs. Adams, leaves the direction of the funds in the competent hands of those in charge. In another memo, the Prime Minister's Office refers a letter to the Department of National War Services from a Mr. O. Limpert of Hespeler, Ontario. Mr. Limpert, on March 6, 1941, wrote directly to Prime Minister King.

> *Most Honourable Sir:*
>
> *I have a strong desire to help the British War Victim Fund. I have a good farm in Alberta on section adjacent to a thriving town, which I would present to the British War Vivtims Fund Committee, or if no*

*such orginization exists, to the Red Cross, to be sold by lottery, proceeds
to go to the B.W.V. fund.*

Would this be permissible?

*As present tenants lease expires end of present month, a reply by air
mail will be appreciated.*

Respectfully yours.

God save the KING.

[signed] *O. Limpert*

I'm not being churlish by including Mr. Limpert's spelling errors,
only hoping to be clear: these were everyday Canadians, in their everyday
lives, who were willing to sacrifice—from giving up a dollar to giving up
an entire working farm—for a war potentially not pressing upon them
in any material way in Nanaimo, or Hespeler, or wherever sweet Mrs.
Adams of no-return-address was writing from. This was the mood and
flavour of total war. It began and it would end, and in between it would
consume lives and livelihoods and imaginations. Even when Jackie wasn't
cowering with her mother in pitch-darkness in her Robie Street basement
during air raid practice, the war inhabited her nights. "I used to go to
bed dreaming about the Germans. You know, they'd come and get you.
And there was no TV, so Germans were great big guys, who were going
to get you."

I'm not being churlish by including Mr. Limpert's spelling errors,
only hoping to be clear.

The war through Jackie's child-eyes was a sometime nightmare. But for
teenager Marjorie Langin? It was an absolute dream—especially when a
knock came at the front door of her parents' Cherry Street home.

"Is this where Clifford Langin lives?" the uniformed lad on the step
would always enquire.

Cherry, a single-block Halifax street lined with trees and three-storey wood-shingled homes, was a half-hour walk from Stadacona and a half-hour walk from the west end's No. 1 "Y" Depot, the Halifax embarkation point for Air Force members heading overseas. A perfect triangulation.

She looked at the stranger, the latest one at the door.

"Yes."

And before Marjorie had a chance to say more, the boy—and they were boys, the whole lot of them who arrived, eighteen and nineteen years old, their first time away from home—piped up.

"Herb Langin in Cranbrook said when I was at 'Y' Depot that I could come here."

Marjorie's words were the same every time, "Of course, come in." And so were her thoughts: "Oh, ho!" she wondered, slyly. "Who be *that*?"

Her mother, Rita, got the teapot on and ushered the boy in. Moments later came Rita's inevitable, "Of course, you are going to stay and have dinner."

The boy had travelled across Canada from the prairies, experiencing, for the first time, the true vastness of the land. He was destined for certain hardship. And he said, looking at the table and the tea, "This is so amazing."

"All they wanted to do," Marjorie remembers, "was sit at the dinner table, or the kitchen table to have a cup of tea. As a family."

⌣⌒⌒

In her Halifax apartment, Marjorie tells me her story as she, just like her mother used to, puts on the kettle: "Everything tastes better with a cup of tea. Anytime you're by, come in. I don't charge for a cup of tea." Marjorie, who became a Lindsay when she married, was fourteen when the war broke out and didn't have a sweet clue it was coming. But when it arrived, it marked a beautiful upending to her world. Marjorie was the eldest of four and the only girl in a boy-soup of "wild brothers." When we speak, she is in her nineties, and she concedes that her short-term memory is waning. But her long-term memory shines. It also tracks perfectly with a 1975 CBC Radio broadcast reflecting on the situation for young women in Halifax during the Second World War. The unsubtly truthful title? "'Ten men for every girl': women fend off men in WWII Halifax."

"Halifax, Nova Scotia, is just about the most exciting place in Canada for a young woman during the Second World War," the narrator remarks. "The city suddenly doubles in size as the port becomes a key hub for Allied naval forces and merchant shipping. Halifax pulses with activity under the influx of soldiers and sailors, war babies and orphans, prostitutes and crooks. And everywhere you look, young men from a dozen nations are desperate for a dance with a Canadian girl."

That Canadian girl was Marjorie.

Marjorie was in the first graduating class of Halifax's Queen Elizabeth High School, in June 1943. In a black-and-white class photo, the seventy-seven boys and girls stand, along with their teachers, outside on the concrete steps leading up to the brand new school auditorium, their faces staggered seriousness and joy. About-to-turn-eighteen Marjorie stands rod-straight, like her classmates. In a pristine light-coloured dress. Like her classmates. Victory roll hairstyle (think Barbara Stanwyck in *Double Indemnity*), bold lip, and, though her feet are hidden by the rows ahead of her, she's no doubt sporting cap-toe glove pumps, like, you guessed it, so many of her classmates. All of them, by Marjorie's estimation, were volunteers in one way or another, even if it was just by way of a good Saturday night, going to the supper-dance at the Nova Scotian Hotel, or to one of the YMCA men's dances. This wasn't especially hard work. "When you went out with the officers, you could go up to the officers' mess. And you were treated like a queen. Very much impressed were we, Halifax girls. By sixteen, I thought I was very worldly. And at seventeen, I *was* worldly. I had met a lot of people."

Everyone had. Halifax had been convulsed out of its inter-war slumber. A welcome avalanche. Restaurants and theatres were jammed. Beaches were swarmed in the summer and the Halifax Common Egg Pond, along with every other available sheet of ice, swarmed all winter. Every home invited in young servicemen for meals. "Here was this little sleepy city, and then all of a sudden? Inundated," Marjorie says. The issue wasn't only the numbers of people, it was the requisite fecklessness. William D. Naftel writes in *Halifax at War,* "seemingly overnight, the streets of the city, so tranquil and orderly just weeks before, were flooded with thousands of service men with little money and nothing to do." At No. 1 "Y" Depot, troops would gather, sometimes waiting for six or seven weeks before there was a full complement to take overseas. "For we girls, it was wonderful." And Marjorie, at this, claps in delight. The service members were from across the Commonwealth: India, Africa, Britain, Ireland. "From such exciting places, in parochial little Halifax. It was like being transported into New York City. For a young woman, it was a mecca."

Young women of Marjorie's age fell into a curious demographic group—old enough to feel the excitement of the war hitting Halifax, but still too young to truly understand the harm inflicted on the city by the tsunami of men. Too young to see the damage to the young men themselves, really. The nightly homelessness experienced by hundreds of service members was invisible to her. Marjorie's blinders were removed, however, by the war's end. She left Queen Elizabeth High School and attended the Maritime School of Social Work for a two-year course, graduating in 1945. Her first job was with the Children's Aid Society. She didn't merely read about the families living in overcrowded flats, like the one featured in that 1940 photo essay by C. G. Robinson. Those overtaxed parents and filthy children, living in single rooms, were her clients. Poor housing in Halifax wasn't created by the war, but it was exacerbated, significantly, by the war and its pressures. Marjorie calls herself "naive and unprepared" for these realities.

Before these inevitable sorrows muted Marjorie's revelry, before she graduated, before she fully comprehended the difficult and frightening positions of the boys showing up at her Cherry Street door for tea, she absolutely, and without reserve, whooped it up in the spectacular hurly-burly of Halifax. She kept on wondering, "Who be *that*?" when she opened the front door to a uniform. She kept on attending dances. The mother of her dearest high school friend, Joan, was a volunteer, and like any good volunteer, Joan's mother recruited every vertical body she could, including Joan, Marjorie, and all their friends, to do whatever was required. They served coffee and snacks at No. 1 "Y" Depot, at the Navy League dry canteen on the Wanderers Grounds, and at the Allied Merchant Seamen's Club on Hollis Street. On Sundays, after the Baptist sermon she attended, she stayed on for luncheons or coffee with service boys who were there for the morning. She volunteered at a Red Cross mobile canteen at the pier, serving coffee and doughnuts when a troop ship was departing or arriving. "My *darling*, I had a uniform! Oh my god. I had a hat. It had a big red cross on the front. And you had to wear a trench coat. It was wonderful."

When I ask her why she volunteered, how it felt, if she knew the impact she had on these boys' and men's time in the city, knew her small impact on the war's success, she pauses. "I would lie," she says, considering false altruism. But, no. "I am sure that all young women my age and older felt not that they were doing a great thing for the war effort. I think that they were nurturing their own inner souls." Or, perhaps, just having a good Saturday night.

⁓

That a girl—fifteen, sixteen, even seventeen years old—could do any of this was unthinkable before the war. This freedom, in the name of volunteering and in the spirit of total war, allowed Halifax girls to capture life in ways they would otherwise have been denied. There is a Panglossian view of this power, in imagining that the place of girls and women in society somehow changed permanently during the war, that somehow they earned autonomy. Alas, no. Women's lives were still controlled by myriad mores. This brief independence only came about by virtue of the chaos of the time in Halifax, the urgent need to respond, and the fervency with which girls stepped up. Marjorie's father, Clifford, allowed his daughter to volunteer, but he wasn't always happy about the places she went. The Allied Merchant Seamen's Club on Hollis Street is one example. The building was new in December 1941 and beautifully outfitted for concerts and meals. It also provided desperately needed beds for up to three hundred and fifty merchant seamen, multi-national and multi-aged civilians who worked on ships, ferrying arms, fuel, food, relief supplies, and other necessities of life and war from North America to besieged ports in England. Merchant ships could carry crews of fifty, and there could be many dozen merchant vessels in the harbour at any time. Because these sailors were civilians, the federal government wouldn't provide accommodation while they were in port. Those three hundred and fifty beds at the Allied Merchant Seamen's Club were filled in an instant, the spillover adding nightly to the four hundred to eight hundred bedless service members already kicking around. The typical view of this predicament, and of merchant mariners themselves, was unsympathetic. "My father was the most amazing man in the world. A true good person," Marjorie says. "But he didn't like me going down there. Because they were merchant seamen. They were not service boys. They were not coming and saying, 'I knew your brother in Cranbrook, or I knew your aunt.' They were different. And yet they were the men, my darling, who kept the lifeline between England and us." They truly did. Merchant members kept England alive. They were also denied benefits and recognition by the federal government for decades after the war, despite being routinely torpedoed and, according to Veterans Affairs Canada, suffering a casualty rate in the Battle of the Atlantic of one in seven, a higher percentage of casualties than any military branch.

Clifford Langin had an unfair opinion of merchant seamen, but he wasn't wrong to wonder where his teen daughter was headed in the evenings. The September 1942 issue of *Chatelaine* magazine considered, in a feature, the question of "children in wartime." The story blames the population doubling, poor housing stock, social service infrastructure in disarray, and plentiful money for a rise in juvenile delinquency in Halifax. "Truancy and theft have increased," the author writes. "The usual school, recreational and club activities fail to hold the interest of boys and girls alike." The feature considers these war-caused problems across the country, with a focus on the bacchanalian state of Halifax streets. "There is a serious problem regarding older girls and young women," the story says, while failing to note whether this implies unintended pregnancy from consensual sex or sexual assault. There's a book-length inquiry to be done on safety during the Second World War. Men, as would be expected, were less safe because they fought overseas. Their injuries and deaths were closely recorded, and are today easy to find in lists of casualties or databases of war dead. But women may have been less safe, too, because the social dynamic in their communities—and especially in Halifax—changed. Of this, there is scant tracking. Anecdotal evidence suggests women were propositioned much more during the war than before. Is verbal harassment a safety issue? Yes. Yes it is. Being free of verbal harassment contributes to a feeling of protection and comfort in one's surroundings. A provincial propaganda film released in 1945 to help recognize Halifax's and Nova Scotia's role during the war features interviews with several women's naval auxiliary members who admit they spend their time off getting out of Halifax for the sole reason of getting away from all the men. "You were constantly being proposed to," one woman says. "There were times when you would get three or four marriage proposals in one week."

But, remember, this is long before this kind of attention would be spun as anything other than positive. If women perceived problems with being catcalled, or worse, it was seen as an issue with the women. One former volunteer I interviewed was raped in a room at the Nova Scotian Hotel. She first met her attacker at a dance. He was an officer, so his rank implied trustworthiness. Because of that, she, a teen, accepted his luncheon invite in the hotel restaurant. "The next thing I know, we are in his room." She paused. "That was my first initiation into that," she told me. "I grew up awfully fast." She never reported it.

Women today, seventy-plus years after the war's end and in the age of #MeToo, are still frequently blamed for their own assaults. So, it's no wonder this teen volunteer didn't risk taking the blame for her own. Blame was something women of that time soaked up like dishrags. (They still do today.) They held the bag, too, for wartime truancy and delinquency. With fathers missing at war, women had to double down on parenting. But many also worked. Another *Chatelaine* feature, this one from June 1943, "Is Home Life Breaking Up?" is a shocking account of women's manifold failures in parenting. It tells one story of a four-year-old locked in a room with his mother off to work from morning until late afternoon. The preschooler has "only a few crusts of bread to gnaw, a gas stove within easy reach." Two other children, one a nine-month-old baby, were locked in the attic of a boarding house at night while their mother "stepped out" with a newly acquired boyfriend. "A roomer on the second floor saw wisps of smoke floating down the stairs, broke open the door to the children's room and found the curtains on fire. Little Johnny, the elder boy, had been playing with matches to alleviate his boredom." The author, Adele Saunders, says the two examples are taken from social service workers' files. If true, these sensational stories cannot be generally indicative of real circumstances. Nor, I imagine are the stories of "car babies," that is, infants found locked in vehicles while their mothers worked. Social conditions shifted during the war, but it seems unlikely there was a pandemic of abandoned and neglected children. And while teens had more free rein than in the past, living in the chaotic soup of wartime Halifax, that didn't make them all "fast girls."

And this definitely wasn't Marjorie. She kept in line. Stayed in school. Perfected her Barbara Stanwyck victory rolls and enjoyed the fleeting fame of being a young woman in the absolute thrall of the moment. "You have no idea how sleepy Halifax was. You could roll a cannonball down Barrington Street on Sunday and you would never hit anybody. I really mean it…. And all of a sudden here were hundreds, thousands of people descending on this little city."

John Fisher explains the strain well. "The best way to appraise a situation is to look at it through the eyes of someone else—a stranger, for instance. Of late months, we have had a heavy influx of visitors to our city. Many of them come here to see us and we have talked plainly and listened patiently. Nearly all of them claim that Halifax is dead."

Fisher, a broadcaster, hosted a daily show on Halifax's CHNS Radio during 1940 and 1941 called Noontime Melodies. The music he played is long lost, but his scripts remain. They are free-flowing think pieces, where he speaks directly of the city, and directly into the ears of his individual listeners. His scripts, collected scattershot at Nova Scotia's provincial archives, are missing pages; many are undated. His habit was to type them on legal-size paper, adding occasional hand-written corrections and additions. Double-spaced, but with no paragraph breaks, no periods, and little other punctuation. He must have known what he wanted to get across. He started shows with "Good morning friends of Noontime Melodies! And how are you all this morning?"

On the day he declared that Halifax, from the eyes of the strangers in its midst, was dead, he was reading from an undated script. He mentions that the week before was Dartmouth's one hundred and ninetieth birthday, which pegs the broadcast in the summer of 1940. "They say the services generally speaking are bad," he continues. "Apartment rates are scandalously high. They are not equipped as they should be in a modern city. Food prices are much higher than other Canadian cities. They can't understand why fresh fruits cost so much more here than in inland cities. These same people complain about the lack of entertainment other than theatres and the occasional dance. They claim Halifax is the worst city to drive in they have ever experienced. They say the traffic moves pitifully slow. Never have they seen a city serving a population of one hundred thousand people without a modern traffic light."

There's that traffic light again…

Marjorie acknowledges the smallness of pre-war Halifax, the utter crushing weight of the war on its tiny shoulders. She also saw Halifax trying its very best to make it work. "You only had one bedroom for the guest," she surmises. "How many guests are you going to put in there!?"

Turns out, it was on the shoulders of Halifax women to figure that out.

Chapter Three

WE MUST ALL STICK TOGETHER

In November 1939, Queen Elizabeth called on women "in every corner of the Empire" to step up.

"The last time that I broadcast a message," she said in this early-war radio address, "was at Halifax, Nova Scotia, when I said the few words of farewell to the women and children who had welcomed the king and myself so kindly." Halifax had been the last stop in a May–June four-week royal tour by King George VI and Queen Elizabeth in 1939 (you might know her better as the Queen Mother).

"We, no less than men, have real and vital work to do," she told women. "In carrying on your home duties and in meeting all these worries so cheerfully, you are giving real service to the country. You are taking your part." And in that, Elizabeth, a thirty-nine-year-old mother of two who had never cleaned a toilet, boiled laundry, or ordered groceries, launched the battle of housewife versus hausfrau.

Women weren't merely asked to help fight the war; total war required their participation. And at least Elizabeth was transparent about the ask. She called on women, specifically. And for specific work—maintain your home, maintain your positivity, and volunteer outside the home as much as you can. Simply put: meet the needs of your community and country.

But too frequently in Canadian federal government documents, even in memos from one cabinet minister to another, the volunteer work that the Second World War's success required was framed as gender neutral. That this unconscripted army of helpers that rose up with the call of war was mostly women remained largely un-noted.

A January 1942 federal government memo from J. T. Thorson, the Minister of National War Services, proposed a restructuring of the way military members returning from or awaiting deployment would be supported in Halifax and other Canadian cities. A slew of auxiliary services, including recreation centres, hostels, and entertainment, should, he suggested, be provided by "citizens committees on a voluntary basis." The missing context? These services were chiefly provided by women. Thorson merely refers to them as "citizens of these communities." You might be thinking: who cares? Everyone understood, and understands, that it was mostly women who were left at home. The language of a government memo isn't that important. Except, it *is*. The language, in its imprecision, is meaningful. Perhaps it was a nod at inclusivity. But I would argue that it was far more likely a failure to acknowledge women. Oh, sure, the outliers got a nod—the women who took on war work, the women who took on traditional male industrial roles. They were worth attention; women doing so-called women's work were unremarkable. Even if they doubled or tripled their labour. No matter the salient impact of the work they did. They were collected, in the public consciousness, then and still, as part of the non-gendered swell of "citizens" who held up the roof while the war rained down.

There's something else particularly vexing about Thorson's memo, and the press release he sent out six weeks later, in February 1942, formalizing the plan and putting a finer point on the idea that these citizen committees would be "charged with the responsibility of seeing that the members of the armed forces are adequately provided for in the urban centres and that funds will be found for such necessary auxiliary services." The communiqué implied that to this point, the federal government was actually competently taking on this auxiliary work. Uh…no. The feds supported war preparedness. They neglected or came up short on the rest. Halifax and its blitzkrieg of people, its difficulty keeping food on shelves and water running through taps, was the proof. And women? Women had already stepped up. Halifax women, starting in September 1939, were living the spiralling effects of the feds' laser focus on battle and battle-readiness. I try to imagine myself as a woman in 1942, hearing of Thorson's brilliant idea to shift the responsibility of these services to volunteers, and hearing the passive promise that "funds will be found." I imagine myself having already spent two and a half years trying desperately to stem the tide of need caused by my once-slow city being cannonballed into a role it never chose and was unequipped to handle. And I take a deep breath and I try to imagine how I would control my incandescent rage. It gets worse: Minister of National Defence James Ralston wrote a letter to Thorson, angry that he wasn't consulted before this restructuring of War Services work. "I just want to record now that I have the gravest doubts," he wrote, about the capabilities of citizen committees. "Morale is a pretty important factor in connection with the maintenance of the efficiency of the Armed Forces, and facilities in urban centres are, I think, definitely necessary for the maintenance of morale." Ralston, plainly, doubted that something Halifax women were, in fact, already doing could actually be done.

But maybe Ralston deserves some credit. Like Thorson, he fails, in his letter, to acknowledge that these citizens were, materially, women, but he also gets at a point. The provision of auxiliary services like entertainment and recreation and lodging and meals (inasmuch as food and shelter can be considered "auxiliary" in any context) was no cakewalk. They were complex and costly to organize and provide. They were also serious-as-a-heart-attack essential to the success of the war. And this has everything to do with morale.

The emphasis that was placed on maintaining morale during the Second World War cannot be understated. High morale, it was reinforced again and again, would win the war. But the subtly ranging definitions of wartime morale, and whose morale, exactly, was being given prime consideration, deserves a deeper look. Minister of National Defence Ralston wanted to ensure military morale. This did not apply to military families. Service wives had no special concern paid to them by their husbands' employers. Indeed, these women were treated quite cruelly, as Katherine Anne Ling points out in her 1994 thesis, *Servicewives in Wartime Halifax, 1939–1945*. An example is the double standard of marital fidelity. "Promiscuity among servicemen was an expected part of war and condoms and venereal disease information were regularly distributed to men before their scheduled leaves. The same behaviour in their wives was referred to as immoral conduct and subject to harsh punitive policies." Even an anonymous and unproven accusation of cheating could result in being cut off by the Dependents' Allowance Board.

While the limit of Ralston's zeal for morale was strictly dictated by uniform, Minister of National War Services Thorson saw the opportunity for volunteering as a benefit to civilian morale. Without civilians supporting the war, he felt, it was lost. The question, never settled: which flavour of morale was more important for the win? Did members of the armed forces need, for example, letters written from home to get up in the morning and keep on task? The idea's absurd. These were men who signed up willingly to fight, whatever that required of them. They were paid to do a job. A difficult and high-stakes job, a job tied up in national identity and duty, but a job, nonetheless. Letters from home were not a condition of service. But letter-writing campaigns, such as those organized across Canada by women's groups, formal and informal, boosted service members' morale.

To open an envelope and find a kind and encouraging word from a stranger back home didn't mean everything. But it patently meant *something*. It was a piece of the complex puzzle of morale. And morale helped soldiers, sailors, and Air Force personnel to continue the fight.

Civilian morale, on the other hand, accomplished this for the country as a whole. It burnished the idea that the country would support the war and all its significant challenges over the long haul. Civilian morale is perhaps best encapsulated in the British wartime saying (and ever-metastasizing pop-cultural cliché) "Keep Calm and Carry On." While this famous slogan—you know it: white all-caps on tomato-red—wasn't ever released on a poster during the war, it epitomizes "Blitz spirit"—the idea that morale had to remain high, and Britons unflappable, in the face of a seemingly unending conflict. This enforced optimism carried over to Canada in spades, and it was habitually framed as a function of the domain of women. "Home defense [*sic*] begins in the kitchen and Canada expects every housekeeper to do her duty there," read an article in the Housekeeping section of the November 1939 issue of *Chatelaine*. "It's practical patriotism to feed the family nutritious, properly balanced meals based on dietetic values as well as economy and sound common sense. For health is important to a stiff upper lip and high morale an effective weapon against the enemy." All housekeeping roads, it seems, led to improved home-front morale.

And morale was indeed considered a weapon. This is an essential thesis in Canadian historian Randall Hansen's epic 2009 book *Fire and Fury: The Allied Bombing of Germany, 1942–1945*. In it, Hansen considers the success and ethics of the British and American bombing campaigns against Germany, in part through the lens of German morale depletion. The brutal bombing of German cities (fair warning: Hansen's account is a gut-punch of creative nonfiction, bringing horrifying death to life) was aimed to reduce civilian morale and thereby crack the resolve of Hitler's entire war machine. In fact, as Hansen looks at it, the bombing emboldened the Germans. Even as their cities were nightly laid to waste, they dug in. Civilian morale, and the will to keep up the fight, was indeed strong.

But there's a third idea I think is worth reflecting on, particularly considering the experience and actions of women during the war: morale as social well-being.

The work of women volunteers during the war was certainly war support. And it boosted morale, both military and civilian. Think about those letter-writing campaigns. Thorson was right—both the recipients of letters from home *and* the senders benefitted from the work. But it was more than a simple morale boost. It was war work that was about more than the war. The work of women, in feeding and clothing and caring for those needing care, in providing help, hope, and healing, concerned itself with the well-being of society. I would argue this was the primary work of Halifax women volunteers. They weren't doing their part only for the good of the forces. They weren't doing it only for their own good. They saw need—in Halifax, tremendous need—and they simply and quietly met that need. They worked tirelessly to clean up the mess that was being made and remade around them by the war. They were harnessing the power of maternal and housekeeping and organizational skills for the greater good.

But there's a dark side. It goes back to the problem of Jackie Wrixon and her little girlfriends knitting on Friday afternoons with the Junior Red Cross, while the boys were out practicing their marching. Some older girls marched, certainly. But I've seen no evidence of the boys practicing their stocking stitch. The entire exercise represents the wholesale reinforcement of gender roles. It's the same with Queen Elizabeth's address to the empire's women. The same when Minister Thorson, in November 1941, stood in the House of Commons and reminded Parliament that "the women who keep the heart of the nation sound by doing their daily tasks in the homes and the communities are doing war service of the highest possible order." That sounds nice and all, but it was work then, and still today, not given its due. The lack of recognition of women's volunteer labour, according to historian

Jay White in his 1994 thesis, *Conscripted City: Halifax and the Second World War*, "reflected cultural biases that viewed volunteer work as the extension of a woman's 'natural' role as maternal caregiver." In other words, no big deal. These same women, Thorson continued in his Parliamentary address, were "responsible for maintaining the morale of men in the armed forces and in the factories." Responsible!? There's a contradiction here of the highest order, to turn Thorson's phrase back on him. These deeds were both ordinary and, it seems, extraordinary. In one sense, mere "daily tasks," akin to tossing another chicken breast in the oven for an unexpected guest. Simultaneously, it carries the responsibility for the morale of not merely some men, but both forces members *and* civilians, and at a time when the stakes had never been higher. No pressure there, Thorson.

By the way, who was responsible for the morale of women? Zero evidence suggests servicemen, or men working in the factories or shipyards, were told they were "responsible" for the well-being of women as they endured the travails of the war. Apparently the morale of women was on the backs of, yep...women.

It was just what women did, I suppose. And no surprise. It's what women do now. Many of my friends, those who are cisgender women partnered with cisgender men, talk about the overwhelming volume of "emotional labour" they undertake in the run of a week. Gen X, my generation, embraced, in our twenties, the fully formed culture of riot grrrls and girl power. We were third-wave feminists—rolling our eyes at the idea of crusty suffragettes, long over the sexual revolution of our Baby Boomer mothers. We expected equality, expected our male partners to take on half the load. But the ensuing thirty years has proven that the load hasn't ended up split so evenly. The Organisation for Economic Co-operation and Development's *Better Life Index* finds that Canadian women today spend, on average, 37 percent more time than male partners cooking, cleaning, and caring for children. That's gutting. And it's not even counting emotional labour—that is, all the tasks that comprise being the household manager, such as organizing parent-teacher meetings, arranging play dates, knowing when the house insurance needs to be paid and how much toilet paper there is in the upstairs linen closet. Longitudinal studies show women do the bulk of this work as well. I only hope that my own daughters can better the numbers.

⁓ᴧᴧ⁓

Today, when most of us think of women in the war, we are programmed to think of the outliers—women joining auxiliary military and women working in factories. Fact is, there were only about seven thousand members of the Women's Royal Canadian Naval Service. The Canadian Women's Army Corps represented a force of about twenty-two thousand; the women's division of the Royal Canadian Air Force enlisted seventeen thousand. None were permitted to take on combat roles. They provided support, heavy on the cleaning, clerical, and cooking end of things. Yet more gendered work. The reason women were even allowed to take on these tasks was because it was an emergency. Total war. Bodies were urgently needed to fight, but the only acceptable bodies for the task were male ones. So the forces—individually, and not without significant hemming and hawing—each agreed to the creation of a women's corps, freeing up those essential male bodies from operational roles so they could move into battle. The Royal Canadian Air Force Women's Division, for one, never got a chance to forget this condition of their service. Their motto was "We Serve that Men May Fly."

Even before these women were officially allowed in as auxiliary members, they anticipated the need for their contributions and readied themselves. Author Jean Bruce highlights the early-war work of about two hundred and fifty Halifax women in her book, *Back the Attack! Canadian Women During the Second World War—at Home and Abroad*. They trained several nights a week in drilling, signalling, shooting, transport driving, and motorcycle riding. They did this without pay for upwards of two years. They even supplied their own uniforms. Once the forces begrudgingly agreed to women's divisions, women's pay was set at two-thirds that of men, based on the sexist calculus that it took three women to do the work of two men. (I'm not making this up.) In 1943, the ratio was boosted to four-fifths the pay. (I wonder what happened to women in the interim that boosted their abilities by 20 percent.) Women were also not permitted to join if they had dependents. Imagine, for a moment, the same restrictions being put on men:

"Hello, I'm able and willing; I hear the situation in Europe is grim and I'd like to help."

"Wonderful, sir. Do you have children?"

"I do."

"Fingers crossed Hitler just eases off, then. NEXT!"

Women with children were also less preferred when it came to employment in war industries, or in traditional male labour roles. The National Selective Service, established in 1941 to address the shortage of workers created by the droves of men going to war, recruited both women and men to fill these roles. The National Selective Service recruited single, childless women first, then moved to married, childless women as need grew desperate. Many women, according to Ruth Roach Pierson in her book *Canadian Women and the Second World War*, lied. "It was discovered in September 1942," she writes, "that many mothers working in Montreal's war plants had told their employers that they were single, because they had been afraid that they would not get jobs otherwise." Remember how badly some women may have needed these jobs. In 1939, Canada comprised about four million adult women. Roughly six hundred thousand, only about 15 percent, were employed outside the home. And two hundred thousand of those worked as domestic servants. The country was still recovering from the Great Depression. Throughout the 1930s, the birthrate was low, immigration was low, production was low, exports were low. People's economic prospects were, at best, stalled. The war's jobs provided a chance not just for immediate cash but for people to rebuild what had been lost over the previous decade.

Yet the glass through which we so often consider women's war work is one-way—women sacrificed during war to help the nation and the war effort. The country needed women to work; women met the need. But the flip side must also be true. The women needed the work; the jobs met *their* needs. It sped the country out of a decade-deep financial drag, yes, but jobs are more than money. Jobs provide emotional fulfillment, the challenge of mastering new skills, the opportunity to be social and meet new people. To feel accomplished. Think of all the benefits we derive from work. Women during the war derived them, too. Jobs during the war for women, viewed like this, ran along the same lines as morale. The benefits went both ways. In this context, it's fascinating that the National Selective Service even existed. Given the myriad benefits and the demonstrated need, it stands to reason that women would jump at the chance to work outside the home. But many needed coaxing. They needed recruiting. They needed to be told they were needed. The cumulative impact of centuries where women had been told they were best suited for the kitchen and the nursery, that their work in the home was the only right and good thing, was strong. Once women started to accept the value of their contributions, they stepped up. Eventually, the number of women working in jobs outside the home doubled to 1.2 million.

And then as quickly as it sped up, it slowed. The war ended and repatriation brought more and more men back, and the vast majority of women were thanked for their work and sent packing. Women first were persuaded to take jobs, and then were persuaded to give them up. The federal government and patriarchal propaganda machine that managed this feat was powerful. A 1943 Gallup poll cited in an issue of *Canadian Affairs*, a periodical from the Wartime Information Board, found that in the event of competition for a job, 68 percent of *women* surveyed felt men should have automatic priority. Only 27 percent felt men and women should even have an equal chance. "Women," pamphlet author Renée Morin writes, "evidently don't think it right to take jobs away from men." Or, at least, only 5 percent of those surveyed dared believe a more qualified woman should take a job from a less qualified man. That is an absolute triumph of perverse communications.

By December 1946, the last of the three arms of women's auxiliary services had been disbanded. Herds of women left the labour market, or sought what was considered acceptable employment for women: teaching, hairstyling, women's retail, or domestic positions. This ramping up and ramping down of women's involvement in the labour force epitomizes the desperate-times-call-for-desperate-measures flavour of the war. Women were lured into the labour market and to the auxiliary forces because of the emergency. When the emergency ended, women chose or were forced to, as the saying went, leave careers for kitchens. The impact of this on women's future economic gains is complex. But here's the nut of it: the revolutionary social change that might have come about through women's broad entry into wage-earning never materialized. Turns out, women's jobs, civilian or military, actually belonged to men the whole time.

All told, nearly seven hundred thousand women were recruited to war and industrial work by the National Selective Service. Another fifty thousand Canadian women served in the auxiliary forces. That's nothing to sneeze at. A lot of women who stepped up and helped make the war winnable. But women who contributed in other ways, volunteers who sold War Savings Stamps, served coffee to deploying service members, or made sandwiches at canteens, numbered, in the estimate of Ruth Roach Pierson in *They're Still Women After All: The Second World War and Canadian Womanhood*, about three million. (And let's get real here: many of those women who were working all day were *also* volunteering in their spare time.) Even using the simplistic view, for every one woman in an Army,

Veronica Foster, known as "The Bren Gun Girl" poses with a finished Bren gun at the John Inglis Co. plant. (**LIBRARY AND ARCHIVES CANADA**)

Air Force, or Naval uniform or wearing coveralls in a factory, there were four others spending evenings knitting socks, making bandages, or visiting war-wounded. Even still, the monolithic cultural imagery of women during the war is women in uniform or the American iconography of Rosie the Riveter. (The Canadian version, who actually came first, was Ronnie the Bren Gun Girl, who worked at John Inglis Co. in Toronto and, in May 1941, appeared on a series of posters encouraging women to take jobs in war industries. American Rosie, with her blue collar, red polka-dot bandana, and bicep flex, didn't appear until 1942, and Norman Rockwell's famous version of her not until 1943, but when's the last time you saw a Ronnie the Bren Gun Girl Halloween costume?) Women's volunteering is often confused with war industry employment or auxiliary military service. A common refrain I heard when I told someone I was working on a book about women volunteers during the Second World War in Halifax was, "Oh! My mother was a nurse…" or "My grandmother worked at…" such-and-such factory or office, or "My mother was a Wren…" (that is, a member of the Women's Royal Canadian Naval Service).

I get it. It's what we've been shown and told. It's the air we've been breathing for eighty-odd years. And, visually, there's no difference between the image of a woman knitting socks for her husband who works at the sugar refinery and the same woman knitting socks for service members overseas, or for bombed-out Britons. As far as fodder for propaganda goes, it's a dead end. Images of women in uniforms or coveralls? Shocking. Exotic. Ronnie the Bren Gun Girl, in her hallmark image (there was a series, featuring her at work and at leisure), sits on a stainless counter at John Inglis Co. in a bandana and coveralls that fail to contain her breasts, exhaling smoke from her mouth and nose. There's a languid and satisfied air about the nineteen-year-old. Two fingers of her right hand hold a cigarette. Two lean on the barrel of the three-and-a-half-foot-long light machine gun she has just had a role in finishing. This is no matron knitting socks in her living room with an afghan over her knees to protect against the chill. This is a young, nubile woman admiring a deadly weapon. The image is about as far as can be imagined from women's supposedly "natural" role as caregivers. Because of that contradiction, as Jay White puts it in *Conscripted City*, "the acceptance of women into traditionally male roles in the armed forces and in civilian occupations garnered far more public attention."

Funny thing is, that wasn't how most women saw themselves. Statistically, they were more likely to volunteer in the home than to work in industry or the forces. Not only that: Ruth Roach Pierson's *They're Still Women After All* cites a wartime study that asked Canadian women how they felt they could best serve Canada's war effort; 26 percent of respondents ranked "maintaining home life" at the top, the most-cited answer. Queen Elizabeth, for one, would have been pleased to hear it.

"Maintaining home life" sounds as if it were nothing more than keeping the status quo intact—making sure the kids got off to school in the morning and the bills got paid. But it was really so much more. The war didn't lessen women's domestic responsibilities. Monday was still washing day. Friday dinner was still fish. On Sunday, you went to church. In Halifax? Tea with every meal. Maintaining home life during the war wasn't so much about carrying on as it was about doing much more in the home, and in life, but with far fewer resources. As Jean Bruce points out in *Back the Attack!*, for most women the war represented years of grinding work, caring for children as a solo parent (and one with, more likely, the 1940 Canadian average of 2.7 children, rather than today's average of 1.5) or taking over a family farm or a small business with a husband, father, brother, or son away at war. Sometimes both. For women, as Bruce puts it, "the war was an endurance test."

There was money around, certainly, for women who could add jobs to their already overloaded mix. But extra money went toward purchasing War Savings Stamps and Victory Bonds. The social pressure to support the war effort through disposable, and not-so-disposable, income didn't abate. A *Halifax Chronicle* ad from June 1941 asks civilians directly to invest both their savings and a regular portion of their weekly wages in Victory Bonds, which were purchased at 10 percent down, with the balance in monthly installments through payroll deductions. "You are not asked to give, but to lend," the ad implores. "All of Canada is your security for repayment. A good rate of interest and a gratified sense of loyalty are your rewards. Invest generously and cheerfully. Act now. Make sure your dollars will have a glorious share in helping to crush the barbaric power that would make slaves of free men." War Savings Stamps were the smaller-potatoes version. After all, the minimum bond purchase was $50. That's almost $800 today. Stamps were more affordable at a quarter each. Even children, like Jackie Wrixon, had them. Like Victory Bonds, War Savings Stamps were redeemable after the war with interest. Sixteen stamps, licked and carefully stuck in a war savings booklet, could be exchanged for a $5 certificate.

This civilian funding of the government's war effort wasn't a hopeful campaign of budgetary palliation. It was policy. "Pay-As-We-Go," as it was called, was adopted by Prime Minister Mackenzie King's government in its first war budget and seeded among the Canadian owner class through speeches by Finance Minister J. L. Ilsley at tony locales such as the Seigniory Club, a resort halfway between Ottawa and Montreal on the Ottawa River (it's still tony, but now it's called Le Château Montebello). The all-on-board messaging would filter down to everyday Canadian wage earners through news media and propaganda. The idea? "Tax to the limit and borrow all we can," in the words of Ilsley in an Edmonton address in September 1941. But the debt wouldn't be held by other nations. "We shall owe the debt to ourselves—to millions of Canadians in one form or another." That's where women—who were rarely, I suspect, the sit-down audience for Ilsley's exhortations—came into the equation in a big way. Women were a burgeoning class of wage earners who contributed to the coffers, and they also did the lion's share of the selling of this idea, through one of its central products—War Savings Stamps. So, in a turn of events familiar to any parent tasked with contributing to their child's sport fundraising, women and girls in many cases both *bought* the stamps and *sold* the stamps. This was by no means only the work of women, but it was largely the domain of "Miss Canada" volunteers, who traipsed around during campaigns dressed in bright red, three-pocket pinafore aprons with a white maple leaf emblem and "Miss Canada" in cursive. They topped them with jaunty rowboat-style side caps. Girls as young as eleven were eligible to be "Miss Canada" volunteers. It's important to read into that age eligibility the unspoken burden this added to women. Sending uniformed children off into the neighbourhood with stamps and cash may have been a different beast in the 1940s than today, but there's no getting around that these were children. Their volunteer work required oversight from parents. And parents, typically, meant mothers. By the end of the War Savings Stamps program, according to exhibit material from the Canadian War Museum, women and girls had raised $318 million through stamp sales alone. That's 1.272 billion, with a B, stamps at a quarter a pop. Miss Canada, indeed.

⁓

Women weren't only engaged in outreach work when it came to earmarking spare change for the war effort. Redirecting resources was their job, too, mostly through salvage and rationing. At war's start, the need to ration, while foreseeable, wasn't yet dire. Resource requirements were ramping up over the months of the phoney war, but women were still serving coffee and tea at gatherings. All during the fall of 1939, the *Chatelaine* magazine Housekeeping section, written by Helen G. Campbell, regaled readers with the kinds of parties that might be held to support the troops—for instance, a bridge party with the winner's proceeds going to the war effort. But the focus was still squarely on menu suggestions for these events. Another early war feature questioned: "Will war affect our fashions?" Uh… yeah. By 1942, *Chatelaine* was reporting that silk was no longer available for stockings and other garments; linen, flannelette, and cotton supplies were waning. Rubber was a no-go as well, which meant no new girdles or corsets (a blessing in disguise?). Hot water bottles were available only by prescription and surgeons alone had access to rubber gloves. Umbrellas and lipstick tubes used metal, so they were limited or discontinued. By May 1942, the federal government's Wartime Prices and Trade Board clamped down and spoke out. Quoted in the *Halifax Chronicle*, Wartime Prices and Trade Board chair Donald Gordon said, "Ships and sailors' lives must not be risked to bring in from abroad a single pound of supplies which we

the VOLUNTEERS

can do without." No more tea and coffee at women's gatherings. No more serving refreshments at club meetings or garden parties. These things were all contrary to the spirit of rationing.

They were also, soon after Donald Gordon's chastisement and *Chatelaine*'s lamentations, contrary to regulation. The first shades of government-controlled rationing hit Canada in December 1941—a universal price freeze that came after months of precipitous spikes in the cost of everyday groceries, caused by equally precipitous and unpredictable food shortages. Women, almost exclusively in charge of food shopping and cooking, weathered these market storms and likely welcomed the price freezes. Coupon rationing, which allotted tickets to individuals for food items and fuel, was a more daunting prospect. The notion of food rationing had been baked into war support from the start, but before the summer of 1942, it was on honour—followed by the patriotic, but still notional. Up to that point, if a woman could manage to get her hands on a pound of sugar to make treats for a Victoria Day garden party, she had a choice. She could follow the spirit of the moment and leave the sugar alone, or she could damn the torpedoes and start whipping cream and rolling out pastry. By Dominion Day 1942, she no longer had the choice. Sugar was the first food item on the ration list in July 1942. This is another case, much like War Savings Stamps, where women were prominent on both sides of the volunteer exchange. When the sugar ration began, every Canadian needed a ration card. A call went out from the Wartime Prices and Trade Board to women's organizations across the country. Chairman Donald Gordon wanted the cards, which needed to be recorded by hand, completed in less than a week. Some eighty thousand Canadian women stepped up for the "gigantic clerical task," according to Marietta McPherson in the August 1942 issue of *Chatelaine*. "Working one, two or three shifts a day according to the local need, the women virtually finished the job in the four days allotted." Chairman Gordon thanked this mob of anonymous women, who, as women had done and would do so many times over the course of the war, silently rose up, conquered, and receded. Gordon noted that their "magnificent contribution" had saved the nation at least half a million dollars. A proud McPherson, in her editorial, wrote, "And now the question is: What other national job do you want done, Ottawa—done well and quickly, and at no cost to the country?"

Those painstakingly recorded cards allotted Canadian adults two hundred grams of sugar each per week, if it was available at all. That's about one cup per person. For perspective, Canadian adults today, on average, eat about a half a cup of sugar every single day. Hopefully those Haligonians liked their every-meal tea strong and not sweet. Anyway, within a month, they'd be glad to have a cup at all; with August came rations on coffee and tea. By December, butter. By March 1943, meat. This was all in the name of ensuring Canadians had an equal share of scarce resources, and that priority went to those fighting, and to bombed-out—and in some cases starving—Britons. Canadians heartily backed these measures. A survey conducted by the Wartime Information Board in 1945 found that 90 percent of Canadians felt that rationing had done a good or fair job of giving Canadians access to food. Given this, few Canadians likely cheated. For those who did, the penalty was fines or imprisonment. But there was a penalty for women either way. If they cheated, they risked the consequences, legal and social. By following the rules, they were forced to feed families without adequate supplies, and to keep up the appearance of womanly perfection and perseverance, as if nothing at all was amiss at the grocery store. How, you ask?

It is here that I have the unfortunate task of telling you about tomato soup cake.

The styled versions of this cake, found on vintage food blogs, make it look like a delicious, if disturbingly reddish, spice cake. Sort of: *Hmmm… red velvet? No, no…that's not quite it….* The grimmer and more realistic online images of this culinary make-do often sport a pinky-orange frosting. (Clearly some present-day bakers have decided to lean in to the tomatoiness.)

I'm no gastronomic prude. It's simply that tomato soup cake, which includes a can of tomato soup, is a symbol of the pretzels into which Second World War women twisted themselves to make it seem as if everything was totally normal. Tomato soup cake was a ration-era favourite not because of the tomato soup, but because it contained only two tablespoons of butter and no eggs. It was a way to make a cake when there was no reasonable way to make a cake. Even when the expectation on women was that they would, nevertheless, make a cake.

Understanding the existence of tomato soup cake, the uninspiringly titled "eggless, butterless, milkless cake," or a recipe for mock brains (a fried meatless puck of onion, flour, egg, thyme, and leftover porridge) isn't merely understanding a culinary conundrum. These recipes help convey the general circumstance of women during the war. Women weren't under less strain than men. No one's saying men had it easy. Pressure isn't a pie with only so many slices to go around. (Or, in keeping with the theme here, pressure isn't mock black pudding.) Men were under unbelievable distress during the war. And women were too. They were coping with family members—often the sole source of family income—away at war and at risk, coping with children and aging family members, coping with the fear of invasion, coping with volunteer, and sometimes paid, work. In Halifax, specifically, they were coping with overcrowding and legitimate fears of German attack, coping with taxed resources and mobs of strangers. Coping with a city that had transformed overnight. This is wholly different anxiety than that faced by the 9th Canadian Infantry Brigade landing on Juno Beach. But as we honour that male strain and sacrifice, we so often categorically fail to recognize that "endurance test" women were put through during war. Women did everything while men worked at war. On top of it all? They had to make a damn cake!

And they had to make it healthful, too. (Well, okay, maybe not the cake, but everything else, and all the time.) Along with the pressure to keep up the appearance that groceries were plentiful and access to them unfettered, there was also pressure on women to keep families healthy. Nutrition was central to this idea. So, even as the availability of food wavered—often failed—and was limited by government decree, the importance of providing food, in adequate amounts and in healthful recipes, not only grew but became a central measure of women's patriotism and commitment to the cause of war.

In 1942, the federal government launched Canada's Official Food Rules, a precursor to Canada's Food Guide. The rules urged citizens, "Eat right, feel right—Canada needs you strong" and enshrined for the first time the daily consumption of specific food groups to meet that end: milk, fruits, vegetables, eggs, cereals and bread, and "meat, fish, etc." This buttressing of health was needed, without question. In 1941, doctors estimated that some 60 percent of Canadians were suffering from vitamin and mineral deficiencies. Rationally, these nutritional shortfalls can't have started with the war. There were shortages of food, yes, but rationing wasn't yet in place. There was no mass starvation that might have created population nutritional deficiencies over a matter of a year and a half. But regardless of when Canadians became vitamin and mineral deficient, the condition wouldn't be tolerated during wartime. "Food is a weapon. Don't waste it!" was one popular American poster aimed at women. "Canada's Faulty Diet is Adolf Hitler's Ally," screamed a *Saturday Night* magazine headline, typical of the time. The messaging was patent: eating well helped the cause. And who determined more than anyone whether their families ate well and followed the food rules? Women. It was the militarization of housework and domestic duties. And it only amped up the pressure on women to do it all with less.

⌒◟ᴧ◞⌒

Economizing didn't only come in the form of saving leftover oatmeal for mock brains. (Sorry, but I just need to say it one last time: *mock brains*.) It came as well in the form of salvage—the collection of myriad household items donated or sold to the war effort, a scrounging made necessary by war production gobbling up added resources at a time when the importation of many raw materials was reduced or halted. "Yet again," wrote Sharon MacDonald in *Hidden Costs, Hidden Labours*, "government relied on women to take charge."

Salvage was another of those wartime endeavours that was multi-levelled. It was decreed by government. But it was organized by community or city committee and enacted in the home. Salvage wouldn't have happened without government deciding it was necessary and important enough to pay for, and without the feds having the money to cough up to make it real. The so-often forgotten half of the equation is that these items would never have made it to the war effort at all without community organizing, and without women in their homes, day after day after day, doing the actual work. It's the nature of that work that makes it invisible. A woman cooks a chicken for dinner. She heats up the oven and puts the bird in, she peels and boils potatoes, she dumps a container of beans she canned the fall before into a pot on the stove; she carves the chicken, makes the gravy, sets the table; she clears the table, scrapes the plates, sets aside the bones and cleans them, does the dishes, and on and on and on. Only one part of that process serves salvage—cleaning the bones. It's...well, it's kind of nothing. She was saving the bones anyway, probably, for stock. But that tiny measure makes everything up the chain of salvage possible. Salvage, seen this way, is understood for what it was: a deed slipped into the run of the everyday that, over years, and repeated by millions of women, made the entire practice possible. Without those bones saved and cleaned, the country's capacity to make war is hampered or halted.

The chicken bones, and those from other animals (bad news for Atlantic Canada: fish bones weren't on the national salvage list), were needed to make glue for aircraft. Animal fats were essential for making glycerine for explosives. Prepping these fats was no enviable task. Salvage depots paid four cents per pound, but drippings had to be rendered. The messy rendering of animal fat was probably the worst salvage task, but, generally, the list of salvage items was stupefying.

Plus, there was a national list as well as individual area lists. In many cases, proper preparation was complex. Of use? Newspaper, scrap paper, wrapping paper, boxes and cartons, old tires, waste rubber (think: a leaking hot water bottle), leather, old shoes, string, and cork. Rags were collected, as well as old clothing and carpets. Intact and broken glass was salvaged, as well as stoneware jars. Each quality and kind of glass had to be separate and each commanded a different price from the salvage depot. Magazines and books were saved to be distributed as reading material for troop ships, in hospitals, and in hostels where service members were waiting to ship out. A vast number made their way from all across the country to Halifax where they were best put to use. Tin cans were, at one point in the war, only collected in the Toronto area; according to a National Salvage Division memo, that was the only place they could be "advantageously salvaged." The metal in other kinds of disposable containers, like toothpaste and shaving cream tubes, also depended on what the memo called "local considerations." But the foil from cigarette packaging, the kind Jackie Wrixon saved from her parents, was on the nationally needed list, along with other kinds of tinfoil, all of which were flattened, never rolled. Anything made of iron, steel, aluminum, brass, copper, bronze, lead, or zinc was of use, so items in the home that were no longer needed or working were handed over.

A poster produced by Ottawa's National Salvage Office shows three determined-looking women (plus a Scottie dog!) marching forward with their salvage in arm—a cast iron pan, pots, spatulas, and a stovetop coffee percolator included. One of the women carries a metal bridge lamp that I would very much like to see in my living room, and which she no doubt wanted to continue to see in hers as well. But the message here is clear. This is duty. Even the dog carries her bone to the salvage depot. "We're in the army now," the poster reads. This was the same flavour of militarization of the volunteer and domestic efforts of women seen with food rationing and keeping families healthy. *Chatelaine* declared: "Canada's Housewives are Canada's Housesoldiers!"

One thing's for certain: these women, while "soldiers," were the grunts and not the officers in this grand brigade. The breakdown of salvage labour follows a familiar pattern. The tip of the pyramid is government. In other words, a handful of men, paid for their work (the first woman ever to serve in a Canadian federal cabinet role wasn't until 1957, so set that notion aside). These pyramid-topping men set in motion the massive machine of salvage. Next, salvage committees formed across the country in cities and rural areas. Again, almost exclusively men, a handful in each locale, who volunteered their time in organizing the receipt of items. The base of this pyramid? Volunteer women, doing the actual salvaging, holding the whole thing up. Sometimes women and children took the salvage items to regulated depots themselves, as Jackie Eisner did. Sometimes, especially in rural areas, salvage committees would organize transport by vehicle.

The feds understood the pyramid. They understood it even if, during the war and in the years after, the specific contributions of women went publicly unnoticed. In a confidential letter from May 1943, Hector B. McKinnon, a member of the Wartime Prices and Trade Board, wrote to National War Services deputy minister Chester Payne about the critical shortage of salvage fats for war production and his desire to collect "every drop" from Canadian homes. "During the past four months," he writes, "this Department has already spent some $90,000 on advertising designed to express this necessity on housewives. It is vitally necessary to continue this campaign to overcome public inertia and to keep the housewife conscious of the urgency of conserving waste fats regularly, on a large scale basis."

Money wasn't only spent on campaigns to urge women to save fat. Harvey Norman Mckenzie Stanbury, salvage organizer for all of the Maritimes, wrote in March 1943 to Charles LaFerle, the National Salvage Division director, about two hundred and fifty posters he had received from the manager of the Casino Theatre in Halifax, promoting the new Noël Coward film, *In Which We Serve*. The film was released in the UK in fall 1942 and made its way to Halifax in spring 1943, screening at the thousand-seat Casino on Gottingen Street. Stanbury writes that he knows the Boy Scouts are planning a rubber drive for the following month and informs his boss that he's handed over the posters to them to put up.

In Which We Serve could charitably be called patriotic, but it was, in fact, developed in cahoots with the propaganda arm of the British government, the Ministry of Information. One of the many posters for the movie shows a uniformed man, kneeling in front of his stricken wife and children. In an adjacent shot, he and two others are in the waves. "A few days after Commander Kinross said goodbye to his family," the poster reads, "his ship, the *Torrin*, was hit by a Stuka diver and went to the bottom of the sea. He and some of his men swam in the Mediterranean, clinging to a rubber float." In case the connection to salvage is unclear, the poster drills home the italics-laden message that these men owe their lives to that hunk of rubber. "That is why you ought to turn in *more scrap rubber* than you have been turning in. The bathmat that you yank out of your tub may turn up as part of a life belt in the Pacific. Maybe you didn't think of it like that—but that's how it is—exactly! Will you *right now* (not tomorrow or the day after) go once more through every room in your house—will you once again look to see if you can't find still one or two more pieces of rubber that you can do without? Glance once more at that picture above—and then *try* to say no!" Not subtle. But, then, there was no room for subtlety. The country needed rubber. And to get rubber, the same pattern of labour would play out as it did with War Savings Stamps. Women would help oversee their Boy Scout children putting up posters, then women would help oversee their

Boy Scout children collecting rubber, and then, as the poster suggests, women would scour their homes for...rubber. The voluntary work of women was piled on by the voluntary work of their children.

⌒ᨆ⌒

Scrimping, in all forms, was the work of women during war.

And that message was never more overt than in media. Examples abound beyond the *In Which We Serve* poster. CBC Radio aired features that targeted Canadian women and taught them how to "make do with less." Antigonish, Nova Scotia's *The Maritime Co-Operator* (written, edited, and managed by women and for women) produced numerous editorials on proper salvage techniques. *Chatelaine* pitched belt-tightening as an Allies-versus-Axis competition with catchy headlines like, "Housewife Versus Hausfrau in the Battle of Salvage!"

When Finance Minister J. L. Ilsley was touring around, delivering his early-war "Pay-As-We-Go" pitches to chambers of commerce and various men's clubs, he was talking to men. But he was speaking to women. "We must work harder, deny ourselves luxuries, reduce our average national standard of living," he told one Calgary audience. "Judge each object on which you may wish to make an expenditure not by whether it is good, but rather by whether it is indispensable." This exhortation implies something: that the majority of Canadians had disposable income to spend on luxuries. In reality, most women did not. Certainly, there was a generation of affluent women during the war newly faced with the question of need-versus-want. (As Ruth Roach Pierson writes in *They're Still Women After All*, during the war, "wealthier women learned for the first time during the war to remake old clothes into new outfits and to curtail their buying of consumer products.") But most Canadian women had already been forced to practice severe economies during the Depression. The war was largely a continuation of that.

The National Selective Service, a new federal government department founded by Prime Minister King in 1941, made coordinated efforts to encourage women to work in war industries and to enlist in women's divisions of the Army, Navy, and Air Force. Women needed persuading to engage in this work, which was new to them, and which had been at best frowned upon and at worst prohibited before the war. But volunteering? Totally different. Volunteering was back-of-their-hand familiar. The norm. Governments didn't have to nudge women to step up to help. Women just did it. Sharon MacDonald reports in *Hidden Costs, Hidden Labours*, for example, that immediately at the war's outset, salvage initiatives were launched by myriad women's groups. "By the time the government created the National Salvage Division [in January 1941], many community salvage projects were already in place."

By the time the feds got around to formalizing matters—by the time it asked civilians to take part—women were already on top of it. They had been for almost a year and a half.

Chapter Four

MA, I MISS YOUR APPLE PIE

October 20, 1944. It was a big night, an absolute flurry, at the North End Services Canteen.

Joyce Ripley was working the desserts window, serving, she's pretty sure, Jell-O, to three hundred and seventy-five servicemen, one after another, polite as all get out. They were mostly naval personnel, and some merchant mariners, who were desperate for friendly faces and a good meal. And a good meal this was—roast beef, mashed potatoes with gravy—"always gravy," Joyce says—plus another vegetable: carrots or peas. The North End Services Canteen was a dry establishment. That meant milk or tomato juice to drink. After the meal? Tea or coffee. Nothing stronger. The women in the heat of the kitchen were north-end Halifax locals: a cook and two assistant cooks, who would prepare, at the canteen's busiest time, two hot meals a day, seven days a week. Normally three hundred men at a time. Some nights, like October 20, 1944, there were more. During 1944 alone, the North End Services Canteen served 220,462 meals, plus sandwiches to order at all hours, and free coffee and doughnuts on Sundays. "I don't know," Joyce says, "how in the *world* they managed."

At the desserts window, the third of three purpose-built passthroughs in the giant hall on Barrington Street, Joyce, then seventeen,

Servicemen gathered around the desserts window at the North End Services Canteen. (NS ARCHIVES)

knew the drill. She had been volunteering at the canteen since late August and had logged forty-four hours by then, in four-hour shifts. She was there almost every Friday, plus the occasional Sunday when she was called upon. Other volunteers worked other shifts, and might not even see each other. There were about 130 in all. There was a lot to get done. Through its tenure, the canteen would feed, entertain, and provide everyday kindnesses to service members. Early on, the women leaders organized one-off afternoon tea or ice cream parties, and bilingual concerts for French ships' companies, hiring, on one occasion, two Birney Cars, or electric tram cars, to return the French naval ratings to their ships at evening's end. How? All of it was by reaching out to friends and organizations to see who could help. Who had a car to take groups of naval ratings (any member who wasn't an officer) for country drives? Who could find a supply of candy for a special

the VOLUNTEERS

occasion? Who knew someone at some organization who might sponsor a movie night? Who had an extra set of Christmas wreaths? An extra set of hands? Many times, organizers simply paid out of their own pockets.

Joyce and two other volunteers would don their North End Services Canteen smocks and smile and pass, smile and pass, smile and pass as the men came up to each successive serving window from their long communal tables. The jukebox, a favourite among the men, provided the dinner entertainment. Sometimes they played Vera Lynn, but tonight it was a Deanna Durbin song on repeat. "They played it over and over," Joyce says. It was probably the Irving Berlin classic "Always," which was enjoying a resurgence after Durbin sang it in *Christmas Holiday*, a June 1944 film release co-starring Gene Kelly.

Joyce and her friends Glorena and Honey arrived every Friday for their shift at 4:00 P.M., to help set up. They set the tables with salt and pepper and ketchup and did whatever else they were called on to take care of by the convener—their volunteer supervisor, who was also in charge of taking tickets as the men filed in. The girls didn't clear, and they didn't load the dishwasher, an eight-foot-long hooded conveyor belt that pelted soapy water at the china and glasses. Some evenings, Joyce served the vegetables. The cooks would plate the meat—only the cooks were permitted to do this—and pass it on to the vegetable servers. The men could indicate their preferences at each window. Usually that preference was dead simple: as much as possible of everything on offer. "Not any of them refused." The men lined up outside, in any weather, for these dinners. It was an irony, decidedly. Both the men and the volunteers were serving the war effort, but while the men sought the simple pleasures of stability, a home-cooked meal, and conversation, teen volunteers like Joyce Ripley, who later married and became Joyce Purchase, sought the opposite—excitement and being part of the action. And each group found what they were after, without question, at the North End Services Canteen.

In fact, there were two North End Services Canteens; the first was held together by spit and baling wire.

That canteen was launched, hastily, in the parish hall behind Gottingen Street's St. Mark's Anglican Church, conveniently close to Stadacona. The entrance was on Russell Street—two steps up to a single wooden door leading to a large, one-and-a-half-storey assembly hall. There was a small stage with a piano at one end, a pot-belly stove with a prominent pipe, and on an adjacent wall, a single six-foot-long pass-through window to the kitchen. They cooked on what organizer Dolly McEuen called "a miserable little four-ring gas cooker" and a small second-hand coal stove, a "temperamental affair." Somehow, these women fed hundreds, daily, on materially less cooking power and reliability than I have in my kitchen today. For dinners, the volunteer women set up three long tables with plastic covers, two dozen to a table. The rest sat at circular tables, six or eight a bunch, or on chairs alone, balancing plates on their laps. After the meal, the tables would be cleared and piled onto the stage. Musicians crammed up there, too, accordionists working not to clang elbows against a forest of up-turned wooden table legs. This scrappy space, where decorations were cheap and cheerful (and in most cases probably begged and borrowed), was where my grandparents, Ted and Marie, met.

The women of the North End Services Canteen created the first voluntary organization in Halifax to serve Navy, Air Force, and Army members, as well as merchant mariners, that wasn't a branch of a larger national organization. The canteen was defiantly grassroots. It also wasn't merely first; it was first and *fast*. War came to Canada on September 10, 1939. A Sunday. Five weeks less a day later, on Saturday, October 14, Hugh "Uncle Mel" Mills was master of ceremonies for the opening night dance. There were 450 attendees, including local women and men from Allied nation forces and the Merchant Navy. On offer? Chocolate bars and cigarettes, purchased by the organizers with one hundred dollars in seed money from the Royal Canadian Navy. The women had a wooden banner made to hang above the door frame and had another hanging sign installed perpendicular to the building that could be seen from Gottingen Street. They chose a motto. "Welcome, Jack, Where Hast Thou Been?" It was a fitting welcome, with "Jack" standing in for any anonymous service member who might be lured through the threshold. But it's also a line from Shakespeare's *Henry IV*, Part 1, Act 2, Scene 4, in which the war-obsessed and pugnacious Hotspur musters for battle, while his sharp-tempered, and politically savvy wife, Lady Percy, questions his preparation and reasoning. She suggests that he might be better prepared for war if he had rest, recreation, and a good meal. Whether this was a morsel of rich coincidence, or a sly dig at the federal organizers of a massive war effort, there is no record. But it's still delicious.

The immediate ramping-up of the canteen's work is a case study in the contrast between the lumbering movements of the federal government when it came to matters that didn't have to do with battle and supply, and the nimbleness and effectiveness of small bands of word-of-mouth–organized women who were accustomed to seeing need, stepping up, and who didn't have bureaucracy to bind them. Whether the feds were too busy to look or wilfully blind, "women were already there," notes Sharon MacDonald in *Hidden Costs, Hidden Labours*, "organized and ready to work, and then some." The need women saw was, in fact, all around them. It was Halifax's deluge of service members and merchant mariners, who, when off-duty, trawled the streets around downtown, Stadacona, and the north end with nothing but time on their hands. "There was little for them to do," writes William D. Naftel in *Halifax at War*, "but wander aimlessly up and down the main streets of the city quite at a loss about how to cope with them."

Luckily, a klatch of naval officers' wives, led by the indomitable Dolly McEuen, had some ideas. Where the feds stalled, the women stepped up.

Sunday theatrical and concert performances—care of the Halifax Concert Party Guild—were organized weekly for between five hundred and eight hundred men. Other times, they showed movies. During the days, while women prepped and cooked, the dining tables were used for games, and desks with stationery were available for letter-writing. There was Ping-Pong. Then they started daily lunches. Dances carried on and increased in popularity: they were held every Tuesday, Thursday, and Saturday. In fact, they were so popular, the floor collapsed. This was all before the end of 1939—within ten weeks of opening. While the repairs were made (at a cost of $1,250, covered by the Canadian Legion War Services), the women, undeterred, picked up the whole operation and moved to the Dalhousie University gymnasium for a Christmas dinner-dance. These were not women who halted in the face of challenge. They didn't endlessly assess. They enacted Plan B, called in favours—such as soliciting the Legion to pay for the new floor and petitioning the Dalhousie Board of Governors to grant the use of the gym—and got on with the work. As Lorna Inness reported in the *Halifax Mail-Star* in an October 1969 retrospective, at one point, when the city's north end was without water for forty-eight hours, the canteen managed by getting Farmers Dairy and the Dalhousie University department of biochemistry to give them drums of potable water. When shortages saw them go three weeks without eggs, the cooks served marmalade, cheese, or peanut butter sandwiches instead of the usual egg salad.

This was, in broad strokes, the yeoman's work of the many Halifax women volunteers who were unaffiliated, such as those who simply welcomed service members into their homes for tea or meals, or those who worked with grassroots and small organizations like the North End Services Canteen. It was meeting those in need where they were and providing what was called for. These were often small comforts, but crucial ones, such as care packages. Often the goods or funds were donated by larger organizations, and local women came together to create them.

For example, with the financial support of fundraising groups like the Australian Comforts Fund and the New Zealand Patriotic Funds Club, Halifax women put together care packages for each member of the Australian and New Zealand armed forces stationed in the city. They were a combination of necessities and luxuries: soap, razor blades, shoelaces, toothbrushes, tobacco, canned fruit, honey, and writing paper.

"Mothers' corners" are another good example of this small-but-essential labour. These booths were set up inside larger organizations, usually recreation centres or hostels. At them, servicemen could have a button sewn on a jacket, have a shirt pressed, or just enjoy a tea and a chat—no small matter to a nineteen-year-old from a small town half a continent from home, alone, and away for the first time awaiting deployment. The mothers' corner at the Argyle Street Hostel, one of several in the city, was staffed by volunteer women for three shifts weekly for the entire duration of the war. The women there had in excess of forty-three thousand interactions with service members. What else to call them? Connections? Contacts? No word quite captures the spirit. And the numbers make it sound clinical, meaningless. But these fleeting relationships mattered, even if few outside those affected or involved understood the value, and fewer still recognized it, then or today.

⌒⌒⌒

Back in the kitchen at the North End Services Canteen, cook Annie Henneberry held hostage a glistening brown roast turkey, legs up in the shallow pan in front of her. Two women behind her, one likely her assistant cook, Maud Robinson, carved one of several other turkeys while other volunteers worked at the same long harvest table. Annie's grey-streaked hair was pulled back tightly in a bun. She wielded her own large knife over the bird in front of her. Though a nearby four-tier shelf was filled with plated foods, probably desserts, there was a lot yet to be done. Condiments and tablecloths still needed to be put out. It was Christmas and the shipment of birds for the big dinner was delayed, only arriving a few hours before. Beside a three-foot-high white sign with bold all-caps: NO SMOKING ALLOWED IN THE KITCHEN, a gaggle of servicemen leaned through the pass-through window. They could smell what had just come out of the oven. Annie came on as a paid staff member at the canteen in April 1940. She oversaw kitchen operations—the making and serving of fourteen hundred sandwiches daily, plus another thousand for a dance, the pouring of three hundred quarts of milk, the roasting of one hundred pounds of meat. In two years, Annie Henneberry cooked four hundred thousand hot meals.

I know practically nothing about her.

Annie might have been Annie Permelia Henneberry, who was born a Cole, in either 1884 or 1885. That birthdate would track with her possible age at the time she was a cook at the canteen. Or, then again, maybe that's not her. Annie is a mystery. Likewise, her assistant, Maud Robinson. Was she Maud Amelia Robinson, who perhaps never married and was born in 1895? Was she Maud M. Beaver, who married in 1919 and moved to the north end from Mushaboom, Nova Scotia? Or was she any of the other Maud Robinsons in the Nova Scotia Vital Statistics database? Another enigma: Miss Alice O'Brian, or O'Brien, listed early on as co-controller of the canteen. As a "Miss," she wouldn't have been a naval officer's wife from another province, as many of the North End Services Canteen organizers were. So, then, who was she? Mrs. V. S. Godfrey was the canteen's inaugural president—the one who oversaw the floor replacement after the collapse. Godfrey's case illustrates a frequent problem with identifying women of the past: the "Mrs." tells us she's married. Good start. But it also tells us that her husband's name is V. S. Godfrey, not hers. There's no V. S. Godfrey in the Vital Statistics database for Nova Scotia, which represents a dead end. But it turns out Godfrey was a prominent naval officer, and, so, traceable, which at least points in the direction of his wife. Commander Valentine "Val" Stuart Godfrey arrived in Halifax in 1936 or 1937 as an inspector of naval ordnance. He acted as Aide de Camp to the Lieutenant Governor. Because he was an officer, he would have had permanent and comfortable accommodations in Halifax, unlike the scores of enlisted men hanging hammocks any place they could find space. That means Godfrey's wife was practically certain to be with him during this time, and her name was…Margaret Horton Hardie Godfrey. As the wife of an officer, Margaret Godfrey would have known and socialized with other officers' wives, and she may likely have run in the same circles as Haligonians like Hugh and Jean Mills. Hugh, the co-owner of Mills Brothers (the city's poshest department store, on Spring Garden Road), ran the Halifax Concert Party Guild. Jean was on the North End Services Canteen's executive and was the liaison for entertainment. It's almost certain that Godfrey would have been drawn into volunteering through one or another, or all, of these women.

Primary among them was Dolly McEuen. You'll want to remember that name.

———∿———

Dolly came to Halifax from Montreal in 1939. I would write, "following" her husband Charles Stuart McEuen, a surgeon and acting Lieutenant-Commander, but I've spent a few years thinking about, researching, and, frankly, admiring Dolly, and I don't think she abided much in the way of following anyone. Dolly landed in a suite at the upscale Lord Nelson Hotel, overlooking the Halifax Public Gardens, in September 1939. She promptly threw herself in. You have to wonder if she even unpacked before she started what would be the whirlwind, and occasional hurricane, of her personal volunteer mission.

Dolly's first stop was the North End Services Canteen, which she co-founded. At the canteen, Dolly, who wasn't out of place in a fox stole shoulder wrap with leg clasps, went to work. She served as co-controller and on the food committee, among other roles. She made tea; she made sandwiches. In a letter to canteen fund donors, she wrote, "I have myself washed up over 600 dishes at the end of a busy shift." She also notes that during the time of writing, which, while undated, must be in early 1940, after Christmas but before Annie Henneberry came on as cook in April, that there was simply no money in the canteen's "slim bank account" to consider paid help. Indeed, she notes that deficits have been covered by a special fund, "gifts from ourselves and friends." She had a habit of paying for things herself, and of calling in financial favours from central Canadians. She knew how to get shit done. In the letter, Dolly mentions a "Thé dansant" and a high tea with ice cream, both held for Boy Seamen off British battleships, the expense of which was shouldered by "Halifax friends." It's clear Dolly wasn't only up to her elbows in grey, greasy dishwater. The woman was a master-class networker. One thing, though. Dolly says something in her letter that tips her as a come-from-away: "I do not hesitate to say that this work which we are doing is outstanding." No Nova Scotian would ever declare that so boldly. It was true, of course. And someone needed to say it, to give voice to the endless work of these women. But it's not in the culture now, nor was it in the culture then, to speak those kinds of truths. She went further. "I feel very strongly that the rest of Canada is quite unaware of our problems and the work which we are doing." This forthrightness was indicative of Dolly's character. And it makes me admire her all the more; not only for her hard work, but for her shaking up of this wet blanket town, with its stodginess and blinkered mores. But Dolly's frankness and fearlessness would set her up for unfair attack in her next, even larger, volunteer venture, the Ajax Club. We'll get to that. But during late 1939 and through 1940, Dolly would be insulated from criticism by way of her joint leadership of the canteen with members of Halifax's "Old 400s," an informal term for the city's wealthy, WASPy establishment families. Chief among them: the Macneills.

Murray Macneill and Kathleen Holmes Macneill had three daughters. Each lived a life writ large. Edith and Janet would become officers' wives. That characterization, seen alone, does these women a decided disservice, but it helps explain their seats at the North End Services Canteen executive table. Isabel, the middle sister, never married, instead becoming a naval officer herself. All three sisters befriended Dolly and joined the canteen in a variety of roles: treasurer, secretary, promotions. All three sisters no doubt made their share of sandwiches, as well as calling in their share of favours from family friends and other Old 400s. Isabel pulled back from her volunteer duties when she became part of the first Women's Royal Canadian Naval Service trainees. She rose to the rank of Lieutenant-Commander in June 1944, the first woman to do so, and the only woman to hold that rank during the war. Janet carried on as a volunteer through the war. Edith would go on to found the local chapter of the Women's Voluntary Services.

We know these women today largely because of their social status. Murray Macneill—Edith, Isabel, and Janet's father—was a prominent professor and registrar at Dalhousie. He skipped the Nova Scotia provincial curling team that won the inaugural Brier tournament. His first cousin was Lucy Maud Montgomery. Yes, *that* Lucy Maud Montgomery, of *Anne of Green Gables* fame. His daughters studied at prestigious schools and had the advantage of money and connections. Janet's first husband was Peter Aitken, the son of William Maxwell Aitken, 1st Baron Beaverbrook.

None of this privilege takes away from these women's work, but it's important to recognize that their toil was matched in intensity and commitment by many. We simply don't know the names or the stories of the scads of other women putting in time. (And, look, it's not like Edith Macneill or Dolly McEuen are household names, even in Halifax feminist circles.)

In Annie Henneberry and Maud Robinson's North End Services Canteen kitchen, for example, there were twenty-one weekly volunteer kitchen-helper shifts. Each shift required the commitment of a cook and an assistant, usually Annie and her sidekick Maud, plus eight others. That's 168 additional volunteer shifts every single week, and we don't have a sweet clue who did that work. The shifts were filled by friends and friends of friends, by word of mouth, and by those who signed on to be farmed out for volunteer hours through the Canadian Legion, the Red Cross, the Women's Voluntary Services, and other larger organizations. It was different for men. Even the lowest-ranked soldiers, sailors or airmen were on unit, ship, or squadron lists. We can pin them down today. Merchant mariners, notoriously difficult to trace because they lack official federal employment files, can still be found through crew registers if the name of the vessel is known. Women volunteers? We know only a few.

Class divisions often determined hierarchies within organizations, and so the names and stories of some were prioritized over the names and stories of others. But consider the intersectionality, too. All the workers who volunteered at the North End Services Canteen, and all the servicemen and merchant mariners who visited the canteen, were white. Black service members spent their off-duty time at Gerrish Street Hall, where they could hear music and enjoy dances and games and meals, and where workers were Black and African Nova Scotian. The official record contains comparatively little about the volunteers at Gerrish Street Hall and their work. (It was the same with other communities. Greek and Jewish women held dinners for members of their communities who were awaiting deployment or on leave, mostly in churches and synagogues.) This strict, if unspoken, segregation was at the time accepted as the norm. It's not like there was an official list of what families comprised the establishment and what families didn't. And there were, of course, prominent African Nova Scotian families in twentieth-century Halifax—such as those of William Pearly Oliver, a community organizer, preacher, and educator, and Portia White, the international opera singer, whose father, William Andrew White, was the second African Nova Scotian to obtain a degree from Acadia University and who, in the First World War, helped form the famous No. 2 Construction Battalion.

But I can all but guarantee: the Old 400s didn't include families that were Black.

—⌣⋏⌣—

"One can assume that women have always found opportunities and reasons to work together informally in single-sex groupings," writes Sharon MacDonald in *Hidden Costs, Hidden Labours*. "To know exactly when they first started organizing in formal ways would be difficult to determine." MacDonald, in her research, tracked the earliest written records in Nova Scotia to women's organizations of the nineteenth century—benevolent societies "aimed at helping the sick, the poor, the orphaned and the widowed." But, as she concedes, this is far from believable as the *start* of women's volunteering.

Women have always helped stitch communities together. And that work has often been dismissed by those in power and in charge. Remember the dual insult of National War Services Minister J. T. Thorson's January 1942 scheme to ask citizen committees to take on volunteer work, and Defence Minister James Ralston's "gravest doubts" that these committees were up to the task? Ralston questioned the capability of women to support those in their midst; Thorson didn't even know the extent of the work women had already taken on. And those two weren't the first or the only men to brand women's grassroots voluntary labour as some kind of new or half-hearted enterprise. In *Hidden Costs, Hidden Labours*, MacDonald cites Prime Minister Mackenzie King's "patronizing attitude," when he initiated, in the fall of 1941, the Canadian Women's Voluntary Services organization, noting in an address to the House of Commons that "the department will be entrusted with the duty of directing and mobilizing the activities of thousands of our citizens who are seeking practical and useful outlets for their enthusiasm and patriotism"—as if women were sitting on their hands, desperate for King to tell them their next move.

So, before King's speech and after, women did the volunteering they had always been doing. But there was a tension—subtle—between the work of national organizations and smaller groups of unaffiliated volunteers. This friction is evident in several documents at Library and Archives Canada's Voluntary and Auxiliary Services files. For example, Mrs. Edith Angus, of the Winnipeg branch of the Imperial Order Daughters of the Empire (IODE), an international women's charitable organization, wrote on May 11, 1944, to National War Services Minister Léo Richer LaFlèche, complaining about the "untimely interference of local citizens committees disrupting the continuity of programmes of National Organizations." Petty squabble or fair criticism? Whatever the case, Angus is deeply irked about these unaffiliated volunteers. Where the enmity came from isn't clear. Nationally unaffiliated groups had somewhat greater freedom, which may have ruffled the feathers of those who were part of bigger organizations with deeper layers of bureaucracy. Co-controller Dolly McEuen, for example, didn't register the North End Services Canteen Fund under the War Charities Act until November 1939, a month after the canteen was fully operational and serving thousands. Technically, they couldn't collect money for operations without that okay. But urgency (and, frankly, common sense) moved them to prefer forgiveness-begging over permission-asking. They collected the money they needed and got themselves to work. That action, to people more constrained by or interested in procedure, may have seemed like the canteen and its executive were playing fast and loose with the rules.

National organizations like the IODE, the Red Cross, the St. John Ambulance Brigade, and others had been in existence before the war. In fact, before the First World War. These groups were well-funded, well-oiled, and well-populated with volunteers. They knew what they were doing. But it wasn't all clear sailing. As far back as 1941, there was mounting conflict between the Red Cross and the St. John Ambulance Brigade because both wanted to be included in coordinated national fundraising appeals. According to archival documents, there was concern on both sides about the duplication of their volunteer efforts and how that might affect the funds they would collect in any appeals. A federal memo indicates that they eventually, with a good dose of mediation from the federal government, agreed to split duties—the St. John Ambulance Brigade would take care of the instruction of first aid, home nursing, and stretcher-bearing. The Red Cross would, among other established duties, collect relief funds and materials, and supervise the distribution of these goods and money. A May 26, 1942, memo to Thorson from National War Services Deputy Minister T. C. Davis contains twenty-one points outlining infighting among national organizations. This memo may have sprung from a January 16, 1942, personal letter Davis received from G. D. Conant, the Ontario attorney general. The letter is a relaxed—"Dear Tom"—rebuke of several national volunteer organizations Conant knows are at each other's throats (and who were also facing internal strife, though that wasn't one of Conant's complaints on this day). "These are not waters in which I care to swim," Conant wrote. "I see nothing but trouble for anybody who undertakes it. As it is not my duty in any event, I have decided to keep out of it."

The documentation of these battles and tensions pales, in Library and Archives Canada files, in comparison to the layers of challenges faced by the federal government in dealing with fundraising, and the fragile egos, or specific demands, of some donors. Mobile canteens were greatly needed in Britain because of bombing campaigns, including the Blitz. (A moment's disambiguation. There are two types of mobile canteens: a trailer-type, used to supply coffee, tea, and sandwiches, which could be found in wartime Halifax at the port when ships were arriving and departing, as well

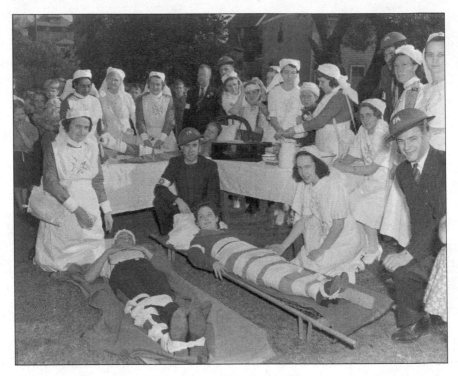

A training day for members of the Halifax North (Women's) Division of the St. John Ambulance Brigade, September 1942. (NS ARCHIVES)

as at outposts; and a mobile kitchen-type canteen, used for emergency food where people were bombed out of their homes.) Pages and pages of federal government memos from 1941 comprise correspondence about the volunteer funding of these mini-kitchen canteens, and various attendant snags and onerousness. In a December 17, 1941, confidential letter, Norman Robertson, the Under-Secretary of State for External Affairs, fills in minister T. C. Davis on a letter recently intercepted by Canadian postal censors. The missive was flagged because it contained an outline of "the shortcomings of the Canadian and United Kingdom authorities," on the topic of mobile canteen gifts. The gist of the criticism: people are not being thanked enough.

It wasn't only mobile canteens. Two days later, on December 19, 1941, Davis wrote Colonel A. A. Magee, executive assistant to the national defence minister. Davis was following up on a $1,750 cheque he recently handed to Magee from the warden of the County of Pontiac, northwest of Ottawa, to fund an ambulance in the UK. He writes that the warden requests recognition, painted on the ambulance, that the gift has been purchased by the people of Pontiac. The year before, it seems, the Association of Rural Municipalities of Saskatchewan funded a mobile canteen and had similar recognition painted on the canteen's side. When a photo of the painted recognition was printed in the local paper, it resulted in an additional $4,000 being donated. Davis, a mercenary with a cause, writes that he is fully behind the request for Pontiac to be recognized. This is the finicky business of so much of the work of the National War Services department—the delicate dance of keeping donors happy and of wading through the bureaucracy of government. And because of their size and government affiliation, similar bureaucracy afflicted larger national organizations like the Red Cross, St. John Ambulance Brigade, and the IODE. I can understand why many women preferred to remain unaffiliated in their voluntary work.

Red tape and protocol aside, the work of these national volunteer bodies is astounding. There were thirteen nursing divisions of the St. John Ambulance Brigade in Halifax alone, who contributed more than two hundred thousand hours of nursing aid over the war. The output of knitted comforts from the Red Cross was prodigious. For 1945 alone, 42,282 pairs of mittens and scarves were produced, 4,664 quilts were sewn for civilian relief, and 33,263 surgical dressings were created for field hospitals. The Red Cross also staffed hospital and troop trains leaving Halifax. During the war, 411 such trains departed, with a Red Cross representative on board every single one, distributing writing supplies and stamps, snacks such as chocolate bars, fruit, and gum, and diversions like newspapers, magazines, and games. Each service member also received a small comfort kit, which volunteer women had put together; it included a razor, shaving cream, blades, a toothbrush and toothpaste, a styptic pencil, comb, Band-Aids, and a "housewife"—the unfortunate term for a small mending kit.

This book focusses more on the stories of smaller organizations and unaffiliated women volunteers, even though there's much more documentation of nationally affiliated groups. But in a sense, it's part of the same parcel. In all cases, whether it's a church auxiliary under the auspices of the Red Cross sewing thousands of quilts, or the solitary act of a woman welcoming a service member into her home for tea, these are individual acts on behalf of individual women. The big service organizations moved mountains, but relying on those massive numbers, where they exist, also somewhat negates the idea of the self-moving individual as the power behind the volunteering. I would argue that's the piece that needs remembering, like the story of an Annapolis Valley woman who saved $150 to send overseas for distribution to war-affected citizens in England by doing housekeeping for others. What also needs cementing is that so much of the work was undertaken by women, at home, doing bits and bobs with the leftover moments of their days. In reality, many Halifax women did double duty, assisting both big organizations and small ones, just as there was significant cooperation between the national groups and local ones, at times. Affiliated and unaffiliated volunteer work weren't competing measures, but complementary. Big organizations knew what was needed in broad strokes, on national and international levels, and they got the work done. Smaller groups and unaffiliated women knew what was needed in their communities, and on their streets and doorsteps. And they, likewise, got the work done. They knew what to do. And they did it.

⌣⌢⌣

Back at the North End Services Canteen, Dolly, Isabel, Edith and the gang knew this: they needed more space. Even before the floor collapse, which happened within weeks of its late 1939 opening, the canteen was already overtaxed. The replacement and repairs took place relatively swiftly and operations barely blinked, as evidenced by the Christmas dinner-dance in the Dalhousie University gymnasium. But the organizers were daily living and breathing the need they saw among Allied service members and merchant mariners. They had no reason to think the war would be over in mere months. They knew what was needed.

Who didn't know what was needed? George Pifher, the Voluntary and Auxiliary Services director, under the National War Services department. Pifher told his boss, T. C. Davis, in an April 24, 1941, communiqué, that the North End Services Canteen was just fine where it was in the old church hall. This memo seems likely to have been part of the internal discussions around a funding request from the canteen, which had struck a new building committee in December 1940, in recognition of the significant overcrowding and ever-mounting need for services. Pifher noted that the Red Cross was donating $20,000 toward a new canteen, but, to his mind, "The facilities of the hall are equal to the facilities of any recreation hut operated by the National Organizations in any of the camps I visited." More than anything, perhaps, this spoke to the dire state of recreation services on offer. He conceded to Davis that the space was "at one time condemned because the floor gave way," but since the floor's replacement, he said, "the hall is now satisfactory for the services rendered." Despite Pifher's from-afar shoot-down, the women cracked on, determined to one day celebrate cooking their last meal on that miserable little four-ring gas cooker.

The canteen executive secured a triangle of land, donated by Halifax Shipyards Limited, and the services of prominent architect Sydney Perry Dumaresq. They raised $54,261 for construction. That they pooh-poohed Pifher and took matters into their own hands was not only a function of the fact that they believed in their cause and deeply understood the needs the canteen met. They also had the benefit of being well-heeled and well-connected. But there's another factor as well: they were toiling outside the more rule- and bureaucracy-bound confines of the government or large volunteer organizations. They were a force unto themselves. And, in as diplomatic a manner as possible, they created the playbook themselves.

The new building opened on September 15, 1941, a grey wood-clad industrial hall, on Barrington Street between Devonshire Avenue and Young Street, almost right at the waterfront and still close to Stadacona. Any service member who accidentally wound up at the old canteen would only need to walk two blocks east down Russell Street, where it spilled onto Barrington. The new canteen would be in sight. A beacon, with four—*four*—new stoves. In their roughly two years in St. Mark's Church Hall, the North End Services Canteen had, in addition to providing entertainment, served some four hundred thousand meals. And the work was only heating up. Even when food rationing started in the summer of 1942, according to journalist Lorna Inness, "the women at the North End managed to work miracles, and there was always something for the men." The dances could now accommodate one thousand guests, up from a cap of three hundred at the old canteen. They continued to have stage shows, as well, on the new and bigger stage, plus concerts, men's-only movie nights, and Ping-Pong. They added a dedicated reading and writing room and billiards; they also started up a camera club and a bridge club. The kitchen served two meals a day and still offered free coffee and doughnuts on Sundays, plus sandwiches to order at all hours. On average, through 1942, fifteen hundred to eighteen hundred visitors were coming through the door, looking for a diversion, a chat, or a meal. By 1944, according to historian Jay White, the canteen had a paid staff of 8 women, and a stable of 130 volunteers.

Seventeen-year-old Joyce Ripley was one.

Joyce Ripley loved the trip to Gottingen Street—didn't matter when or for what. Her family travelled regularly to shop there—for anything more than groceries, really, which they could get near home in one of the grocery stores in Rockingham, a small suburb outside peninsular Halifax overlooking Bedford Basin. Most Halifax suburbs then, when the footprint of the municipality was smaller, overlooked the Bedford Basin and Halifax Harbour. This is not only because it's a truly massive body of water; the basin is about eight kilometres from its innermost tip to the mid-harbour Narrows where the Halifax Explosion took place, and another seven kilometres to the harbour side of McNabs Island, now a four hundred–hectare provincial park at the harbour entrance. Saying something "overlooks the harbour" in Halifax is like saying something in Toronto is "in sight of the CN Tower." It's hard not to at least have a sliver in view. Joyce usually hopped on the train at the bottom of Rockingham to head into town, or on the Pender bus. Occasionally, her dad would take the family in the car. On this day, he had something to pick up at Allen's Hardware on Gottingen Street near Cunard Street, so he drove everyone in on the bouncy, unpaved Bedford Highway; Joyce and her sister in the back, her mother in the front. Today, they wouldn't stop at Simpson's, the big department store on Mumford Road. While Joyce's mother went to the fishmonger to buy enough oysters for chowder, Joyce and her sister ogled the dresses in the windows at the New York Dress Shop.

Living in Rockingham meant Joyce was partly outside the melee of wartime Halifax. She was twelve when the war kicked off. "It was coming," she says, "but I never really noticed that it was coming." Soon, she saw the basin crammed with convoy vessels; felt, by osmosis, the buzz and electricity. But her father was too old to sign up and her age and location off the peninsula largely saved her from the murky soup of shortages and crowding, except on two fronts: she liked a lot of sugar in her tea and that was a no-go after 1942, and she had to move in with her sister so her bedroom could be let out for war visitors. Joyce loved the guests, a rotating assortment of women and couples who made friends with her mother and played Rummoli with Joyce. She hated sharing a bed with her sister, who was five-and-a-half years younger. "She always thrashed around."

A wider world lit up for Joyce when she walked through the doors of Queen Elizabeth High School on September 2, 1942, the new school's opening day. She was now heading into town five days a week for school and could see, better, what Halifax was going through. The monthly blackout practices—which seemed to always happen while she was studying, so her mother would light a little candle for her—made more sense. She saw the lineups at the movie theatres and restaurants. At QEH, as the school was known, Joyce and her friends noticed all the young teachers had disappeared. "We were left with elderly ladies coming back from retirement." Or, at least, "they seemed to me to be very old." She completed home nursing training with the St. John Ambulance Brigade in Rockingham—learning how to properly make up beds for the wounded in an emergency and how to put on a sling, and she sold War Savings Stamps. In April 1944, near the end of grade eleven, Joyce went to the waterfront to watch the launch of HMCS *Nootka*.

In August 1944, she arrived for her first shift at the North End Services Canteen.

August 27, 1944, to be precise. How does she know? Joyce is a lifelong journaller and she filled five little diaries over the course of the war. Now in her mid-nineties—"I said to my doctor, I've never been old before. And I'm not really sure I can handle this!"—these valuable books flesh out the details of her teen years in Halifax during the Second World War. That summer before school started, she and a school friend, Pat, popped down to the offices of the Women's Voluntary Services, an organization that matched up volunteers seeking opportunities and organizations in need. After their interview, Pat decided she didn't love the idea of canteen work, but Joyce was in. "I thought, well, I am old enough, I should do some work." She inveigled two others to join her: Glorena Hoadley and Helen Read, whom Joyce always called "Honey." She worked a second afternoon shift, 4:00 P.M. to 8:00 P.M., on September 1.

There was no slapdash matching of volunteers and slots when it came to the Women's Voluntary Services. The fit had to be right from both the perspective of the volunteer and her overseers, and there are many cases where the fit, in fact, wasn't right. Correspondence abounds in the Women's Voluntary Services files at the Halifax Municipal Archives detailing the wonder and woes of volunteer interactions. A letter to Mrs. Baillie, who ran the Blue Triangle—a canteen for women's auxiliary service members run by the YWCA out of the Waverley Inn on Barrington Street—notes that a volunteer server had been given "a little talk" about her behaviour, which included being "unruly" and "trying to tell people how to do things." I am pleased to report to you that there are no such notes on file about Joyce. After her two shifts at the North End Services Canteen, she worked a shift for the very same Mrs. Baillie at the Blue Triangle Canteen. This was on September 2, after school on her first day at QEH. The next day, she was at the YMCA Canteen, farther south along Barrington Street, at Harvey Street. On September 8, Joyce took on another shift at the North End Services Canteen, "trying out in various spots." This one stuck. It became her regular Friday activity. School finished early and she would head down to her canteen set-up duty. Sometimes on a Sunday, too. She kept at it all through the fall of 1944, over Christmas, and into the first half of 1945. She eventually earned a smock, with a little label on the front that showed that she was a volunteer. Joyce was proud. She looked very smart. (Perhaps a smidgen less so after February 19, 1945, the day Joyce's diary reminds her of a tragic event: "picked last pr. Stockings!" Girls grew up wearing ribbed, knit brown cotton stockings and graduated to nylon back-seamed stockings, worn with a garter belt. But nylon was a prized war material and a new pair would have been all but impossible to find in 1945. Joyce bought a pair of lisle stockings, a type of thicker cotton, as a not-up-to-snuff replacement for the nylons.)

That Christmas, 1944, would be the last at the North End Services Canteen. The women couldn't have known, of course, that victory in Europe was a little more than four months away, but they seemed to nonetheless go all-out that year. Rationing and shortages were significant, so the shoppers' committee began gathering supplies starting in October, hitting up friends and businesses, as was the way—"cadging and wheedling and borrowing," in the words of William D. Naftel in *Halifax at War*, "all of which became more necessary as the war dragged on." Indeed, 1944 was the height of attendance at the canteen. "Our capacities," Mrs. E. G. Young, who was head cook at that time, later reported to the *Mail-Star*'s Lorna Inness, "were taxed almost beyond endurance." Almost. This holiday, impossibly, there were donations of fruit and cigarettes for the men. The real coup comprised the soft drinks and one hundred pounds of candy—almost unheard of, given the sugar ration. The day before the big event, the kitchen staff prepped peas, and peeled and chopped two bushels of carrots (about one hundred pounds) and enough potatoes to match. They mashed fifty pounds of cranberries into sauce. The morning of, they roasted the turkeys and hams and cut and buttered fifty loaves of bread. The meal, at noon, was free. "As the men finished their dinner, Chief Petty Officer Cunningham proposed a vote of thanks to the ladies and three rousing cheers shook the hall," wrote Inness. "The ladies smiled, and promptly went back to work clearing up, washing dishes, and getting ready to repeat the whole procedure at suppertime."

⌒〜∧〜⌒

They needed no commendation. They had been at it for more than five long years by then; they probably could have been at it for another five more. And, the thing is, they were special. But they also were not special at all.

Halifax was inordinately pressed upon by the war, and the volunteer organizations that supported the bulging mass of service personnel and administrative staff, dignitaries, war workers, and family members seeing loved ones off were not like the volunteer organizations in other Canadian cities. Halifax felt more, worked harder. But it wasn't just the North End Services Canteen that outdid itself. Work that deserved three rousing, hall-shaking cheers went on all over the bustling city. Much, perhaps most, of this work gets some attention in this book—some, inevitably, will not; some for reasons of space or interest, some because it's untraceable. That work may never see daylight. But whether nationally backed and well-established, federal government–sanctioned and well-heeled, local and mighty, or individual, it all added up. And in terms of adding up the numbers of individuals served, it would be difficult to find an organization that tops the Central Magazine Exchange.

The Central Magazine Exchange was simple. It was a collection point and clearinghouse for reading materials. It started with magazines, newspapers, and books. It grew to include playing card packs, board games, darts, and stationery. Anything ships and troops could carry with them. After all, as a letter of appreciation from an Allied naval ship notes: "war conditions are nine-tenths boredom." Eventually, the exchange branched out into other comforts: toys for merchant mariners to take home to their children, boiled sweets for men on submarines, and warm clothing and oranges for those on rescue ships. Mostly, though, it was about the reading. Radio host John Fisher, in June 1942, profiled the exchange on his Thursday night national CBC program *East Coast Reporter* (the former CHNS broadcaster had moved to the CBC that year). The "nine-tenths boredom" letter was quoted by him in his report. He also explained that picture magazines were in highest demand. (Presumably because of language barriers; merchant mariners might be from any commonwealth nation.) *Life* magazine, Fisher said, was the most requested. Digest magazines were also popular, followed by westerns, detective stories, and thrillers. English sailors apparently preferred American magazines, and no one was interested in women's mags or publications from before the war. "Magazines as old as 1885 have been received." I'll say it here for John: yikes!

The Central Magazine Exchange was similar in many ways to the North End Services Canteen. Both were paramount to the well-being of service members and merchant mariners, unspeakably busy, and staffed by a force of almost exclusively anonymous, dedicated Halifax women. The exchange operated six days a week, helmed by volunteers who did two day shifts and one night shift weekly. These women, Fisher noted, were also self-supporting. "Each make[s] a weekly financial contribution to the fund. With this, and with revenue from the sale of old newspapers, they are able to finance an organization that has done much to cheer and to occupy the minds of democracy's heroes." The exchange, then, like the canteen, did not receive stable funding from the government. The canteen and the exchange both started off small, and swelled to meet need, changing what was on offer as necessity arose. One provincial government publication called the Central Magazine Exchange's bundling and distributing "the first voluntary war work taken on by women of Halifax." This isn't quite accurate. Certainly, men heading overseas on those early ships in the fall of 1939 and would have been given reading materials, but as far as an organized approach goes, the exchange probably started after the canteen, or at best simultaneously. It's not definitive, but the exchange registered under the War Charities Act in March 1940, four months after the canteen.

The work at the exchange was strictly physical and administrative, rather than partly emotional. Volunteers would receive materials from across Canada and the US, and from farther afield. Within Canada, the magazines were shipped to Halifax for free by the Canadian National and Canadian Pacific Railways. They came from service groups such as the

Canadian Women's Club of New York City, the Women's Naval Auxiliary of Ottawa, and Kiwanis Clubs, as well as from individuals. Fisher cited a regular shipment from a Mrs. Dearden of Hamilton, in memory of her son; a Halifax tram car conductor also popped by weekly with a stack of magazines. The women would classify, wire-bundle, and then ship or dole out goods. This all happened at a shed on the Pickford and Black Wharf. The main Pickford and Black building today is an upscale retail storefront on Upper Water Street in the beautifully restored Historic Properties. In the 1940s, the locale was much less grand and much grubbier. Pickford and Black (the firm, that is; founding partners Pickford and Black died in 1914 and 1934, respectively) was a ship chandler's outfit, with offices on the street side, and business—the transport of passengers, mail, and freight—around the back on the water side. Lucking into the shed—a three-storey industrial tarpaper-clad building—worked well for friends Amy Jones and Una Smith, who established and ran the Central Magazine Exchange over the course of the war. The Central Magazine Exchange shared its space in 1941 with the office of the Maple Leaf Milling Company. The exchange must have been a loud neighbour. At the height of its operations, it had 150 different volunteers coming and going, as well as non-stop waves of people arriving with pickup trucks and station wagons to pick up materials for troop ships, Air Force depot stations, merchant ships, hospitals, hostels, and canteens. Outposts were also supplied, some within Nova Scotia, others in Allied and neutral territories such as Newfoundland, Greenland, and Iceland. A 1941 photo from the E. A. Bollinger Archives, held by the Nova Scotia Archives, shows three naval ratings picking up a load of magazines, *Maclean's* among them, that swamp the back of a 1936 two-door Buick Special—so many magazines there's barely space for their black, tartan-collared Scottish terrier pal who's come along on the errand.

By 1942, other magazine exchanges were popping up in Canadian centres. Halifax's Central Magazine Exchange wasn't only the first exchange by about two years, it was also, arguably, the most important

Naval ratings load magazines into the back of a 1936 Buick Special—leaving barely enough room for their Scottish terrier. (NS ARCHIVES)

because of the broad range of mariners and service members it supplied. It was, decidedly, the busiest. The need for materials increased through the war, and George Pifher, the National War Services department's voluntary and auxiliary services director, worked consistently to boost the volume. Quotas were set for each zone and Pifher fostered competition among depots, the results of which were sent out in monthly bulletins. The January 1944 edition, which may have been the first of such bulletins, noted monthly totals, in the thousands, for cities including Ottawa, Montreal, Regina, and Calgary. Halifax has a special notation: "none for overseas other than local requirements for Navy and Merchant Marine."

Amy Jones wasn't going to let that stand.

Jones knew that Halifax women volunteers were handling an average weekly distribution of 42,000, with 6,000 staying in the province and 36,000 going abroad. Other cities were shipping 2,000 to 50,000 articles every month. In other words, Halifax was processing more magazines weekly than Toronto, a city ten times its size, was shipping out every *month*. Jones wrote E. L. Miller of the Halifax Citizens War Services Committee. Miller, in turn, wrote Chester Payne, National War Services deputy minister, who replied with what amounted to a sorry-not-sorry apology. This was a rare moment of indignation from a woman volunteer in Halifax, though it's worth noting that Jones was looking to correct the record, not to get some kind of award. (You've read this far, so it will come as no big surprise that Jones never received one, anyway.) Future bulletins correctly listed the distribution numbers for Halifax, which were consistently high. Higher, even, than those January 1944 numbers—regularly processing 125,000 articles monthly. The Central Magazine Exchange was by no means the only organization that supported the truth that Halifax and the province consistently punched above their weight. In February 1940, the provincial Red Cross made note that Nova Scotia had, in five months since the war's start, already raised $512,000—146 percent of its quota for that time frame.

Joyce looked at each diner kindly as he moved along the line, following his plate from window to window at the North End Services Canteen. When their eyes met, and she got the nod or the "yes, please," she ladled thick gravy onto the meat, before passing the plate up the line to the next volunteer. Sometimes the men would lean on the long counter in front of the potato-veg-gravy window to get a better look inside the kitchen. It wouldn't be like home, of course, but it was a kitchen, this was hot and delicious food, and they were far from the places and people they loved. It would definitely do. It was January 1945. The Christmas rush had passed, but the leagues of service members and merchant mariners were still showing up day after day after day. Volunteers, some days, were hard to come by and Joyce, who had now spent half a year at the canteen, sometimes arrived at her shift to act as convener, taking meal tickets and helping lead operations on the non-kitchen side. On March 23, she didn't take tickets, but did triple serving duty, scooping out beans, potatoes, and the day's second vegetable. A week later, on Good Friday, only one hundred men showed up for the evening meal. Maybe it was because the men knew that the meal wouldn't include meat, a nod to Catholic service members. In any case, she and the other volunteers were glad of the rest. One hundred men was, in the scope of the canteen, nothing. But need kept up. And the women's stamina kept on. This was a marathon. And while they were close, they hadn't yet hit the wall.

Did Joyce have an understanding of what she was accomplishing during these months? Did she view her work as important? Did she have a sense of it being bigger than "I'm going to put this ketchup out"? She most certainly did not. "We weren't serving in the war itself. I just got on with the work, as most people did." No one ever told her this. It was just understood.

She was in Mr. Wheatley's Monday morning English class when the church bells started pealing. Every bell in the city, it seemed. Indeed, the sound must have carried easily from the south and west ends of the city and across the Halifax Commons from the north toward QEH. An announcement came over the school's public address system: the war was over. (It wasn't quite, technically. Hitler was dead and the Germans had put down their guns. The German surrender didn't take effect until the following day, on May 8, 1945.) In any case, class was dismissed. Joyce collected her belongings and caught the next bus home to Rockingham. A little later, when she and a gaggle of friends tried to board the bus to head back into downtown to celebrate, the driver refused to let them board. This was the same Pender bus driver who had ferried these girls back and forth to Queen Elizabeth for the entire school year. He knew them, and on this day, he looked after them, because he had seen the riots and looting happening in the core—vicious revelry that would last two days. "We were nonplussed, I think, is the word," Joyce says. They weren't going to walk into town from Rockingham, so that was the end of that.

While Women's Voluntary Services called on her twice during September 1945 to help pass out cigarettes, chocolate bars, ice cream, and bottles of Coke to repatriated service members at the Navy League Recreation Centre, Joyce worked her last shift at the North End Services Canteen on June 27. The canteen had stopped serving full meals as service members made their way more quickly in and out of the city. And that was it. From its October 1939 launch through VE day, where the counting ends, the canteen served 850,000 sit-down meals and more than 725,000 short-order lunches. Averaged out, that's 417 hot meals and 356 lunches a day. When it was over, Joyce thought, "Well, that's that. All very ordinary."

A few years after, when Joyce was married and in her own home, she returned to her parents' place in Rockingham to collect her canteen uniform, the smock she dutifully and proudly put on every shift that said "North End Services Canteen" on the front. She had left it hanging on the back of the dining room door. But it was gone. "I think," she said, "my father threw it out."

Chapter Five

YOU'D BE SO NICE TO COME HOME TO

The naval rating lies on his side. He's half on a rug, on top of a terrazzo floor, front-to-back with about a dozen others in front of a fireplace. His cap hits at a jaunty angle where it's slipped off his head. He's asleep, half-fetal. It's easy, if a fallacy, to read emotion into his positioning—emotional or physical exhaustion? Boredom or drunkenness? In any case, he's dog-tired. And he had no other place to go than the floor of the YMCA on Barrington Street in the old Ladies' College. Halifax in April is not warm. The average high is only 6.8°C. It's good that he was inside. Sadly, his figure might have been ignored by the media and the city if he had been a shabbily dressed civilian. But it's the first week of April 1941. And he's in uniform. And, so, quite unaware, this side-lying kid winds up on the front page of the *Halifax Mail*, under the headline "Disgrace To Canada."

A year and seven months into the war, it had come to this.

This disgrace might have been news to the rest of the country, but everyone in Halifax knew much sooner than April 1941 how bad things had gotten. From the time the federal government turned Halifax, unasked, from tiny town into world war–launching pad, the strain had been building and the population swelling. And this strain was exerting itself in ways truly not even calculable given the transience of military members and their families, and the nonstop arrival of war workers and their families. The shipyards begged for employees. It needed five times as many skilled workers as it had on hand. Civilians were scrambling to keep up. Halifax's mayor, William Edward Donovan, had the luckless task of chairing the Halifax Hostels Committee when this story ran. He knew well the extant problems of bedless service members. He knew many spent their nights walking the city, or resting in downtown doorways. He had been an alderman in his previous term in municipal government and had run again in the April 24, 1940, election, this time for mayor. His bid was unopposed. Donovan, apparently, enjoyed a challenge. He would both inherit one and watch it balloon like a sickly boil as the feds continued to pile military and merchant mariners into the city, continued to demand the presence of dockyard workers, and continued to do little to nothing to staunch the flow of families following their loved ones to the city. Accommodations were falling short for service members alone to the tune of four hundred to eight hundred bodies a night. Then, a fire at the dockyard on December 24, 1940, took down a block of barracks where service members could at least hang hammocks. Merry Christmas, Halifax.

Four months later, the "Disgrace To Canada" story ran, and five days after that, an evidently frantic Donovan sent a telegram to James Garfield Gardiner, the minister of national war services.

…AT MEETING HOSTELS COMMITTEE REGARDING OVERNIGHT ACCOMMODATION NOW TEN TWENTY SIX BEDS ALL SERVICES STOP DURING PAST FORTNIGHT HUNDRED FIFTY ADDITIONAL SLEEPING ON MATTRESSES SIX HUNDRED TURNED AWAY NIGHTLY ABSOLUTELY NO ACCOMMODATION STOP…

Things were not going well. The atmosphere in Halifax was like a kid's birthday party gone sour: everyone having a good time until suddenly the pizza's eaten, the clown's gone home, and the cake is ground into the carpet. And still the guests kept arriving.

Housing was far and away the biggest issue facing Halifax at this time. But it wasn't the only municipal gremlin. Naval members and merchant mariners who returned from sea duty needed to get off their ships. Not only were they sent away from their berths, but they wanted to get away. Of course they did. These were cramped quarters, and the men's stressful workplaces. Doctors don't want to bed down in emergency rooms; teachers have no desire to curl up in their classrooms. Army and Air Force personnel were in similar positions. Spending long days and endless nights sitting in the same depot where they worked did not appeal. It's no wonder the North End Services Canteen so quickly added games and tables for cards and short-order sandwiches to their menu during the day. The same services were available at scores of facilities all over the city. There was a paucity of restaurants. Food prices were steep, anyway. The Council of Social Agencies reported early in the war that food prices in Halifax were the highest in the country, and twice that of Toronto. Practically every church opened its doors nightly for service members and merchant mariners. But churches weren't for sleeping. At the Church of England Institute on Barrington Street, the doors closed at 11:00 P.M. "You don't take a room in Halifax," Trent Frayne wrote in the *Globe and Mail* in May 1943, "you take a bed." Increasing numbers of newcomers would have been happy to have one. Katherine Anne Ling reports in *Servicewives in Wartime Halifax* that in 1942, the Children's Aid Society, after years of rising numbers of children arriving in their temporary care because parents new to the city could find no accommodation whatsoever, stopped placing children. There were too many. What this meant for these children, I cannot begin to imagine.

When Marjorie Langin graduated from the Maritime School of Social Work in 1945, her first job was with the Children's Aid Society. "The slums in Halifax at that time, darling, were so utterly unbelievable." A series of photographs held by the Nova Scotia Archives shows the state of a few shacks torn down by the Board of Health in 1941. Their location is unclear, but it has to be somewhere on the edge of the city, given the surrounding scrubby brush and the lack of anything else close by. They are cobbled-together windowless hovels. Whoever nailed the boards relied on discarded wood and dispatched with the notion of a floor. It doesn't seem possible these are inhabited, but the insides show platforms on the earthen floors and bent metal bed frames. Rags and blankets stand in for mattresses, more nests than beds. This is definitely someone's home. There's a tweed hat on a nail on the wall and clothing hanging from the rafters; there are gloves and a lunch pail. An iron kettle rests on a small wood-fired cooking stove.

One of the demolition shots shows a man whacking at a half-toppled structure. He's wearing a suit and polished shoes; this is for cruel show. Beside him there's a uniformed police officer smiling at the camera and holding a two-headed axe. There's no telling if the inhabitants had a chance to remove wanted belongings first, nor if they were relocated or left to fend on their own. And in any case, the urban core wasn't necessarily a material improvement on conditions such as these. One of Marjorie's first working experiences was at a tenement on Water Street, where all the families on a single floor shared one dripping water tap. The tenants had no choice but to put diapers on the oven door and dry them, unwashed. "You would see these little ones with the most awful rashes," she says. "Thank god for the VON and the public health nurses."

As for the Victorian Order of Nurses (VON), one representative from the organization reported to the Halifax Council of Social Agencies in 1944 that many north-end Halifax houses were of poor and rapidly deteriorating quality—with no central heating and exterior doors with large gaps. There were leaky roofs and drippy plumbing, leading to damp floors and walls missing plaster. The majority had shared toilets, located "in cellars, in hallways, or off kitchens." In addition, "hallways," the report stated, "are dark, damp, and smelly, for the most part, with

A shack being torn down by the Board of Health in 1941. (NS ARCHIVES)

stairways rickety, and in some cases dangerous, because of loose boards." There were no fire escapes. Ling notes that in 1943, city inspectors counted approximately thirty-five dwellings in the middle of the city with outdoor privies; they counted 140 cesspools. Newspapers reported water shortages. In the summer of 1942, and in the summer and fall of 1943, parts of Halifax were under boil-water orders. In Halifax's deep north end, in the Black community of Africville, householders were in a decidedly worse position. The city had never extended water and sewer service into the area, even though properties there were assessed and residents paid taxes for these municipal services. Because the city refused to build appropriate infrastructure, outdoor privies were the only option. Residents drew water from wells, which were under near-permanent boil-water orders.

Racist municipal decisions undermining livability was Africville's status quo. In the nineteenth century, a rail line had been installed through the middle of the community, and an infectious diseases hospital and prison were constructed nearby. Post–Second World War, the city built an open-pit dump on the settlement's edge. Soon after, throughout the 1960s, it bought out residents, expropriated land, demolished the church, and razed what was a vibrant and proud community. Africville never mattered to Halifax. It faced historic neglect and civic hostility—racism always trumped the city's bust and boom cycles. But then, boom times aren't always kind to working-class housing. During the First World War, when the waterfront was buzzing and the downtown core growing, many homes were torn down for, or converted to, industrial and commercial use. The remaining north-end housing stock was described by Hugh MacLennan in *Barometer Rising*: "Houses were like cracker boxes standing in rows on the shelf. In some cases the foundations were so cockeyed it looked as though the houses they supported might tip over and sprawl into the street."

In 1917, the Halifax Explosion would eliminate swaths of these homes. This was by far the worst, but not the only, disaster to affect working-class housing in the city core. Thomas H. Raddall, in *Halifax: Warden of the North*, writes that in 1857 an inferno swept through Hollis Street, and two years later another destroyed much of Granville Street.

> *The two fires made a great clearance in the heart of the town, and modern structures went up to replace the old. In truth, fire was a benefactor in the old crowded wooden city, whatever the momentary suffering. The irony of later days was that twentieth-century alarm systems and fire-fighting apparatus perpetuated the wooden slum which in the old days was swept away at least once in each generation, and which long defied the efforts of hopeful committees dedicated to slum clearance.*

I'm not sure losing family members and all one's worldly possessions, however meagre, is "momentary suffering," but we'll yield Raddall his callous assertion and take the point it supports: there were only so many ways this could go for the working class. Either the existing housing stock would hang on until long after its best-before date, putting residents at risk, or it would be intentionally razed or inadvertently destroyed. Too often it was replaced with more modern housing outside the residents' financial reach. It was into this mix that the federal government dumped the Second World War. Soon, servicemen and their families and war workers began open, often desperate, competition for the city's remaining cracker-box housing stock.

The only immediate solution to the shortage was sharing space, which usually involved doubling-up children. This was the plight of both Joyce Ripley, who moved into the bed with her wriggling younger sister, and Jackie Wrixon, who moved into the room with her new baby brother. (Billeting with a baby was a pain, but she did like that her brother came with a ration book.) Her mother registered Jackie's room with the Wartime Prices and Trade Board on August 6, 1943, certifying that the price was not more that she had charged on October 11, 1941. The board took seriously the issue of price gouging, but it fought a rearguard action. The Rentals Committee routinely heard complaints of apartments and rooms being let out at rates 30 percent higher than they had been for previous tenants, a practice that was illegal after that October 1941 Wartime Prices and Trade Board rate freeze. In scope, overpaying was probably a somewhat better option than the alternative, which was sharing a rented space meant for one family with two others, resorting to a tenement firetrap, or trying to eke out an existence in one of those Health Board-condemned shacks. No matter how it was sliced, the overcrowding was, in a word, horrendous. Then it got worse.

"Diphtheria came first."

It's an ignominious three-word sentence in *The New York Times*. But it was also a statement of fact. Diphtheria was in Halifax.

Twenty Norwegian whaling ships had spent the summer of 1940 off Antarctica and were diverted to Halifax that fall after Norway's June 10, 1940, surrender to the Germans, who had invaded the Scandinavian country two months earlier. The Norwegian whalers carried with them a nocuous strain of diphtheria. Over that fall, it advanced through Halifax's crammed-together population, which was both previously untouched by the strain and, according to a Harvard medical team member who travelled from Boston to investigate and treat the outbreak in January, scantily immunized. And there wasn't only diphtheria. Halifax's doubled-in-an-instant population, according to the *Times*, was "overcrowded and over-tired," with one of every three of its doctors called into military or naval service. Schools were thronged, with forty to fifty in a classroom, and seventy students to a wash basin, Katherine Anne Ling writes in *Servicewives in Wartime Halifax*. Children, crammed in, suffered head lice, scabies, and impetigo. "Into [Halifax's] busy harbor [*sic*] steamed ships carrying the infections of the world." There were measles. Meningitis was spreading. Plus, a new and virulent strain of scarlet fever. Halifax, one of the visiting Harvard medical team members declared, was "a hell-hole of infection."

———∿∿———

It's not that nothing was done.

Halifax was in dire need of more accommodation. The emergent public health and social crises were interwoven with the lack of sufficient housing in the city and the unrelenting influx of bodies being layered in, one day's worth on top of the next, and the next, and the next. So, starting in the fall of 1939, city officials worked with the federal government and service organizations to arrange for the transformation of two existing institutional buildings to hostels, providing beds for the night as well as recreation activities and meals. The Salvation Army would run a

Red Shield War Service Centre on Hollis Street, which would house 200 to 250 nightly. The Salvation Army operated these kinds of centres in many cities and welcomed all service members, active and returned. Its rooms for reading and writing were free. Patrons could purchase refreshments and meals. Beds cost thirty cents a night, sometimes more. A larger hostel was funded by the Red Cross and operated by the YMCA in the Barrington Street campus of the Halifax Ladies' College, not far from the Nova Scotian Hotel. It was in this building that the naval rating featured in the "Disgrace To Canada" story found a clear spot on a floor to bed down. The dormitories and other spaces accommodated 310 to 350, but certainly not every seeker who came through the door. Given the building's previous life as the Ladies' College, it offered showers, a gym, space for concerts, and a library reading room. Just like the Salvation Army, the YMCA operated hostels in many Canadian cities, called Red Triangle Huts (as opposed to the Blue Triangle version, which was for women). Active service members could attend, as well as those within six months of discharge. These two facilities were Halifax's first stab at providing beds outside of barracks. A good start. But not nearly enough.

Rolling into the first full year of the war, 1940, expropriation was increasingly used to help find bed and recreation space, though mostly it seems it was a mutually agreed-upon commandeering of needed buildings. (Though not in all cases. A memo from Voluntary and Auxiliary Services director George Pifher to Léo Richer LaFlèche from December 14, 1942, alerts the National War Services minister that the Halifax YWCA has the option to buy the Waverley Inn on Barrington Street for $30,000, with the offer expiring the following day at noon. "It is occupied by elderly residents," Pifher writes, "who will need to be evicted."

Apparently they were. (Who knows what happened to the residents who were left to find another situation in the city's worst housing crisis on record?) The building became the Blue Triangle Canteen, where Joyce Ripley worked when she started volunteering. The Navy took over part of the Halifax Exhibition Grounds on Almon Street. Pier 21 became the home to an Army regiment. Personnel stayed at No. 1 "Y" Depot, the Air Force embarkation point in the city's west end, which was later known as HMCS *Peregrine*. The Navy, which would add some twenty thousand members to the city's population in revolving waves over the course of the war, booted out the students and took over the campus of the University of King's College as an officers' training station.

By November 1941, the feds started to put up prefabricated ("prefab") houses in the deep north end on the site of Mulgrave Park. A tenants' manual from July 1943 notes that the federal agency in charge of the housing has constructed them "as quickly and as cheaply as possible" (not exactly a ringing endorsement) for "workers engaged in the production of armaments and munitions." In other words, these houses would not help struggling Haligonians, merchant mariners, or service members looking for a few nights' accommodation, nor newly arrived service families. Also, there weren't enough. John Fisher reported on *East Coast Reporter* that more than one hundred prefabs were built between November 1941 and May 1942. Another nine hundred were planned or under construction at that time. They were needed. Desperately.

By April 1941, when the "Disgrace To Canada" story ran on the front page of the *Halifax Mail* and Mayor Donovan sent his panicky telegram to Ottawa, beds were still needed—somewhere in the range of three hundred on a given night to one thousand on another—over and above what these expropriations and early hostels provided. So, more hostels sprung up— partnerships between service organizations and the federal government. They were staffed almost entirely by Halifax women volunteers, which we know from the detailed files of the Women's Voluntary Services.

The Canadian Legion operated Atlantic House, in what Haligonians today know as Keith Hall, a sandstone-front building on Hollis Street built as the home of Alexander Keith, adjacent to his famous Lower Water Street brewery. This had been the Knights of Columbus Hall, until the federal government purchased it for $17,000. Angus L. Macdonald, minister of national defence for naval services, said in an interdepartmental memo to National War Services Deputy Minister T. C. Davis: "I do not think the price paid for this building was excessive." (It's certainly the business of a well-functioning government to control spending, and this comment may have been in response to an earlier query from Davis, but at a time when service members were sleeping on floors and citizens were living in mouldy shacks for lack of housing, assessing value for money might not be the best blush.) The sign on the portico called Atlantic House an "Educational and Recreation Centre for Service Men," but it also slept up to four hundred. Farther south on Hollis (a hostel hotspot), the Knights of Columbus took their $17,000 and opened a hostel and recreation centre at the intersection of Fawson Street (this street is now long gone; it once connected Hollis and Water Streets). That one slept three hundred. There were four hundred beds at the Salvation Army Red Shield Hostel and Centre on Argyle Street, a brick-front three-storey hunk of a building beside the Diamond Taxi stand, where the Neptune Studio Theatre is now located. It served meals and provided recreation as well as beds. The Navy League of Canada, an organization that promoted naval defence and supported merchant mariners, ran the Allied Merchant Seamen's Club, also on Hollis Street, near Salter Street. This hostel served meals as well as beer—a deep oddity in Halifax at the time—and could host three hundred and fifty merchant mariners from all around the world a night, but it could stretch to six hundred by making use of recreation spaces, such as the concert hall and library. This building was a replacement for the Navy League's large building at Barrington and South Streets, which was, in Angus L. Macdonald's words to Davis, "taken by the Air Force at the beginning of the war against the objections of myself and practically all other citizens of Halifax." (Expropriation wasn't only of strictly civilian properties, it seems—service arms took from other service arms, too.) On Barrington, there was also a hostel for women service members at the YWCA, across the street from the at-capacity Halifax Ladies' College campus hostel run by the YMCA. Many smaller and specialized accommodations also sprung up or grew significantly in 1941 and 1942, including residences for service members or mariners of specific nations, run by their governments. Some churches made space for those needing beds as well.

One of the difficulties in counting the city's capacity for bodies in beds during this time is the interchangeability of names when it came to these facilities. Huts and clubs were mostly for leisure activities, such as reading or cards. Some had tea services. Some entertainment. They weren't for sleeping, typically, but the YMCA called its overnight accommodation centres "huts," so that tosses that designation out the window. Another contradiction: huts were also generally temporary constructions, but the Knights of Columbus Hut on Barrington was a giant gothic-revival fortress that was part of the St. Mary's Basilica compound. It preceded the war and survived long past. Recreation centres hosted crafts, tea services, libraries, activities like badminton, and often outdoor games and sports. But some also had beds. Hostels were, as expected, for sleeping. But they were in some cases significant centres for entertainment, leisure, and sport, too. Then there were canteens. Places to get a meal. But there were also concerts at canteens. "Service centre" was a catch-all term. For example, the Quinpool Road Hostel and Jewish Congress Service Centre, at the corner of Monastery Lane, held Passover dinners and dances. It was called a hostel, but it seems not to have had beds. Other centres' offerings are more mysterious. Across the harbour from Halifax, the Dartmouth Services Club, at the corner of Queen and King Streets in downtown Dartmouth, welcomed Army, Navy, Air Force, and merchant mariners. Whether it had overnight accommodations is unknown. It burned to the ground in 1942. No doubt scores of other organizations that provided beds have been lost to memory and record.

Even with all these existing, growing, and coming-into-being hostels, at the time Angus L. Macdonald wrote to Davis, uncounted thousands of personnel were also being billeted in private homes in the city. When more barracks spaces opened up, as two thousand did for naval members around May 1, 1941, the expectation was that these beds would free up. Macdonald wrote: "I should fancy that some of these homes will be able to take in people for a night's lodging." You have to wonder about Macdonald's wording. "I should fancy" doesn't inspire much confidence in the way of strong policy. And, indeed, hundreds of service members every night were still on the streets, or at least on the floor. I should fancy this was cold, harsh, and uncomfortable.

There's a decided sense among all this that the gaggle of federal officials in charge either didn't fully understand the situation on the ground in Halifax, or weren't able to muster the resources—financial, intellectual, emotional, or ethical—to address it. Or perhaps they were hamstrung by the lumbering nature of government. A good example of the glacial pace of bureaucratic manoeuvring is the Argyle Garage. In the summer of 1943, the National War Services department's Voluntary and Auxiliary Services director, George Pifher, came to Halifax to look into the city's manifold war-related problems. He and a real estate advisor toured several buildings that might be purchased for a canteen and recreation centre for service members. To Pifher's eye, the Argyle Garage, the city's first enclosed parking garage, a cavernous 1920s building taking up the entire corner of Argyle, Prince, and Grafton Streets in the downtown core, was the one. Besides, no other locations he viewed were, to him, suitable. If not the Argyle Garage, he reported, "there appears no alternative but new construction." So, let's track his progress. Pifher visited Halifax in the summer of 1943. He returned to Ottawa and delivered his report to the executive committee of the National War Services funds advisory board at a two-day meeting on August 24 and 25. Following that, a series of meetings took place amongst officials from the Department of National Defence and the Army. At the next advisory board meeting, September 20 through 22, 1943, the news was delivered: at sixty thousand square feet and without the option to lease only a portion of the space, the Argyle Garage was too large and too difficult to renovate. The meeting minutes note that the next step was for board members to await an alternative proposal from the Army. Finally, in November, the board approved for construction a temporary "Services' Cafeteria" at $32,000. The timeline for completion was four to five months. "Negotiations," Pifher notes in a memo to the deputy minister, "are continuing in respect to the question of space for additional recreational facilities." To recap: the need for a new canteen and recreation centre in Halifax was acute, but the feds would take nearly a year to make this project happen, and even after all that time, could only manage to get the canteen part included, not the recreation component. One can't help but contrast this with the early days of the North End Services Canteen. Those women took care of the urgent need in front of them, negotiated as they went, and took care of the administration when they had time. So long as it didn't get in the way of the real work, the paperwork could wait. In the case of the Argyle Garage, and so many other attempts by government to provide desperately needed aid, the order of operations was perversely reversed.

It was also simply not viewed as being as important as battle and battle-readiness. Naval Rear-Admiral Leonard Murray, in charge of the Canadian Navy from his base in Halifax, "had little time for—and less interest in—the deteriorating relationship between the Navy and civilian authorities in Halifax," notes Stephen Kimber in *Sailors, Slackers and Blind Pigs*. "The situation was worsening by the week…. But how could anyone compare the city's piddling problems…with his never ending battle to save his sailors and merchant seamen from almost certain death at the hands of German wolf packs? Murray knew what his priorities had to be."

Others around him were more circumspect. Kimber says Murray's sub-commander at Stadacona was pressuring him to take action to provide recreation. And at one point Donovan's successor, Mayor John Lloyd, "was organizing a civic delegation to travel to Ottawa to beg for 'special consideration' of Halifax's needs as Canada's prime wartime city." Given Ottawa's proven inadequacy, there can't have been much hope behind this mission. In the meantime, service organizations and individual women volunteers were continuing to work doggedly to provide diversion.

Dances were at the top of the list. Every night. Church dances, hotel dances, canteen dances, club dances. Dances, dances, dances. During the days, sailors, soldiers, airmen, and merchant mariners with time on their hands could visit huts, where they might spend idle hours reading, playing games, or writing letters. Some recreation centres offered camera and bridge clubs, as the North End Services Canteen did; others offered instruction in handicrafts like linocut printing and leather work. In a rare moment of mental health awareness, the 1942 edition of the provincial government pamphlet "Nova Scotia Helps the Fighting Man," touts a benefit to leisure and recreation beyond quashing boredom or keeping idle hands occupied. "If handicrafts can assist and even a few personnel in finding a satisfactory way of life, or help them to re-assume a normal outlook and a healthy mental attitude, then they are taking their share of responsibility in the development of post war citizens."

There were myriad concerts and movie nights. The Naval Reading Service ran a reading room in the King Edward Hotel at Barrington and North Streets, where service members could lounge on leather armchairs in front of the fireplace and read magazines or books. The service, run by Jean Gow and a clique of women volunteers, also had an arm similar to the Central Magazine Exchange for supplying naval vessels with reading materials. The service's sorting plant, at No. 1 Jetty at the dockyard (roughly where Cunard Street might spill out into the harbour if it extended that far east), received and sorted thousands of publications. There was another

Elaine Tilly, Jean Gow, Claire Sandey, and Irene Griffiths of the Naval Reading Service, 1942. (NS ARCHIVES)

comfortable reading area in the south end, at the Central Legion Library inside Atlantic House on Hollis Street (that's Keith Hall, if you're keeping track). Same for the Navy League's new facilities on the Wanderers Grounds, a recreation centre built in addition to the League's Allied Merchant Seamen's Club on Hollis Street. The Navy League Recreation Centre, built specifically for naval ratings, opened in August 1942, with two buildings housing separate dry and wet canteens, plus comfy couches, lounging areas, and a games room. Mostly, though, the centre's purpose was activity and exercise. There was a field, organized rugby and football games, and a track; inside, showers and changing rooms. There was also, still, the Navy League's Allied Merchant Seamen's Club for merchant

The Naval Reading Service reading room at the King Edward Hotel reading room, 1940. (NS ARCHIVES)

mariners, where volunteers staffed a kitchen, as well as reading and writing rooms, and held concerts and movie nights. The YMCA (not the YMCA-run hostel in the former Ladies' College, but the YMCA proper, farther north on Barrington in the downtown core; it's dizzying, I know...) offered a spa service with massages and a steam bath—one of those seated box-type contraptions, where only the user's head stays outside, wrapped in a towel) as well as badminton, Ping-Pong, rowing machines, and swimming. Well, swimming in theory, anyway. The pool at the YMCA was Halifax's only one and the Air Force frequently claimed it for air rescue training, preventing anyone else from using it to get exercise or to swim a few gentle laps—more of that expropriation mindset, where the priority was not the pursuit of well-being. Specialized clubs existed, too:

The magazine department of the Naval Reading Service, 1940. (NS ARCHIVES)

the Wings Club, off the lobby of the Nova Scotian Hotel, for airmen; Gerrish Street Hall for Black servicemen; Maison Surcouf, on Victoria Road, for Frenchmen; the Anzac Club, for Australians and New Zealanders; the Chinese Seamen's Club. Members-only civilian clubs, like the Waegwoltic in the south end and the Halifax Club downtown, catered to officers, giving them automatic membership and free use of the facilities. The Ajax Hospitality Headquarters on Spring Garden Road, though private, refused to discriminate based on rank.

Of course, servicemen could eschew all these spots for other kinds of leisure and recreation. (Though, given the staggering number of attendees at the centres—they had seven hundred a night for concerts at the Hollis Street Allied Merchant Seamen's Club and don't forget the collapsed floor at the North End Services Canteen—indicates they were, as far as attendance goes, abused beyond capacity.) Service members frequently swam in the Northwest Arm from the small beach at Franklyn Park, just west of Point Pleasant Park, or across the arm at Sir Sandford Flemming Park, known locally as The Dingle, or at popular Black Rock Beach, at the mouth of Halifax Harbour. There were commercial opportunities, as well: movie theatres like the Paramount and the Orpheus, and the Capitol at Spring Garden and Barrington, among others. If photos did not exist of the Marcus Dance Show's run in Halifax, its happening would be, to say the least, improbable. But there they are: images of a metallic-painted woman on a stage, naked except for a bathing cap and short-shorts, dancing to a naval orchestra; others in bikini tops and veil-like flowing skirts, parading in unison to a song called "Patriotic."

This would have been utterly outside the pale for the Halifax that Haligonians knew before 1939. Like, to the core. But with the excitement that this burlesque show brought, and the eye-opening to a broader world it would rend, the flip side was restaurants not merely overcrowded, but engulfed. Outside movie theatres, lines for tickets—in 1941, forty cents, including the provincial amusement tax and the Dominion war excise tax—were hundreds deep, almost all servicemen. Joyce Ripley "couldn't get near a show." The Capitol would run the same film back-to-back-to-back and patrons would line up outside and go in as soon as there was a seat. That could be at any point in the screening. "The usher would come out and say 'there's room for two or four or one or six!' And you walk in during the middle of the show and you'd stay precisely until you'd seen up to that part and then you left so someone else could come in." At first, this must have seemed somewhat amusing. But it wore thin, especially as the civilian population felt, over years and years, its second-in-line position.

This extended even to seemingly inconsequential things like soft drinks. In a 1943 episode, tracked in detail through a series of confidential memos blasting back and forth between Pifher and his boss LaFlèche, the

Marcus Dance Show, 1941. (NS ARCHIVES)

impact of rationing on civilians is clear. The gist: rationing didn't apply to canteens and cafeterias inside military establishments. They got all the sugar, tea, or whatever else, they needed. Outside military establishments—say, at the North End Services Canteen or in Halifax restaurants like the Green Lantern on Barrington Street—strict rations were in place, even though the bulk of patrons were service members. At restaurants, forces members were ordering sugar products such as soft drinks. And servers, because these customers were young men serving their country, hardly felt they could say no. Problem was, every time a server said yes, this depleted civilian supplies. LaFlèche is perhaps overstating the matter when he writes in March 1943 that, "the consumption of soft drinks has become today part and parcel of our civilization," but he makes a point: people are getting fed up.

Shortages also started to grate as the war machine ate up other resources, and not only the ones people might expect. There's an entire folder at Library and Archives Canada detailing the challenges with sports and recreation equipment. Inflatable balls with rubber bladders were in short supply. "The bat situation has been very critical," notes one memo, because there was no ash available. Birch was a second-rate stand-in, but even it would not be available for everyone, one memo revealed. "There will be sufficient bats for the Armed Forces both in Canada and overseas and a moderate supply left over for the civilian trade." Melton cloth for tennis balls was also hard to come by, as were Ping-Pong balls. In 1943, there were nearly ten thousand badminton shuttlecocks manufactured by one company, but the entire supply was taken by the Air Force. Even public recreation spaces were taken away from civilians. They could no longer use the YMCA on Barrington (no more fancy steam box sessions) or Gorsebrook Golf Course in the south end. In stores, there was a double difficulty in Halifax: rationed goods, plus the pressing mob of shoppers, which included all the usual citizens plus the thousands of visitors. "One could buy a fur coat, a diamond necklace, an exquisite watch," writes Thomas H. Raddall in *Halifax: Warden of the North*, "but only the lucky could find a kettle, a shirt, a stove, or a suit of child's underwear for months and years."

The federal government didn't see any of this—or the way it impacted Halifax specifically and acutely—as its problem. Jay White writes in *Conscripted City* that, "Ottawa downplayed the social ramifications of using Halifax and surrounding area as the primary Canadian operational, training, administrative, supply and repair base for naval forces and merchant shipping." This, of course, was a complete abdication of the screaming knowledge that, indeed, Halifax was, and Haligonians were, being deeply affected. And it wasn't only that they were watching movies end-first and not getting enough Coca-Cola. The province's deeply conservative attitudes about alcohol created myriad problems. Booze was not served in restaurants at all; it could be bought legally only in authorized government-run stores and, by law, had to be taken home immediately and consumed there, or at a private club. The issues are clear as day. Thousands of the city's inhabitants were transient. They had no homes to which they could take a bottle of beer. A workaround—that alcohol was legal if served in a private club (this was alcohol purchased by members, brought to the club and stored there, in private lockers)—was an option within reach only of officers. The result of these restrictions had to have been expected: a whole lot of drinking in parks and on the streets. This was, and is today, illegal in Halifax. But as far as crime goes, it had to have been on the light end of the scale. With the caveat that *of course* reading about crime from the reports of night detectives is bound to produce the sense that Halifax was in a desperate way, the wartime police blotters read like a dispatch from the outer rings of hell. Many reports involved service members, and naval ratings, specifically.

There was indecent exposure by a naval rating at 9 Uniacke Street. The complainant was a Sgt. Rogers and his wife, who lived next door. There was common assault by a naval rating. There was a stabbing case involving an American soldier and a Canadian naval rating at Franklyn Park. There was a great deal of "loitering," which, in the context of the city's homelessness and lack of recreation, would be expected. A Canadian naval rating was charged with public drunkenness after a report of a prowler in backyards on Spring Garden Road. An English naval rating named Dempsey was apprehended after breaking into Oxford Jewellers on Barrington Street. In truth, reading through these blotters, as much as service members were the perpetrators in these reports, they were also victims, mostly of violence or theft—often both. No wonder Mayor Lloyd was in Ottawa asking not only for "special consideration," but for money to hire more police. The federal government remained unmoved. "Halifax was accorded no special status," writes White in *Conscripted City*, "on the grounds that all urban centres were undergoing similar difficulties because of the war, and to treat one differently would create a precedent for other cities."

By 1942, this neglect reached a boiling-over point, from the perspective of both the military and civilians. Service members, for their part, were done with Halifax, a place where they couldn't get a beer without buying it from a bootlegger, couldn't count on a night's bed, could barely get into a restaurant or a movie theatre. An anonymous, undated open letter to Halifax in poem form captures well the feelings of many a service member in the city during the war. One stanza (of several doozies) reads:

You don't speak English, you speak Haligonese,
And the stench off the pond is what you call breeze,
You make us pay double for all you can sell
But after the war you can still go to "HELL".
And when you reach Hades and Satan greets you,
You'll feel right at home—he's from here too.

Even as the influx slowed and Halifax's population stabilized starting in late 1943, the city's situation with regard to housing and recreation remained in dire straits. Pifher reported in August to the National War Services funds advisory board that hostels at this time were "over-crowded to the extent that the health of the occupants may be endangered." In the words of one Air Force Wing Commander that Pifher quoted in his report: "Hostel conditions for men in Halifax are deplorable in the extreme." The war was four years on, and the damage in Halifax was irreparable. Halifax's civilians felt trod-upon by the services. Halifax-based service members felt let down by their guests. In truth, neither was to blame. Both suffered because of the neglect of the federal government and its failure to see the interconnectedness of housing, health, crime, and recreation, and its failure to see the correlation between civilian and military well-being. Within twenty months of Pifher's report, Halifax would crumble in a riot, the roots of which lie in this orchestrated indifference. The feds had made Halifax a war city, and then refused to concede that they'd done so. They preached the importance of morale, but failed to adequately provide the means for it to flourish. Instead, they depended on service organizations and leagues of women volunteers to provide those services, all the while creating conditions that made it as difficult as possible for them to do so. No one got out of it unscathed. An anonymous Halifax woman volunteer who worked evenings behind the counter at the YMCA canteen told Jean Bruce for *Back the Attack!*, "It was low-ceilinged and smoky and crowded, and there was always a slightly drunken sailor away in a corner playing the piano. Some nights men told us terrible, terrible stories of bombed-out houses, dead families, occupied countries, Nazi tyranny, torpedoed ships. We'd give them some more coffee and laugh at their jokes, and go home to our comfortable beds and have nightmares, with cold winds blowing through our minds."

The work of supporting well-being was palliation. Food and housing were essential, but also essential for these young men—who had, until they'd arrived back in the city, faced death in a very real way, and who would soon enough face it afresh when they were again deployed—was knowing someone cared. They needed someone who would listen, someone who would show concern. A cup of tea meant more than a cup of tea. A woman at a mothers' corner sewing a hole in a pocket meant more than a mere repair. The feds understood this; they talked the talk of morale, even as they gave it short shrift by their inaction.

But it wasn't only Ottawa that failed service members. It was Halifax, too.

Chapter Six

DARN THAT DREAM

Dolly McEuen laughed heartily over her left shoulder at the antics of Royal Navy Seaman James Reid. Reid stood beside her outside the Ajax Club, mock flexing and carrying a wide grin, comparing biceps with an unidentified fellow crew member of HMS *Jervis Bay*, possibly Samuel Patience, also a seaman and also a Scot. Same as Dolly. Reid and his pal had good reason to smile. They were two survivors of the attack on HMS *Jervis Bay*, a steamship that took heavy shelling on November 5, 1940, while acting as the sole escort for a thirty-seven–ship convoy. Eight days after it left Halifax en route to Britain, the group of merchant ships was spotted smack-dab in the middle of the North Atlantic by the German pocket battleship *Admiral Scheer*. It was suicide, but for an escort ship, it was also duty: HMS *Jervis Bay* steamed toward the *Admiral Scheer* and engaged its less-capable guns, giving the rest of the convoy time to scatter. After a twenty-four-minute battle, *Jervis Bay* was on fire, listing badly to port, its captain dead, its crew members battered or dead, and with no guns left. Those remaining abandoned ship into the 10°C water. Six hours later, in the pitch black and in worsening seas, Captain Sven Olander of the Swedish freighter *Stureholm* picked up survivors from the first of four life rafts. Sixty-eight were pulled from the water; sixty-five of them alive. They buried three at sea and, then, at great risk, Olander and his crew returned the survivors to Halifax, thirteen hundred nautical miles away—the closest port. They were back in the harbour on November 12, 1940.

Dolly McEuen's Ajax Club wasn't in shape to host any kind of gathering. But Dolly wanted to hold an event to commemorate HMS *Jervis Bay* and celebrate the *Stureholm* and its captain's bravery and sacrifice, so the Ajax would bloody well manage. The unofficial inauguration of the Tobin Street...well, what to call the Ajax? A club, yes. It was a vast mansion, with a bar, a library, sitting rooms, and plenty of lawn. But the Ajax was more. It was unique in Halifax: the only place the thousands of ratings looking for a spot to sit and have a drink could order one legally—just beer, mind you; no hard liquor allowed—outside barracks. And the only place they could fit in enough friends. The canteen at Stadacona accommodated too few. This no doubt informed the Ajax club's motto: Nec Quirquam Nisi Ajax—loosely translated from the Latin: "Nothing Except Ajax." (Dolly, who co-founded the North End Services Canteen, had a real thing for mottos.) So, despite the fact that the urinals hadn't arrived and the wallpaper-hangers were standing on ladders above glue pots, Dolly planned a luncheon for HMS *Jervis Bay*'s survivors, Captain Olander, and the members of the *Stureholm* crew. Toasts were raised at the crowded bar, photos were snapped on the steps of the rounded columned portico front entrance. The Ajax interior might have been in a state, but Dolly most certainly was not. She wore her fox stole shoulder wrap over an inverted box-pleat skirt suit, pin curls, and bold lipstick. In her right hand, she gripped the massive paw of Sven Olander. In her left, a lit cigarette. This moment, in front of the Ajax, with the survivors and their rescuers, smiling and waving, ten days post-attack, was what it was all about for Dolly. The Ajax wouldn't be just a club. It wouldn't be just a place for a naval rating to get a beer. And this informal launch party wasn't just a luncheon. It was a welcome. It was an embrace. It was gratitude embodied. It told these men they mattered.

A month later, on December 14, 1940, with the help of voluntary work parties from the Canadian and Royal Navies, the Ajax opened its doors to ratings from either navy. The main lounge fireplace was

SKIPPER TOASTED. He is Capt. Sven Olander, of the Swedish ship Stureholm who turned his ship back to rescue survivors of the Jervis Bay. Proposing the toast is the club's energetic chairman, Mrs. C. Stuart McEuen. Everybody looks happy.

A newspaper clipping shows the Ajax Club's Dolly McEuen toasting Captain Sven Olander of the Swedish ship Stureholm *in November 1940 after his rescue of survivors from HMS* Jervis Bay. (NS ARCHIVES)

surrounded by leather armchairs, chandeliers, and floor-length curtains. Brand new linoleum floors had been installed, a donation to the club. The smoking lounges were set, and the bar polished. Dolly chose a cream-and-Dutch-blue colour scheme for the two thousand–book library, and volunteers made sure small bowls of flowers were kept fresh on the desks and the mantel. The two games rooms' walls had autographed photos of Hollywood stars. One presumes the urinals did, in fact, arrive. The walled garden was dotted with blue and yellow umbrellas for shade and boasted a stone cooking fireplace in a secluded spot under some trees where men could barbecue. There was a tennis court and a horseshoe pitch. Just as she had written updates to sponsors of the North End Services Canteen,

Dolly did the same for the Ajax. "On entering the club, you see a beautiful hall, with a winding staircase," she wrote in the first annual report. "Not a thumb mark mars the delicate wallpaper, this is the only gift which might have been termed impracticable. In the dining rooms are light-coloured enamelled tables and chairs without a scratch, without a burn. Then there is the garden, with its beds of gay flowers; these have proved a great joy to the men, and never has a bed been walked on, or a flower touched." Two weeks after the official opening, for Christmas 1940, Dolly festooned the club with garland, spruce boughs, and bells. Every man who walked through the door got a present, care of the Interallied Hospitality Fund, which was supported by Dolly and her many friends, and fattened without question with the help of her fizz and unending suasion. The Ajax even had a club mascot—Spitfire, a tortoiseshell kitten, named by the survivors of HMS *Jervis Bay*, who lost their own cat, Spitfire, in the attack.

The Ajax Club wasn't only one of the loveliest clubs in the city, it was also impeccably run, with zero financial support from the government. And it helped solve a huge Halifax problem: it gave naval ratings, that is, any member who wasn't an officer, one place in the city of Halifax to get a drink that wasn't questionable bootleg liquor, in a place that wasn't a dive or a urine-drenched alley. The club, and its beer—twelve-ounce bottles for twenty cents and ten-ounce drafts for ten cents, in strictly limited quantities—kept ratings from the Royal, Canadian, and Allied navies safe, comfortable, and comforted.

To this point in our story, I've been largely keeping mention of the Ajax Club from you. Not because it wasn't important, but because it deserves its own close look. The Ajax is a bellwether for the trajectory of the war in Halifax—salvation for the tens of thousands who would come through its doors, yet a salvation that would soon be denied them due to Halifax's pernicious small-mindedness. The Ajax would be shuttered within fourteen months of its official opening. It failed not because it was bad, but because it was too good. And in no small measure because it was managed—not just staffed by, but run, terrifically—by a come-from-away woman.

The motto's question was put to Halifax in the spring of 1942: And nothing if not Ajax? And, as you'll see, Halifax gave its petty, petty answer.

Dolly (properly speaking, Janet Evelyn McEuen) swooped into the Lord Nelson Hotel in fall 1939 along with her husband, Dr. Charles Stuart McEuen, a Navy surgeon. Either then or very soon after, they were joined by their twenty-one-year-old niece, Mhairi Fenton-McEuen, whom Dolly and Stuart had cared for since Mhairi was five years old. Whether Dolly saw her stay in Halifax as temporary, whether she couldn't find appropriate housing (a less likely scenario, given her social status and deeper-than-most pockets), or whether she simply preferred staying in a housekeeping suite in the Lord Nelson (who wouldn't, with its posh two-level lobby, expansive sitting rooms, gold-leaf coffered ceilings, and attentive staff?), that's where she made landfall and that's where she hunkered down for the haul of the war.

It's not clear exactly when the McEuens arrived, but it was at some point before September 12, 1939, the date Stuart was promoted at Stadacona to Acting Surgeon Lieutenant-Commander, two days after the start of the war. For her part, Dolly immediately promoted herself from officer's wife to Halifax mover and shaker. She made the acquaintance of the Macneill sisters—Isabel, Janet, and Edith—and Jean Mills and her husband Hugh, who ran Mills Brothers, as well as the Halifax Concert Party Guild, the city's biggest wartime entertainment outfit. That's how she got Mills to host the opening of the North End Services Canteen. Patently, Dolly knew the crowd to align herself with. She immediately set to working. And to networking. By October 14—voila, she was on hand at the opening of the North End Services Canteen. Seven months later, in May 1940, Stuart shed his "acting" designation and became Surgeon Lieutenant-Commander at Stadacona. By then, Dolly had already registered the Interallied Hospitality Fund under the War Charities Act, with Isabel and Edith listed as the co-administrators of the fund, secretary and treasurer, respectively. (Their sister, Janet, though definitely no slouch, was less involved in executive-level organizing than her sisters; after all, she was at this time the single mother to a just-turned–five-year-old.) All that summer of 1940, Dolly volunteered at the North End Services Canteen and reached out to friends and acquaintances to pad the bank account of the Interallied Hospitality Fund. She was also on the hunt for a home for the club she envisioned might serve a role similar to that of the North End Services Canteen, but go beyond it, too. She would call it the Ajax, after the Royal Navy cruiser that had engaged with and chased a German pocket battleship off the southern coast of Brazil in the first naval battle of the Second World War. In September, she struck gold when she got in contact with the trustees of the Odell Estate.

The house was empty, which was a good start. The Odell Estate had been built sometime before 1874. That was the year the man who had it built, Justice William Blowers Bliss, died there. Why not call it the Bliss Estate, you ask? Actually, its name was "Fort Massey," which must have caused no small amount of confusion, given the nearby church, Fort Massey, and the nearby cemetery, Fort Massey, which grew out of the original, you guessed it…fort, Fort Massey. One of Bliss's daughters, Elizabeth, had married William Hunter Odell, a senator. When Bliss died, Odell and company inherited Fort Massey (the estate), and whether earnestly working to limit confusion or leaning in to the cachet of his new house, the sprawling property at the corner of Tobin and Queen Streets, in Halifax's south end, became known as the Odell Estate. Senator Odell died in 1891, in the house. Elizabeth Odell made it to 1901. Their only son, William, had died young in Rawalpindi, Bengal, in 1894, so the estate was passed into the care of the Senator Odell's spinster daughters—Ella, Frances, and Mary—who, as the twentieth century found its footing, lived it up in the twenty-five room mansion, keeping on the servants, and holding elaborate parties as well as pet funerals, according to the *Montreal Standard*. Ella passed in 1920; Frances in 1934. Mary was the last to shuffle off this mortal (and apparently fabulous, what with the parties and pet funerals) coil, in 1937, aged eighty-one. None of the sisters had children to whom to pass on the mansion, so the estate was henceforth controlled by a trust. And the trustees were more than happy to let Dolly take over, rent-free, for the duration of the war, provided she paid for and completed any renovations on her own dime and time. At the crest of Tobin Street, the house would be easy for naval ratings to find, a straight shot up the hill from the Nova Scotian Hotel, where the liquor flowed freely, if illegally, at weekly supper-dances, having been smuggled in by any means necessary.

Prohibition in Nova Scotia has a messy history. The federal government, bowing to prohibitionist pressure, in 1878 passed the Canada Temperance Act, a weaselly piece of legislation that passed the buck by allowing Canadian cities and counties to hold votes on the availability of alcohol within their borders. By 1882, every county and city in Nova Scotia had held a vote, giving booze the boot. Halifax electors were the sole holdout. In 1910, a seemingly redundant law was passed by the Nova Scotia Legislature that prohibited liquor everywhere except Halifax. But in September 1916, Halifax could hold out no longer. The province forced the city into prohibition—at least for a while. By 1929, Nova Scotians were clamouring for access to the everyday pleasures most other Canadians could lay their hands on, having already crawled their way out of prohibitionist polity (except for Prince Edward Island, which held on through 1948). A plebiscite killed Nova Scotia prohibition the following year.

Nova Scotia's, and especially Halifax's, history with prohibition was also messy because, well, it's not like there was ever, at any point, a dearth of booze in the city. Halifax was a port town. If you wanted something, you could get it. So even though alcohol's legal return saw the province institute extreme measures to restrict its sale, skirting the measures was relatively simple. Alcohol could be purchased legally only from province-owned stores, by those of majority age, but there was no Chianti with a meal at a restaurant or hotel. There was no after-work beer at the pub. And while it was a fact that people were not casually or openly drinking in restaurants or at dances, they sure as hell were drinking, and not only in their homes or private clubs. "This is not difficult in Halifax," wrote the *Montreal Gazette* in March 1942. "Never, even in the depth of prohibition, has it been hard to find a drink in the east coast Canadian port: assuredly it is not hard now." Alcohol was an issue of setting, not access. And so this vast influx of people from other provinces and countries—men and women who were accustomed to having a drink and relaxing—found themselves dealing with the embarrassment of flasks under tables, bootleggers abounding, and drunks in the street. This was the social problem, health problem, public health problem, and morale problem that the Ajax Club was teed up to help solve.

And Dolly set up the club not only to solve it—to allow men to come in and enjoy a beer and let off some steam—but to solve it strategically. One has to imagine that the rules in place at the Ajax around alcohol and other vices were painstakingly crafted as a prophylactic against those who might accuse the club of bringing about the downfall of its patrons. The club was open daily from 2:00 to 11:00 P.M., but the bar itself was only open from 5:00 to 9:00 P.M., and never on Sundays. Patrons used a mandatory free coat- and hat check, and they were not permitted to carry their drinks to other parts of the club, such as the library, garden, or card room. Men could buy tickets for five beers—bottle or glass—and no more. If they hadn't used all their tickets before the bar closed, they could cash them in. One bottle of beer could also be enjoyed as an add-on to the twenty-five-cent full-course cold suppers in the club's restaurant, but these were only available from 6:00 to 8:00 P.M. There was beer, and beer alone. No spirits, no shots. And no gambling allowed, either.

"Dry" ratings who chose not to drink were happily accommodated in the Ajax's second restaurant, called the Pop Shop, where sandwiches were served for five cents, along with soft drinks. This service ran an hour later, from 6:00 to 9:00 P.M. This all seems, perhaps, very regimented, but these were men who were accustomed to regimentation. There's no indication in any of the archival material that men were dissatisfied with the Ajax or its offerings—on the contrary. They loved it. Dolly's revolution in supporting the naval ratings that visited the club was that she worked her best to fit the offerings to the men and their needs. The problem was that her club and its offerings did not fit into Halifax and its social mores.

⌒〜〜⌒

At first, the Ajax enjoyed broad support. Actually, scratch that. All along, the Ajax was beloved by *almost* all.

The Australian, New Zealand, South African, Norwegian, Dutch, Free French, and American navies all supported the club. Same for Halifax's mayor and the superintendent of the RCMP. Halifax's chief of police, the fabulously named Judson J. Conrad, publicly praised the Ajax, as did the Halifax Building and Trades Council. The pot of money from which the Ajax's operations were funded was heavily supported from across the country, and even from other countries, due to Dolly's connections. In 1944, even when the work had shifted away from the Ajax Club itself and on to other ventures, Dolly's Interallied Hospitality Fund raked in the equivalent in 2021 dollars of almost $1.3 million. Obviously the British and Canadian navies were on board. They had sent voluntary work parties to help with the push to finish renovations and open the club in December

1940, and continued to send daily work parties over to complete odd jobs and maintenance, and for cleaning duty. These men assisted the paid staff, including a gardener, part-time furnace man, and handyman, as well as two cooks. Dolly, Isabel, and Edith were full-time volunteers, along with four others. And there were another sixty regular part-time volunteers, all Halifax women. The British Admiralty also provided the Ajax with crowd control and serving help—two leading seamen and a master-at-arms. The Ajax opening was attended by Sir Gerald Campbell, the British high commissioner, who travelled from Ottawa to be at the launch, where he spoke about the great promise of the Ajax and the service gap it would fill. "A great deal of trouble starts with loneliness," he said. All this was important, obviously. But there was one nod of support that was essential, and don't for a moment imagine that an organizer as determined and direct as Dolly failed to obtain it. The Ajax was across Tobin Street from Fort Massey United Church, and for any of this to work, Dolly needed to know that Fort Massey was on board. To that end, she reached out to Reverend John Norrie Anderson. He raised no objection. With that hurdle cleared, Dolly hurtled forward.

The Ajax didn't work because it was posh ("no millionaires' club was ever kept neater," wrote the *Montreal Gazette*), and, really, not even because it was well-funded. It worked because it pivoted to meet ratings' needs and constantly expanded services, just like its sister organization, the North End Services Canteen. While Edna Rogers and Carol Cleather reliably sold beer tickets from giant rolls and Dolly's niece, Mhairi, helped ratings check out books from the library, club driver Moira Drummond pulled around to Tobin Street in the club's station wagon, a donation from Labatt Brewing Company, based in London, Ontario. In the summer, Moira popped by the hospital every day and picked up convalescing service members, six at a time, and took them for two-hour drives outside the city. She dropped them at the club for tea in the garden and then returned them to the hospital. Given the volume of men who enjoyed these drives in the

AJAX LIBRARIAN is Miss Mhairi MacLeod Fenton, of Montreal, who was in France during the Nazi blitzkrieg and was evacuated from Boulogne on a small boat 12 hours before the mass evacuation of British Tommies. Here she previews a novel for a bearded British sailor. Like other members of the staff she gives her time gratis. Library needs more books.

Dolly McEuen's niece, Mhairi, shown here in a March 1941 newspaper clipping, served as the librarian at the Ajax Club. (NS ARCHIVES)

THE AJAX "TAXI" is a station wagon donated by a London, Ontario, firm. Unsalaried chauffeur in the picture is Miss Moira Drummond, of Montreal, daughter of the late celebrated Canadian poet. Here she is about to drive a working party of British Tars back to their ship.

The Ajax Club "taxi," driven by Moira Drummond, in a March 1941 newspaper clipping. (NS ARCHIVES)

summer of 1941—nine hundred, according to Isabel in an Ajax supporters update missive—Moira would have had to commit to daily drives for five months straight. In the winter, Moira donned her kitten-heel boots and a pea coat, white scarf, and chauffeur's cap to act as the club taxi driver, picking up and returning patrons and work parties to their ships. The wagon was outfitted with tire chains to cope with Halifax's slippery and hilly streets. In these, and in so many other offerings, the Ajax proved its efficiency and ability to act directly and quickly. The Ajax started as one thing, and the women there consistently met the patrons where they were and offered them what they said they needed. This matched the ethos of the North End Services Canteen. And it stood in decided contrast to the lurching half-steps of the feds.

Dolly knew the Ajax's work was vital, and she called it such in the July 1941 annual report. The club's object, she said, "is to uphold the morale of the men, to bring warmth and hope into their lives and help them forget, for a few hours at least, the grim realities of war.... In the creation of this naval club, we dared an experiment in social services." It quite literally was. There's no clearer line drawn to that conclusion than that of the five-minute speech made by Petty Officer Arnold Edgar, cited in Stephen Kimber's *Sailors, Slackers and Blind Pigs*. Edgar was addressing the Halifax judge sentencing him for assault on a police constable in the post-Ajax Club era. "Here we are," Edgar explained, "far from home and among strangers.... We come in from a long cruise and we have nowhere to go for entertainment and relaxation and a glass of beer so we are forced to buy liquor from the government stores, and to drink it we have to go to cheap restaurants." (Given the restrictions, Edgar must be referring to an illegal club.) "There, we meet the wrong kinds of people, and sometimes we get into trouble. We used to have a good place to go, a place where we could meet and talk and have our beer and pleasant surroundings. That was the Ajax Club."

But the Ajax Club's days were numbered.

Before its slap-in-the-face closure, which came in February 1942, the Ajax served 170,000 naval ratings, doing the work the government didn't or wouldn't. But all of it would be dismissed, because a handful of influential Haligonians, had a real hate-on for beer. Worse: for women providing beer. And worst of all? For come-from-away women in the business of providing beer.

~⌇⌇~

Dolly opened the anonymous letter and read her accuser's charge. "You are almost a Jezebel," it began. "Read your Bible, and see what follows drunkards and all those who lead the young astray." It called the Ajax a "den," implying iniquity and sin. Another letter was addressed to Edith, also anonymous, but, judging by the writing, from a different author. This concerned citizen was "greatly surprised and ashamed to think that a daughter of Prof. Macneill," would support the immoral work of the Ajax. "God forbid you should ever have a son to bring up to your way of thinking." These gendered attacks were par for the course. Mrs. E. M. Murray wrote to the *Halifax Star* in February 1942, calling the Ajax women volunteers "barmaids." (Hardly a slight today, I know, but this was serious mudslinging in the 1940s.) Murray also implied that Dolly was embezzling funds, or was at least exploiting volunteers and swindling the public, who were paying to support the Navy men on the daily work parties. William D. Naftel, in *Halifax at War*, suggests the small-but-vocal campaign against the Ajax, which began out of the blue in January 1942, was based in resentment over these women's ability to quickly get things done. "The fact that a few local women had established and run a successful organization on such a scale upset, it was said, some national organizations, which felt that their jurisdictions have been invaded." Jay White, in *Conscripted City*, says the rancour was because Dolly wasn't a Haligonian: "When other war service activities were barely off the ground, the Ajax Club was the most lavishly outfitted centre for servicemen in Halifax. The fact that it was organized and financed mainly by wealthy Montrealers and corporate sponsors from Central Canada created resentment among local volunteers who felt that their less grandiose efforts suffered by comparison." Indeed, corporations and individuals sent furnishings and cheques and books and magazines from myriad places, big and small. Donors were in Toronto, the Bahamas, New York, London, England, and Washington, DC. A material volume came from Montreal—Dolly's home base, even if she was living in Halifax for the duration of the war and had shown herself to be deeply committed to the city and to the community she found here. A disdain for the Ajax's come-from-away tinge was even expressed by National Defence for Naval Services minister Angus L. Macdonald, in an April 1, 1942, letter to National War Services Deputy Minister T. C. Davis: "The Ajax Club was formed by a certain lady, Mrs. McEuen, of Montreal, whose husband is a Commander in the Navy at Halifax. I think that this was rather a mistake, but Mrs. McEuen made no public appeal, and evidently collected some money from personal friends."

Nova Scotia's distaste for those who are not from here—"come-from-away" is the common quasi-pejorative—is difficult to explain to, um, those who aren't from here. It's probably a little bit of racism, a little bit of anti-immigration, but it's not explicitly or even completely those things. There is a history in Nova Scotia, and in Atlantic Canada generally, of banding together to overcome geographic isolation and adversity. This goes back a long time. The concept of come-from-away suspicion is rooted in the idea that others can't tell us what to do, because they don't *understand* us, or how we work, or, primarily, what we have been through. Perhaps more simply: those who haven't been here for generations haven't put in the time. Earning the right to call yourself a Nova Scotian is about an unrealistic track record of shared perseverance. (A linked idea is the notion that anyone who moves away, or "goes down the road," is somehow a traitor.) None of this makes a lot of sense, but it's fiercely endemic to this place. It's also completely and sadly devoid of all self-awareness of the fact that, unless you are Mi'kmaq, the Indigenous people on whose stolen land Nova Scotia was created, you are, by definition, a come-from-away.

So, even though most of the women volunteers at the Ajax, and even most of the executive—including two Macneill daughters, entrenched members of Halifax's Old 400s—were Haligonian, the Ajax would always be seen as a come-from-away venture, and would always be judged more harshly by some because of the fact. But there was a complexity to the attacks on the Ajax. It was also about women in positions of capable leadership. It was about Dolly as a come-from-away. But mostly, and most successfully for the temperance zealots at Fort Massey Church, it was about the beer.

In March 1942, H. R. Grant, the Social Service Council and Temperance Alliance of Nova Scotia's general secretary, wrote a letter to the *Halifax Chronicle*. It contained some truth: "Alcohol is alcohol, whether in beer or whiskey" and "science teaches that alcohol when taken as a beverage (causes) diminished efficiency of body and mind." It contained some spurious, if conventional, temperance wisdom: alcohol causes "an enfeeblement of moral control" and "any beverage containing alcohol in any amount is not safe and therefore unfit for use." It also contained an outright lie: The Ajax was working to "intimidate the members of Fort Massey and the members of government." Ultimately, it set up the conceit that Dolly was a purveyor of danger and death and it set up her neighbours at Fort Massey United Church as the frontline of Halifax's protection, "in deadly earnest against all forms of evil." A showdown was in the breeze.

⌒⌒

Dolly wore heels. And she was a fan of skirt suits—thicker for the winter, lighter in the summer. Pumps and a skirt are not the easiest outfit for climbing up onto a bar, yet, no doubt with the help of the seamen around her—who would, by all accounts, have moved mountains to protect their Dolly—up she climbed onto the Ajax's brass rail beer counter. She wanted to be heard.

"After tonight," she announced, looking out over the crowd, "we are unable to serve you beer."

There is no record of the tone in which Dolly read her statement to the men on February 2, 1942. But we know this much: Dolly loved her club. She loved her men. She believed wholly in their right to enjoy the same privileges as any naval officer visiting any of the private Halifax clubs to which that rank automatically made them honorary members. She believed wholly in their right to enjoy the same privileges as civilians who happened to have homes in which to drink a beer. She was called "fiery" in the media (a comment frequently paired with a description of her ginger hair). She was called "pushy" and "persistent" in confidential government memos. What she actually was, in my estimation? Strong. On January 19, 1942, she received two-weeks' notice that the club's beer license would not be renewed by the province and would only move forward on a temporary basis. Technically, the club could, on a shaky footing, and for who knows how long, still sell beer. But Dolly wasn't having it. "I, now, as a citizen," she promised from atop the bar, "intend to take up the cudgels on your behalf."

With a forest of naval ratings looking up at her as she read her statement, Dolly explained that the Ajax's beer license had been suspended after complaints from the apparently deep-suffering congregation of Fort Massey Church. The Canadian Press reported, the following day, that the seamen in front of Dolly "voiced disapproval." No doubt. Dolly's supporters rallied in the early spring of 1942. The letter-writing began— testimonials from the Building and Trades Council, the RCMP, the mayor, the police chief. A shore patrolman assigned to monitor the Ajax area told the Canadian Press that not one brawl had started there, nor had one charge been laid. Haligonians wrote to their papers, Halifax's *Chronicle*, *Mail*, *Herald*, and *Star*. Canadians wrote to publications across Canada. The Ajax situation was even covered in US magazines. Whether endorsing alcohol or abstinence, letters, editorials, and private correspondence, such as Dolly's "Jezebel" letter, became a battleground of opinion on the matter of the Ajax. The only thing everyone might have agreed on? Halifax was intransigent.

The province, on the Ajax file, was fiercely immune to reason and inoculated against recognizing irony. One undated local editorial held at the Nova Scotia Archives points out that Premier A. Stirling MacMillan revoked the Ajax license to protect the congregation of Fort Massey from the nearby presence of beer, when no church, including Fort Massey, had taken action to help children recently discovered living in condemned shacks on Grafton Street. The second irony: the province cannot possibly have been as deeply concerned about protecting Haligonians from booze as it claimed, given that it operated—and profited from—a liquor store on Agricola Street at Bloomfield Street, across from W. S. Fielding School, where "hundreds of children see patrons lined up to buy liquor at the store, which is open all day."

How did the Ajax shift so quickly from admired to admonished?

At a January 2, 1942, meeting—just one month before Dolly stood on the bar—five Fort Massey elders had met in the minister's study for a regular Kirk Session, a meeting of the minister and church leaders. By the end, it was agreed that the church would protest the club's license renewal to the attorney general. At this point, the Ajax had been running for over a year, and problem free, by the independent accounts of the police and shore patrol. And Fort Massey had been run—for nearly exactly the same amount of time—by a new minister, Reverend Gerald Rogers.

Rogers had replaced Reverend John Norrie Anderson, who left his post at the end of 1940, only weeks after Dolly had spoken to him about the Ajax and received his nod of okay on the club's operations. Two things about Anderson: however he felt about alcohol, he understood what it meant to be a service member. He was wounded and gassed in France in 1918 as a member of the Royal Field Artillery. And? When Dolly came to speak to him in the fall of 1940, he had apparently given her the all-clear for beer without having consulted his flock. Then almost immediately, in flies Rogers—a veteran not of war, but of preaching.

There are two points in the Kirk Session minutes that justify the church's protest. First, Dolly was buying the Odell Estate. It was listed for sale by the trustees in November 1941, and Dolly secured first right of purchase for $16,000, intending to donate it to the federal government for the use of naval ratings—on three conditions: that it operate for the duration of the war, that the Canadian Navy have control over honorary membership, and that the name stay. "I make no further conditions," she wrote in her offer letter, "...but I express the wish that upon the cessation of hostilities, the club should continue for the benefit of Royal Canadian Naval ratings, with Royal Naval ratings as honorary members or guests. Should this then not be feasible, I would wish that the premises be used for any club purposes deemed fit by the Royal Canadian Naval authorities, and, failing the latter, that the property be sold and the proceeds be donated to the Royal Canadian Navy Benevolent Fund." Angus L. Macdonald, the National Defence for Naval Services minister, who was negotiating on behalf of the feds, was on board. On December 15, 1941, he sent a telegram to Dolly acknowledging acceptance of the terms. In the eyes of the Kirk Session, this was an indication that the Ajax Club wasn't destined to be a temporary imposition on their godly spheres, but a permanent club. And no matter how well-run it was, that apparently wouldn't do. The complaint was lodged with the attorney general; on January 19, the club received notice that its beer license wasn't being renewed; and one week after that, the apparently spineless Angus L. Macdonald wrote to Dolly rejecting her generous gift.

The second note in the meeting minutes justifying the protest to the attorney general? "Several undesirable incidents." The specifics are left out, but in a later statement, church elders noted a grocery list of indiscretions, as trifling as women and children seeing men entering and exiting the club, and as serious as the time a drunk man wandered into the church in the middle of a children's party and passed out on the floor. In another case, not mentioned in the church's letter, but in Kimber's *Sailors, Slackers and Blind Pigs*, a drunken sailor, who was passed out in the pews one afternoon, roused himself to give a wolf whistle to a woman church member who was walking by. Despite these greater and lesser annoyances, there's no evidence that Reverend Rogers and the Fort Massey congregants were unable to carry out their work or worship because of the beer sales across the street. In any case, the powers that be, including the then-crucial Reverend Anderson, had given their unanimous consent for the Ajax to open in late 1940, as well as their direct and ongoing public support.

All the powers that be, that is, but one: Alexander Stirling MacMillan, Nova Scotia's premier. Or, to put a more accurate point on the matter: the premier's wife, Martha Sinclair MacMillan, head of the Fort Massey Ladies' Association and the woman who had been wolf-whistled at that afternoon while she was walking through the church.

～\\～

To understand the importance of this moment, it's essential to understand Nova Scotia's acute history of political backroom-ing and favour-currying. Consider: before he was a federal cabinet minister, Angus L. Macdonald was the premier of Nova Scotia. He had been in the job since 1933. Prime Minster Mackenzie King wanted Macdonald, a well-liked Nova Scotian and a man in prime professional position vis-à-vis Halifax and the Navy, in his war cabinet. And so, when Norman McLeod Rogers, a cabinet minister (coincidentally, *also* a Nova Scotian, as was Defence Minister James Ralston) died in a plane crash in June 1940, Angus L., as Nova Scotians referred to him, was installed as the member of parliament for Kingston City. (Technically, he ran unopposed in the August 1940 by-election that was triggered by Norman Rogers's death, but you get what I mean.) When Angus L. went to Ottawa, Alexander Stirling MacMillan took over. When the war was over, MacMillan retired from politics so Angus L. could have his old job back. (Nice for Macdonald, but one has to wonder how and if this benefitted Nova Scotians; similarly, how it helped the people of Kingston, Ontario, to have a random Atlantic Canadian premier take over as their MP.)

That her Nova Scotia–premier husband was powerful also conveyed power upon Martha MacMillan. And beyond Nova Scotia, too: in 1943, given the shortages in Halifax stores, Martha was having trouble putting her finger on a film projector for the screenings she wanted to run at the YWCA. She wrote directly to National War Services Minister Léo Richer LaFlèche, the top of the chain. LaFlèche, old boy to old boy, asked John Grierson, the founding (and at that time still) chair of the National Film Board, to send Martha MacMillan something right away. There are no screaming links between Martha and the city's ardent temperance advocates, but it's worth noting that her husband was born in Antigonish, Nova Scotia, where the West River Temperance Society, established in 1827, staked its claim as the first such organization in British North America. Martha herself was a native of Prince Edward Island, whose prohibition law outlasted Nova Scotia's. It was Canada's last holdout by a staggering two decades.

It's impossible to know if Martha or A. S. were at the fateful Kirk Session in Reverend Rogers's study. The minutes list the attendees as Dr. A. E. Kerr, Mr. H. A. Flemming, and Mr. A. R. Rettie, plus an unnamed moderator (this is presumably Reverend Rogers) and an unnamed clerk (this is likely Arthur S. Barnstead, a church elder and elected clerk for the session). It's likewise impossible to know what kinds of conversations went on about the impact of the Ajax, and how great or small was the influence of Martha having been wolf-whistled at in the church. Here's what I would argue *is* known: A. S. MacMillan had it in for the Ajax from the beginning.

Even before the Ajax's official opening in December 1940, MacMillan had sent a letter to Angus L., maligning the club and asking Macdonald to warn British High Commissioner Campbell not to travel from Ottawa to attend the opening. Who deserves the credit for Campbell's eventual attendance and rousing endorsement? Macdonald for refusing to deliver MacMillan's warning? Or Campbell for completely ignoring it and coming to celebrate the Ajax anyway? Who knows? It took fourteen months, but in the end, Premier MacMillan got his way. The temporary license was finally officially cancelled on February 23, 1942. The night before, the Ajax sold its last beer.

———ᴠᴠ——

We don't know if Dolly was standing atop the bar again on the evening of February 22, but she wasn't impressed by "the action of Honourable A. S. MacMillan, the premier of Nova Scotia." Still, she kept her cool, and used her moment to speak to thank those service members around her. "God knows how few of us civilians will ever realize how much you are doing for us and how much we owe you. But at least on my behalf and the lady voluntary workers of this club, I say thank you."

She still had the cudgels in hand. And she wasn't going down without swinging them. Dolly had bought the Odell Estate, even after Angus L. pulled out of the deal that would have seen her donate it to the Navy. She proposed to Fort Massey Church, and Reverend Rogers, a compromise, seeing to it to address the church's issues, even if they were spurious. She invited Rogers, twice, to come visit the club, to recognize how nice it was and how controlled the environment. Rogers, on brand, refused to "cross the threshold as a Christian gentleman." So the reverend wouldn't talk one-on-one? No problem. She offered to move the club entrance to Kent Street, so no churchgoers would see men entering or exiting the Ajax. She would request that the Navies make Tobin Street out of bounds for all personnel. She would also install a high fence on the Tobin Street side of the property. The congregation, then, wouldn't merely be spared seeing naval ratings entering the club; they would neither see the ratings on Tobin Street nor, miraculously, would they even see the estate itself. Those were the specifics. The general idea was to make the Ajax seem, in the eyes of the Fort Massey congregation, less like what the church called it in a prepared statement: "A menace to the life and work of any church in the province."

Dolly no more believed the club was the root of the church's problems than she believed poor Hitler was simply misunderstood. Social ills existed in spades in wartime Halifax. And the Ajax wasn't only granting naval ratings the same civil privileges as anyone else, it was mitigating problems by, in Dolly's words, discouraging drunkenness. It was a coordinated effort in harm reduction. In her own prepared statement, she laid a dose of cold truth on the church, which would ring accurate for any Haligonian who'd been living the reality of Halifax at war for three years at this point: ratings were wandering the streets looking for beer. Finding none, they were buying spirits from the abundant bootleggers. While the Ajax was serving, she said, "this situation did not exist." In a 1966 feature story for *The Atlantic Advocate*, Norman Creighton characterizes the commonplaceness of bootlegging in wartime Halifax and the availability of liquor to servicemen: "You had only to step down a dark alley and knock on the first door. Then, twenty-four hours later, you stumbled back to your ship, with nothing to carry away from the city but a growing distaste for the Canadian way of life." No one ever doubted that the "undesirable incidents" with drunkenness at the church had taken place. But there was likewise never any proof that those men had gotten drunk at the Ajax. All this is not to mention other activities taking place openly in Halifax at the time—from the merely risqué, like the topless dancers at the Marcus Dance Show, to the illicit, like Germaine Pelletier's popular brothel at 51 Hollis Street, at the corner of Salter, positioned conveniently halfway between the Allied Merchant Seamen's Club and the Canadian Legion's Atlantic House hostel and recreation centre in Keith Hall. It's a wonder church elders didn't pin Halifax's uptick of wartime sex work on Dolly and the Ajax, too. But then, it was Dolly herself who had asked the Halifax Police's morality squad to beef up patrols around Tobin and Queen Streets to deter women from peddling their wares to her ratings as they came and went from the club.

Offering to install the fence, move the entrance, and keep the whole of the Canadian and Royal Navies off an entire Halifax street must have felt to Dolly like admitting guilt to a crime she didn't commit. And still, Reverend Rogers refused her overtures. In mid-March, Dolly wrote again to Rogers, the congregation, and the members of Nova Scotia's Legislative Assembly, inviting them to a meeting at the club to find a means of moving forward. Her invitation's opening salvo? "It is apparent that the situation in regard to the Royal Navy in Halifax is back where is was in 1939." Ouch. She dug deeper: come and talk, make an arrangement, or we'll keep fighting, and "bring greater publicity to the situation," calling that eventuality, with bald-faced sarcasm, a plight all involved "earnestly desire to avoid."

Thirty attended the meeting on March 13, 1942. Not to drink beer, which the Ajax could no longer sell, but to talk about why there was no beer on offer. Dolly reiterated her conviction that the Ajax, contrary to exacerbating alcohol abuse, mitigated it. And she spoke about a new, rumoured federal government-funded club that would replicate many of the offerings of the Ajax, including selling beer to naval ratings. Dolly didn't begrudge the Navies this new club. Her criticism hit solidly at the cock-up that characterized the federal authorities' handling of recreation and leisure for service members in Halifax, and the utter disconnect that existed in the mindset of the feds between service members with nothing to do or eat or drink, and the impact of those deprivations on the rest of Halifax.

The new club, she said,

> will take time, during which the men of the navies will walk the streets as they did before the creation of the Ajax Club. It will take money—money that all of you have been urged to lend and save for the government. It will take skilled labour, which is needed for vital defence work. It will take materials, of which there is an admitted shortage. Once opened, it will take more money to support it. ...

The Ajax Club is ready to serve tonight at no cost to the government.
All that is necessary to serve beer to the men who wish it is a license.
Why have we no license? The question is being asked all over Canada.

The Ajax was indeed a hot-button issue—one the federal government, the church, and the province were calculatedly avoiding. Of the thirty in attendance March 13 at the Ajax, only one Fort Massey congregant showed up: Melvin S. Clarke, a church leader, it seems, by virtue of his sitting on the 1945 committee representing the church in the purchase of a manse house. Clarke's single paltry contribution to the discussion was to say that he did not, in fact, represent the church. A sole member of the provincial government came to the meeting: Joseph R. Murphy, the Member of the Legislative Assembly for Halifax South. (A minor point reinforcing the incestuous nature of Nova Scotia politics: Murphy won that seat, unopposed, in the by-election to replace Angus L. when he went down the road to Ottawa to sit in King's war cabinet. Murphy died in office near the end of the war, which was convenient for Angus L., who needed a seat—so he reclaimed both it *and* the premiership.) At the meeting, Murphy said nothing.

The province's silence and the federal government's failure to show up did nothing to help the Ajax impasse. But it did a great deal to further tear apart the relationship between Halifax and the Navy, and to iron-in the image of the city as a backwater burg incapable of or unwilling to meet the challenges before it. This was Halifax's reputation across Canada and beyond. Reverend Rogers took one on the chin from an Edith M. Bacque of Toronto, who wrote to him directly and with "deep and nauseating contempt." Edith might have made a competent scriptwriter for war horror. "What do you know of the screaming torture of the stokers—some killed, many wounded, by live steam, when the boilers explode in (a) wounded ship? Have you dragged your existence through days in an open lifeboat—watching your comrades go—one by one—through madness—thirst—and freezing to death? Have you been at sea in the tropics—and known that hungry monsters await you should you go overboard?" She signs off, "Yours—in righteous disgust."

While Edith sneered at Rogers, most others sneered at Halifax.

"Total abstinence is still good politics Down East," wrote the *Montreal Gazette*, a paper with unequalled writing on the Ajax, given that the bulk of the Interallied Hospitality Fund's financial donations came from Montreal and its surrounds. "Nova Scotia is one of the places, now luckily reduced in number, where people drink wet and vote dry." Hugh MacLennan wrote in the *Star* a subtle but clear indictment of Halifax's priggish habits (given the city's treatment in *Barometer Rising*, this was something of a recurring literary theme for MacLennan). He noted that two former pupils from Lower Canada College in Montreal, one a military policeman and one a naval lieutenant, had separately reported to him the unfortunate closing of the Ajax. "After three months in my old town, they and their comrades had come to hate the place because they saw that a law adapted to peace-time circumstances was gnawing constantly at the self-respect of their men." He continued: "How can people pretend that it is better for the morality of a service man—or any other citizen—to drink slyly or around corners, to wander the streets in an effort to escape his loneliness, than to sit quietly with his friends as he has been accustomed to do at home?" (Two asides here that further the understanding of Halifax culture. First, in this letter, MacLennan is criticizing the city in a manner no Haligonian would normally abide from a come-from-away. It's tolerable, though, because despite MacLennan himself having long ago "gone down the road," he still counts as a Nova Scotian. Second, MacLennan fails here to mention his Old 400s connection and that he is an old family friend of the Macneills—he introduced Janet to her first husband and was a mixed-doubles tennis partner of Edith's. Long story short: MacLennan's criticism is far from arm's-length.) Criticism came from objective parties, too. *Time* magazine scorned Halifax's "Calvinist moral attitude." CBC host John Fisher, meanwhile, tried to mitigate the national censure on *East Coast Reporter*. "This city is carrying a great burden for Canada," he reminded his listeners. "This city has not been fairly represented to the Canadian public. A great work is being done here." It was true. And it was primarily women volunteers who were taking it on, and hustling to mend the tearing fabric as they went.

———

On March 21, 1942, one week after that final community meeting, the now-closed Ajax had its moveable assets frozen by the overseers of the War Charities Act. Dolly, a woman of her word, had followed through on her promise to buy the Odell Estate from its trustees, and was, despite everything she'd been through, still committed to gifting it for the use of naval ratings.

Negotiations started for the transfer of property and equipment to the Navy League. But on April 11, 1942, Navy League president David H. Gibson wrote to National War Services Minister J. T. Thorson and Deputy Minister T. C. Davis. This represented a significant move up the chain of command for anything Ajax-related. Gibson had a serious message to deliver, expressing a "deep conviction that the situation in respect to the naval ratings at Halifax, calls for immediate consideration and decision." Gibson noted that there were ten to twelve thousand naval ratings in port at any one time, seeking a few days of rest after fraught weeks or months at sea. A few, those lucky enough to have families in the city, would have a home for respite. The rest were at wits' end until they left again on the taxing cycle of deployment and return. And since the closure of the Ajax, there had been "recent persistent reports of these naval ratings casting about for a side-street or side-alley of 'dives' where they can take their refreshments." Gibson, with deep regret, informed Davis and Thorson that the Navy League could not be associated, in deed or implication, with taking over the Ajax because it would associate the league with the act of "depriving the rating thereof." The federal government had shuttered the club. In place, it had vaguely offered to help make way for a replacement. But when Gibson wrote his letter, it was almost two months after the Ajax lost its license and there had been no clear movement forward. Perhaps something in the letter hit a nerve. Three days later, the Navy League had the go-ahead to procure the Wanderers Grounds for a new recreation facility, including *two* buildings—one with a wet canteen, one dry.

It would be five long months from the Ajax's last beer to the first served at the Wanderers Grounds.

⁓⋀⋀⌣

Resilient people pivot.

Dolly shifted her skill and ambition, as well as the considerable financial heft of the Interallied Hospitality Fund, to her new endeavour, the Ajax Hospitality Headquarters. The new Ajax moved into a storefront location at 90 Spring Garden Road, in Halifax's main downtown shopping district, near Queen Street, right next door to Mills Brothers. There was no longer a bar, but the Ajax was well-attended nonetheless. The offerings matched, in many ways, what service members could enjoy on Tobin Street—essentially, whatever they reasonably needed. On the menu? Informal use of the Ajax lounge space with tea and snacks, a piano, an open fire, and writing desks, as well as planned parties by request. There was still a car, and still a volunteer chauffeur, so there were excursions for picnics, boating, swimming, and bonfires. Dolly supported a spiderweb of province-wide Ajax branches, including in Musquodoboit Harbour, Chester, Sheet Harbour, and Wolfville, where sailors could enjoy extended stays for convalescence. Volunteers began an "Advice on Shopping Department" that offered men help choosing gifts for loved ones at reasonable prices. They added a "Baby Department" as well, so expectant fathers could bring pre-packed care bundles back to their partners. For her part, Dolly remained simultaneously indefatigable and sartorially fabulous. A photo in the 1944–1945 Ajax annual report shows her, perennial broad smile, awarding the inaugural Royal Navy inter-ship soccer cup, wearing a leopard coat with what looks like a mink front panel and sleeves. Dolly was still working on her experiment in social services, in this Ajax iteration, as an exercise in radical hospitality. And in that, the Ajax continued, unabated, in its volunteer impact. An anonymous sailor who spent time recuperating at the Ajax branch in Hantsport, Nova Scotia, wrote to Dolly in August 1943: "No disrespect to [Halifax], but you do not need to be told how overcrowded it is, and how aimlessly sailors who have to stay here are forced to spend their time."

Apart from the regular financial reporting Dolly completed as a War Charities Act registrant, it seems that the federal government had little or nothing to do with the Ajax's ongoing volunteer work. That is, apart from a telegraph National War Services deputy minister T. C. Davis sent Dolly in May 1942, in the wake of the Ajax beer controversy, and as Dolly considered her next moves.

IN LIGHT OF PAST CONTROVERSY WE CONSIDER IT IN YOUR INTEREST AND IN INTEREST OF ALL CONCERNED THAT YOU CARRY ON UNDER ANOTHER NAME AS WE FEEL THIS WILL PROVIDE FOR HARMONIOUS FEELING IN COMMUNITY STOP

Needless to say, she did not comply.

As far as the club building itself, with its impeccable renovations and thoughtful decorating? There was no chance such a gorgeous and well-outfitted building and grounds would sit empty for long in Halifax's over-taxed climate. Two weeks after the Navy League washed its hands of Davis and Thorson's scheme to have the organization run a club in the former Ajax space, the Norwegian government bought the Odell Estate from Dolly. The federal government gifted the club's moveable assets—the books, the glassware, the furniture, all of it—to the Norwegians. Nothing inside or outside the club changed in any material way. The Odell Estate served as a hostel for Norwegian sailors for the remaining years of the war, with no uproar from Fort Massey or its congregants.

The bar sold schnapps.

Chapter Seven

RUN RABBIT RUN

Edith Macneill? I'd say she needed some schnapps.

Edith removed her coat as she strode into the offices of the Women's Voluntary Services (WVS) on Granville Street. It was winter and this was Halifax, and the four-storey wood-shingled Fisher Building that housed the WVS was only three blocks up from the water. The harbour's icy breeze blew west, slamming into the large storefront window and shivering the old building's timbers. Edith took a moment before the inevitable rush to open the WVS Day Book, wondering, perhaps, what fresh hell awaited her on this day (though she likely didn't think of it as a fresh hell, exactly, but an opportunity to guide Halifax women volunteers to tasks that needed doing and jobs that needed filling). After all, Edith hadn't only chosen this as her ultimate volunteer mission. She had started the whole thing.

The black-covered string-bound WVS Day Book had Edith's office phone number—3-7769—scrawled inside the front cover. She was married now, and no longer a Macneill but instead Mrs. Girouard. Her husband, René, an Army major, was posted overseas, so there was no need to move from her parents' spacious home on Young Avenue in Halifax's deep south end. The WVS Day Books—the organization kept them through the war and past it, though only two of the books survive—were essentially monumental to-do lists, added to daily by Edith or one of the other women volunteers answering the phone, opening the mail, or receiving walk-in visitors at 86 Granville Street. The "doing" part was all Edith's, it seems.

She had her finger on every movement in the office, every single day. She would mark a check beside the items once they were completed, or sometimes cross them out. Beside most, she wrote "E. G.," her checks and initials giant and dark against the cursive missives. One archived WVS Day Book runs from November 30, 1943, to April 26, 1944; the other from July 20, 1944, to October 10 of the same year. So many months and so much work. Some of it utterly inane. All of it necessary to keep the organization running.

Mrs. Girouard! Mrs. Coolen of the (North End Services Canteen) dancing class needs new records. Has tried several times at the Phinney store, but they have no knowledge of the credit she is supposed to have for these. Can she please have it for this weekend?

Mrs. Crouse has free time now any afternoon on Monday or Wednesday evening—canteen preferred.

Junior Red Cross called. More workers needed. They are still in Roy Building.

Mrs. Baker of Navy League phoned stating the Women's Institute of Mahone Bay have offered to knit for the Greek Relief. If the WVS will provide the wool. Please call Mrs. Baker who will provide name and address of party in Mahone Bay [to] whom to send the wool.

Window wash man not paid

Mrs. Read called. Cannot go to Y Canteen this P.M. Called away to nurse a sick friend. Canteen notified.

She had better get to work.

To understand the Women's Voluntary Services centre is to understand the depth and breadth of women's volunteer work in Halifax during the war. WVS branches existed all across Canada, in some forty-four cities. They rippled out from the Canadian Women's Voluntary Services in Ottawa, which was itself modelled on the British WVS, founded in 1938.

Halifax's branch was unique. It was a late-starter, nationally, only getting off the ground in the latter half of 1943. This has to been seen for what it was: a function not of Halifax women failing to engage in volunteering, but of them being too busy working to organize the work they were doing. Halifax was also a WVS outlier, as you'd expect, because it was undoubtedly busier than most. A rusted binder at the Halifax Municipal Archives catalogues WVS placements. This was the central work of the WVS—women registered with the centre, indicating what they could and would take on as volunteer work. Organizations registered, indicating what they wanted and needed. Edith and company were the fast-moving matchmakers. They supplied volunteers to blood donor clinics and the Halifax Concert Party Guild, and dispatched myriad knitters to organizations that knit comforts for servicemen overseas and in hospital locally, like the Lady Ironside Knitting group. Women volunteers were sent to the Barrington Street YMCA, in the former Ladies' College Building, to take calls and make room registry placements. They did the same at the YWCA Blue Triangle Hostel just down the block. They were called on for other light clerical work at the provincial Red Cross, or to help make surgical dressings, or to act as drivers. The Protestant Orphanage nursery school needed help and so did a play therapy class at the children's hospital. None of this even nicks the surface. There was library and sorting work at the Canadian Legion library at Atlantic House, the YMCA library, and the Naval Reading Service. WVS women staffed the hostel at Atlantic House as well, and the Salvation Army Hostels on Argyle and Hollis. Canteens were in great need of servers: the Allied Merchant Seamen's; the Wings Club for Air Force personnel, just off the lobby of the Nova Scotian Hotel; the Blue Triangle for members of the women's auxiliary services at the Waverley Inn on Barrington Street; Stadacona; No. 1 "Y" Depot; the Army, Navy, Air Force Club for Women—basically… all of them. (Well, almost all of them. The WVS supplied the Quinpool Road Hostel and Jewish Congress Service Centre, but not the canteen at

Gerrish Street Hall, which served Black service members.) Notably, huge volumes of WVS volunteers were sent to the Central Magazine Exchange and the North End Services Canteen. The need never ended, because this was Halifax and it was the war. Miss Shand begged for office help at the Hollis Street Council of Social Agencies office. Miss Pearson needed volunteers to entertain children in the nursery school at the Jost Mission. Mrs. Murphy at the Red Cross had ten regular sewing volunteers but was desperate for more. Mrs. Guy Little from the St. John Ambulance Brigade had an immediate need for volunteers to work in hospitals and at the Allied Merchant Seamen's Club. Edith helped them all. No organization had more impact on Halifax's volunteer heavy lifting than the WVS. And the WVS, start to finish, was Edith Girouard.

—⁓⁓—

But let's go back to the days before she was worried about assigning volunteers and paying the window washer and chasing record store credits. Edith, seated in the house of her parents, Murray and Kathleen Macneill, on tree-lined Young Avenue in Halifax's south end, pulled a sheet of Dominion Bureau of Statistics letterhead from her desk. She had started working for the Dominion Bureau of Statistics, a federal agency which was the precursor to Statistics Canada, after her marriage in August 1941. Most Halifax women worked before marriage and not after. Edith, like my grandmother, Marie, did both. She had graduated from Dalhousie University with a science undergraduate degree back in 1926 and had become a teacher and dean at the now-closed Fairmont Junior College in Washington, DC. She had thrown herself into volunteering when she returned to Halifax on the cusp of war in 1939. With her new husband, René, posted in Europe, it seemed like a good enough time as any to take on a job with the regional office of the Dominion Bureau of Statistics.

At the office, in the Dominion Public Building on Bedford Row, Edith worked on the Cost of Living Index. And she still had—or made—time for the WVS.

Before rolling it into her typewriter, Edith flipped the letterhead twice—so that the Dominion Bureau of Statistics logo was at the bottom and on the opposite side from where she wrote. She frequently used the letterhead when she was starting up the WVS in the summer of 1943—perhaps paper was difficult to come by, though paper salvage concerned itself mainly with newspaper. In any case, Edith made use of the privilege of having a federal government job and used the paper. She wrote many letters that summer from her cozy little office at her parents' house on Young Avenue. The space was upstairs in the half of the house she shared with her younger sister Janet and Janet's daughter, Anne. Isabel, the middle Macneill daughter, who had tirelessly volunteered and organized with her sisters at both the North End Services Canteen and the Ajax Club, had left Halifax in 1942, joining up with the Women's Royal Canadian Naval Service (WRCNS or, in informally, "Wrens") at its founding. Isabel would attain the rank of Lieutenant-Commander and become captain of HMCS *Conestoga*, a so-called "stone frigate" or land establishment and WRCNS training station in Galt, Ontario. Isabel was the first and only female commander during the Second World War in the entire British Commonwealth. While Janet and Edith lived upstairs at 102 Young, their parents commanded the downstairs, which they almost certainly shared with naval officers seeking accommodation in the overtaxed city. The house's current owner, Anja Pearre, can point out where small plates had been nailed on doors on the main floor; other neighbours know that their houses were shared during the war, too. "Do you see this?" Pearre says, pointing at a painted-over ridge. "They were numbers."

In her east-facing office, Edith had a terracotta-tiled fireplace and a built-in bookshelf. Today, the room's window overlooks the house's circular driveway and a monster purple-flowering rhododendron. I don't know if it was there when Edith looked out that window, but rhododendrons can live for a century or more, so I like to imagine her taking a break from her work and looking down at it, just a small bush in the 1940s. Much of 102 Young remains intact from when the Macneills bought the house in 1935—the Douglas fir floors, the ceiling medallions and crown mouldings, the Victorian slag glass pendant in the front hallway, and the French doors leading into the living room where the Macneills kept their grand piano. The piano is still in the same spot; beside it, in the expansive Macneill living room, Edith had married Army Second Lieutenant René de la Bruère Girouard on the Friday of the Labour Day long weekend in 1941. René left soon after. Edith didn't begin her volunteer journey when René was posted overseas, but rather stayed on the fast-moving volunteer freight train she had been riding since the fall of 1939, when she'd met Dolly McEuen and co-founded the North End Services Canteen and then swiftly transitioned to her founding executive role with the Ajax Club. She rode with Dolly through the Ajax's untimely execution at the hands of MacMillan, Angus L., and the Fort Massey haters, and helped Dolly open and establish the Ajax Hospitality Headquarters on Spring Garden Road. She did all this through 1942 and into the start of 1943. Then? Then Edith attended a three-day conference in Ottawa that changed everything.

The conference took place June 28–30, 1943—three days of lectures and discussions on the value of women's voluntary efforts across Canada. A keynote address was given by Princess Alice, a granddaughter of Queen Victoria and the wife of Major General Alexander Cambridge, the 1st Earl of Athlone, and Canada's wartime Governor General. Edith was mesmerized, not by the royalty, but the possibility in front of her. From her hotel room at Ottawa's Château Laurier, she wrote a six-page cursive missive to a friend about the value of "woman-power," which she felt could be harnessed for the war but put to great use in peacetime "to make the world a better place." She was also humiliated that women at the conference, one after another, from Winnipeg, Fort Erie, Kingston, and other places, delivered reports on their work and on their WVS centres, while Halifax had no centre of its own to brag about. On balance, she left Ottawa energized. "I feel rather overstuffed with new ideas—but I hope I am not too idealistic when I say that if every woman heard what I have heard, and acted on it, the postwar world would be a much better place to live in."

⌒〰⌒

The Canadian Women's Voluntary Services was a division of the Department of National War Services. The Order in Council that created it on October 31, 1941, aimed to coordinate the voluntary efforts of the women of Canada "with a view to their best utilization for the needs of their communities, the maintenance of national morale and the furtherance of the welfare of the nation." The WVS was a British movement, and had already made its way to Canada with neither this Privy Council dictum, nor the nod of the King government in Ottawa. But an April 1941 preliminary report for the cabinet war committee reveals why the government felt the federal nod was important. The nut of it? Women were working "spontaneously" and "not recognized by any branch of the government." The government, apparently, didn't much like spontaneous women. A large number of volunteers, the report notes, were "engaged in the operation of canteens, lunch rooms, and serving men of the Armed Forces. Others are engaged in knitting and sewing and producing material benefits of this kind for the use of the Armed Forces and victims of the war." Here, the report-writer adds a derisive note: "The type of women usually engaged in this is a woman past middle age." But age wasn't their only supposed sin. "The majority wear uniforms, which, strictly speaking, is contrary to the law, and they try to make their uniforms as nearly as possible like the uniforms of different branches of the Armed Service." A national WVS, then, would control the work of these women. It would control the attire of these women. Indeed, it would control the women, maintaining that minutely crafted "you're in the forces now" sentiment that kept women feeling like their work was patriotic, while simultaneously making sure they never got too big for their britches or too close to the actual military. The WVS would also solve the problem of where to put women who were anxious to help. There were many. Elizabeth Linton of Toronto sent a plaintive hand-written letter to National War Services minister J. T. Thorson, begging to be sent overseas to assist in the war effort. "I shall be willing to enter any service, without remuneration." Linton's husband was overseas and her daughter was in Scotland, volunteering as an auxiliary nurse. "I live alone and would be ready and willing to pick up and leave to go overseas at very short notice should the opportunity arise." So many women were writing to Alberta Senator W. A. Buchanan that the senator wrote a personal and confidential letter to National War Services deputy minister T. C. Davis complaining about them. "I am being deluged with demands from the women who want to serve. If Lethbridge is any criterion, the women are more anxious to serve than the men." His tone suggests exasperation at the notion. One woman, Buchanan noted scoffingly, was offering to be a spy. I can only imagine how deflated she must have felt when she was, in all likelihood, sent to volunteer at a daycare.

Many of the initial Canadian WVS volunteers were given a twelve-hour training course in childcare, according to Ruth Roach Pierson in *They're Still Women After All*. They were then asked to spend either one full day or two half-days a week at nurseries, which were set up for women working in war industries. This was entirely new. Women who were married were expected to stop work, produce children, and stay home to make sure the little ones were cared for there. Once children arrived in a marriage, the likelihood of the woman working outside the home was contingent upon help found either in the home, by way of relatives who lived there, or some other arrangement. There were no other options. WVS workers shuttled into childcare centres were eventually reluctantly or gratefully boosted out. "It was soon found," Roach Pierson writes, "that day nurseries had to be fully staffed by paid workers." (All I think of here is how it was probably automatically assumed that all women would be good at, or interested in, caring for children. And the tandem faulty assumption: that working in a daycare is a cakewalk, requiring little to no training.) Luckily for volunteers, there was plenty more to do than look after kids. The WVS acted as a labour pool for huge nationwide campaigns like the National Clothing Collection program, which gathered millions of pounds of relief clothing, and the selling of War Savings Stamps, as well as jobs that were really extensions of government administration, such as the distribution of ration cards and the completion of forms for the federal government's new Family Allowance project. But the bulk of the WVS's work was in its role as community-level volunteer fixer—the matchmaking work of knowing who needed help and who was on hand to provide it. And in Halifax, more than any other city in Canada, this need was staggering. Edith came away from that June 1943 conference in Ottawa with more than a plan to create a Halifax WVS. She aimed to set up an organization that would outlive the conflict, and that would make the future city a better place. She decided to take the summer to get the project off the ground.

But first? First she needed money.

———— ∿ ————

"Dear Warren…"

Edith sat in her home office and typed up one of her first requests for funding in August 1943. She fired it off to 14 Wall Street, New York. The recipient was Warren Publicover of the Newmont Mining Corporation. Publicover was treasurer of the British War Relief Society's Maple Leaf Division, a Canadian branch of the US relief organization. Under Publicover's helmsmanship, the society provided financial aid and materials to civilians affected by the war, and by conflict's end would have funnelled more than $2 million in cash and provisions to various organizations. But it wasn't exactly Warren Publicover, treasurer, to whom Edith was reaching out, nor was it Warren Publicover, lawyer at one of the world's largest mining companies. Edith wrote to Warren Publicover, friend. Warren grew up in Lunenburg, an hour's drive from Halifax, but he would have been at Dalhousie at the same time as Edith before carrying on to earn postgraduate degrees from NYU and Columbia University. He and his wife, Anita, also from Lunenburg, visited Nova Scotia frequently and were friends of the Macneill daughters. Edith wrote Warren not for money—yet—from the British War Relief Society, but for guidance about how and when to ask the British War Relief Society for support. Edith was canny.

The administrative board was already set up for the WVS, she explained to Publicover in her letter, with Edith as chair and representatives from local women-run organizations such as the Red Cross, the Navy League, and others. Edith planned that the WVS would be run much like the WVS centres in England and other parts of Canada, but "Halifax," she wrote, referring to the impact of war activities on the city, "as usual, has a unique problem with which only Halifax can deal." Part of the problem was financial. Other cities' WVS branches were in part funded by municipal contributions. But Halifax, she explained, was in a position of ironic defeat. Its swollen transient population paid no direct property taxes, Edith explained, while at the same time putting a heavy strain on civic facilities. On top of that, an ever-growing amount of property was being purchased by the federal government, which was exempt from municipal taxation. "Our city treasury is not very healthy," she wrote. Could he advise her on the best approach to the British War Relief Society? He could, in fact: just put his name down as treasurer, he said. She did. She was promptly sent $275 in seed money. And so it went from there. Privilege at work.

Edith secured free office space for the WVS's first two weeks from the Victory Loan Committee, located in the Tramway Building at the southwest corner of Sackville and Barrington Streets. And soon enough,

Moirs Chocolate on Argyle Street gave her $500; so did William Stairs, Son & Morrow, a shipping company. Maritime National Fish Limited gave $100, as did Robert Simpson Eastern Limited, who also threw in "a clock of some significance," according to Edith's notes. There were a smattering of smaller corporate donations, in the $10 to $20 range, and many in-kind contributions, which went toward the WVS's move into its permanent home in the Fisher Building at 86 Granville Street, where the rent was $20 per month. Martin and Moore Limited provided exterior paint. The storefront, opposite the provincial legislature, was painted black with blue trim and a blue door. The Navy donated a street sign, black with yellow letters and trimmed with blue. Edith wrote countless letters, showing what may have been her greatest skill: combining equal measures of mercenary zeal and politeness. In May 1945, she wrote a letter to Murray's, a popular restaurant chain in Montreal, Ottawa, and Toronto. "I would be most grateful," she typed, "if you could supply me with the reasons why you have not opened a restaurant in Halifax." She wrote to Beckford Furniture on Agricola Street, urging them to create a window display to encourage women who shop on Agricola to register with the WVS, as women who shop on Barrington and Gottingen already did. "I will call on you personally when I am next on Agricola," she promised/warned. She wrote to Henry Birks and Sons around the corner on Barrington and George Streets to say that the Birks window that had been donated to promoting the Ajax Hospitality Headquarters would be of much better use to her, instead, since the WVS supplied volunteers to the Ajax. This was, without doubt, with Dolly's permission. They kept up their tight friendship through the war.

Indeed, there are significant shades, here, of the Ajax Club, which benefitted immensely from corporate and private donations and what many saw as Dolly's "pushy" ways. She never shied from asking friends and acquaintances for money and goods. She reached out to anyone and everyone and expected support for the good work she undertook. And, truly, Edith was her equal in this in this. One epic missive in the Halifax

Municipal Archives is a carbon copy of a letter to the mayor after the May 1945 VE day riots, in which Edith lays out her suggestion for identifying and punishing the looters. Edith also mirrored Dolly's propensity for eschewing red tape and asking for forgiveness rather than permission. Looking over the National Archives files of the Canadian WVS is to be slapped in the face by bureaucracy—there are memos discussing the finer points of stationery wording and paper stock, and debating the best photos of Princess Alice to accompany promotional material. There was the question of smocks versus uniforms for voluntary workers.

The Halifax WVS found itself in the weeds at times, to be sure, but the whole endeavour was working on a different plane from the national organization. It was scrappy and meaningful. Edith was on the ground. Decidedly. She just wanted to get things done. A letter to Edith from T. J. Moore, Halifax's clerk of works, informs her that the sign (this must be the one the Navy donated) she has applied to install above the Granville WVS storefront does not meet city specifications. She writes back, ever diplomatic, and with a decided Dolly-esque tone, basically saying, *Oh, dear; well, it's already up there now!* Edith wasn't bossy. She was the boss.

Whether Edith learned from Dolly or Dolly learned from Edith through their friendship and peas-in-a-pod work at the North End Services Canteen and the Ajax, or whether they were simply two well-connected women who naturally understood how to exploit their privilege, I don't know. But the drive and networking skills of these friends was matched, even if their volunteer work was different.

⌒∿⌒

The Ajax, in both its iterations, was all about hospitality. The WVS was a clearinghouse, plain and simple. Its work was getting as many women registered as possible, quickly figuring out where they could do their best work, and getting them immediately out the door. As I write this, I'm thinking about COVID-19 and the massive volunteer efforts in Nova Scotia to help stamp out the spread of the virus. Nova Scotia has led the country in asymptomatic rapid testing. During the height of the third wave, at most places in the province anyone could access a convenient fifteen-minutes-or-less test for COVID-19, for free. This service was largely staffed by an army of volunteers at community testing sites. Any volunteers who wanted to help just filled out a simple web-based form and their email was added to a mailing list. Every three days or so, a spreadsheet was sent out and volunteers could select the days and times and jobs they wanted. One of my daughters was a volunteer nose-swabber; the other was a volunteer sample tester. During the war, they would have been connected with opportunities like these through the WVS.

Instead of an online database of email addresses and spreadsheets, the WVS had registration cards and, later, registration pages. (And, make no mistake, they also juggled their fair share of scraps of paper with names, addresses, phone numbers, and availability.) Women registered by approaching a WVS booth—set up at places like Zellers on Barrington—or by walking in to the Granville Street office. This is how Joyce Ripley, who worked at the North End Services Canteen, got her start. Joyce had registered with her friends Glorena and Honey. And that was common: gaggles of high school or university students would register together. Many names listed had matching addresses, such as Shirreff Hall, a women's residence at Dalhousie University.

Registration cards often contain notes about volunteers who want to work together. The card for Pamela Smith indicates: "This girl is anxious for something to do, and will go anywhere, prefers to work with Audrey Shaw." Happily, the adjacent entry is for Audrey Shaw, and it reads: "This girl is anxious to have work, will go anywhere, with Pamela Smith." Experience was a key element—"has volunteered as a canteen worker" or "has a first aid certificate." Edith made a special note on the card for Jean

Boswell, a student at Dalhousie: "Dancing—Square. Can teach it." Esther Greenblatt, another Dalhousie student, was flagged as a French speaker. Same with Mrs. Barbara Heward. Mrs. Mary Patterson had her driver's licence. Notes on availability were useful, of course, and especially when women needed to be removed from the volunteer pool. Suzanne Bryant Raney's card said, "Having baby soon—do not call." Medora Berrigan "got married and went west." Some notes referred to success—Nancy Moir was reported by Mrs. G. to be "very satisfactory." Others to temperament: "I told you about young Miss Whitman. She has had two good reports lately, one from the North End, and one from the YMCA after I had given her a little talk. At first she was criticized for trying to tell people how to do things, and for being a little unruly. However, she is so eager to work, that we would appreciate it if you would give her another chance. This is not the Miss Margaret Whitman we sent to you before, but Miss Bernice Whitman." We can only hope young Miss Whitman got another chance. Many notations are patently irrelevant, or, at least, seem so today.

I can't imagine why it would matter whether a woman helping the Girl Guides and Boy Scouts run a medicine bottle collection centre was Jewish, Protestant, Catholic, British, a housewife, or had a bachelor's degree. These are the overt categorizations of volunteers that seem to have little to do with their ability to help. But there are other hinted-at notions contained in the WVS Day Books: "Miss Dorothy Nelson is coming in at 11:45 to discuss some difficulties she has had at the (Salvation Army) Canteen Hollis Street. She + three friends have left there" and, simply, "Mrs. Nichols is a stranger in town." It's tough to know if these are derisive toward the women mentioned or supportive of what are evidently difficulties. Does someone need to know if Mrs. Nichols is a stranger in town because she may need a hand with navigating the city to get to her volunteer duties, or is that code for some darker meaning? Is the problem at the Salvation Army Canteen the women volunteers, or are the difficulties being caused by someone at the facility? We don't know.

Although administration was the thrust, much of the work of the WVS was, indeed, relationship navigation and soothing. A letter to Mrs. J. D. Prentice at the North End Services Canteen addresses a prickly problem with dance classes: the girls who volunteer as practice partners don't understand they're there to help those who cannot dance, not to spend time with the men who do. Someone was going to have to break the news to these eager beavers. Other jobs simply showed up at the door, and the door, it seems, was always open, no matter how mystifying the ask. "A gentleman was sent here by Kinleys Drug Store," a WVS office volunteer, Mrs. A. Dickson, writes to Edith in the WVS Day Book. He wanted to know "where he could buy 2 thumb guards for a baby that sucks its thumbs. I located one at Medical & Hosp. Supplies."

But, truly, the lion's share of work was cat-herding. Volunteers would move out of the city or stop volunteering without informing the WVS, so they would need to be tracked down. Some women had no phones, and the WVS routinely called neighbours. Registration cards would say: "nearest phone, next door neighbor Jean 2810." Meanwhile, organizations were mailing and calling 'round the clock to say that they required more workers. The volunteer need in Halifax was like a monster whose appetite could never be sated. What had to have made this worse is that, in all the documentation, there's no evidence of delegation. The WVS was a clearinghouse, and every little thing in the house was cleared through Edith. Everything. An insect infestation in July 1944 saw Edith write in the WVS Day Book, "There is a Flit gun to be used if any small flies appear, as they did on Wed. These may be ground fleas and are being attended to. Dept of Health states that they are not serious, but if the Flit does not exterminate them permanently we will get 'Woods Odorless Insecticide.' They are from heat and dry weather." Soon, the G. H. Woods exterminator came around and Edith reported: "Insects are from plants and are ants" (with the "ants" underlined and the "plants" double underlined). Soon? "Flit gun now contains especially deadly pesticide." Finally, another person's handwriting weighs in on the matter: "Can't hope to compete with fleas or ants." No matter; I'm sure Edith took care of them, whatever they were.

Despite, or perhaps because of, all this micromanaging, the WVS became, under Edith's hand, a runaway success. She would indeed have a worthy report to deliver from Halifax at the next WVS conference in Ottawa, showing up the Fort Eries, Kingstons, and Winnipegs of the world. Within six months of its launch, the Halifax branch of the WVS had signed up five hundred women volunteers.

∼⌒⌒

Still, Edith had her eyes on a bigger prize. She saw the WVS not simply as helping to fill Halifax's volunteer gap during an emergency, but as a means of bettering the city she loved, long-term. In June 1944, she sent to a Mrs. Worthylake in Shelburne, Nova Scotia, a de facto guide for starting a WVS branch. Along with the requisite how-tos (one, particularly endearing, speaks to the broader social mandate at play for Edith. She mentions that in Toronto—and no doubt in Halifax—several women "of questionable occupation" had registered for canteen work. But Edith doesn't recommend turning them away: "Such people can always be used in something and it might help them a great deal to give them such work.") She tells Mrs. Worthylake the WVS is "really a movement, and not an organization." One that seeks "to stimulate an interest in all women in making the country a better place, and in inviting every woman to offer her time, even if she has very little."

Edith cannot have had very much of that precious resource herself. Day to day, she was managing her life, her job, and the WVS. And she was also running out of time in another sense: her husband's return date, while unknown, was imminent with the end of the war and the couple planned to leave Halifax soon after. As early as 1944, she wrote to several of the organizations that had served as the advisory board for the WVS, confirming their commitment and noting that the organization's strength was in the long haul. Soon enough, she became more explicit, asking organizations, such as the Junior League of Halifax, in April 1945 to take over WVS operations. Secretary Allison Conrod wrote back to say the board believed it would not be "financially possible." And soon, another resource was becoming slimmer: money.

When the VE day riots erupted in Halifax, only three days after Allison Conrod wrote her letter declining to take over for Edith, the businesses that supported many of the ongoing expenses of the WVS were significantly damaged and looted. Downtown was a sea of glass. Merchandise that hadn't been stolen littered the streets. These businesses, which had contributed to the WVS's financial solvency since its founding, were no longer in a position to help. Warren Publicover's British War Relief Society's Maple Leaf Division was wrapping up its work in preparation for dissolution and could no longer help fund the WVS. When the Fisher Building lease ran out that summer, the WVS had $250 in the bank. The organization was, in Edith's words to George Davidson, the federal Welfare Department deputy minister, in mid-June 1945, in "desperate financial straits." Edith was writing to Davidson seeking a free room in the federal offices at 80 Sackville Street, at the corner of Market Street. She figured the $250 in savings would last the WVS another year if it were only paying for office supplies and a telephone. "If we could obtain permission to move immediately, I would be most grateful, as I would like to supervise the move myself, and my future movements are uncertain, as my husband may return shortly." Davidson wrote back to say that he would help.

I've never been able to determine if the WVS made the move to Sackville Street. In the *1945 Halifax–Dartmouth City Directories*, the WVS is still listed at 86 Granville Street. But by 1946, it's gone from the Fisher Building. The National Health and Welfare Family Allowances department is listed that year at 80 Sackville, but the directory makes no mention of the WVS at that address. Edith disappeared, too. Once she married in 1941, René was listed at 102 Young Street, and Edith, like other married women of the time, became invisible in the directory. But by 1946, René is no longer listed at the Macneill house either. He had returned from the war and he and Edith had left Halifax, settling in Quebec and later Ontario. The WVS documents—all the Day Books and scraps of paper, all the carbon-copied correspondence to and correspondence from, all the registration cards and sheets, all the federal WVS promotional material—were, at some point, boxed and stashed. They were donated to the municipal archives by Leslie Pezzack, who inherited them from her aunt, Zilpha Linkletter. Zilpha was born in 1915; Leslie told me that she had a strong belief in preserving historical artifacts and documents and was an excellent record-keeper.

Without these boxes of ephemera, the minutiae of the WVS's work would be lost. And the tendrils of its impact, which crept to every possible corner of Halifax's volunteer ecosystem, would be, like the work of the women who supported the WVS, practically unknown.

Chapter Eight

SING AS WE GO

There was Pearl Adams. There was Arthur Sampson. And there was Walter "Duck" Johnson. Serious gaze. Jacket and tie. Johnson was leaned over the porch bannister, his right hand crossed over his left wrist. He gently clasped a pencil, but there was nothing gentle about his eyes. It was as if he were sizing up the situation, ready to write you up in the dog-eared notebook in his breast pocket. Johnson was a warden; Adams and Sampson, fire wardens—the three, together with sixteen others from the uptown area surrounding Creighton, Maynard, Gottingen, and Agricola Streets, were members of the Halifax Civil Emergency Corps, Platoon 7E. The group comprised wardens, who took on auxiliary policing, blackout compliance, first aid, and emergency rescue training, as well as fire wardens, who were trained in fire suppression and the use of pumps, hoses, and special scoop shovels. This was a time when there were no Black members of the Halifax Fire Department. The city's first African Nova Scotian firefighter, Billy Carter, wouldn't be accepted into the ranks until 1957. He died in 1973 in the line of duty. Platoon 7E's metal helmets—bearing FW stamps for fire wardens or W stamps for wardens, as appropriate—were standard issue and, on some, ill-fitting. Members wore white armbands while on duty. They wore them, too, when they gathered for a photo in July 1943. Paragons of voluntary neighbourhood protection, from grandparents to teens—all Black Haligonians from the uptown neighbourhood—some wore three-piece suits, others, jackets and ties; the three women wore single-breasted knee-length coats, and pumps. One sported a corsage.

Members of the Halifax Civil Emergency Corps, Platoon 7E. (NS ARCHIVES)

This group played a central voluntary role during the war. The ranks of career police and firefighters became depleted as those men signed up to fight, and the gap needed to be filled by volunteers. There were additional duties, too—routine air-raid practice monitoring, and being ready in the case of enemy attack. This was a real risk in a country at war, and more in Halifax—a strategic linchpin at the western end of the Battle of the Atlantic—than anywhere else. Civil Emergency Corps platoons existed all over the city, and the province. There was another all-Black group in Africville, four kilometres north, and evidence of a third in New Glasgow. The platoons, community members protecting community members, were commonly known as the "home guard." And, here, for this photo, on the steps of Gerrish Street Hall, they were at home.

It's no wonder this photo was taken on the steps of Gerrish Street Hall. The dance and meeting space—a wood-shingled building on the north side of Gerrish Street between Gottingen and Creighton—was a dedicated community hub during the Second World War. In fact, the building at 107 Gerrish Street enjoyed a number of community-based incarnations. Before and during the First World War, it was the Salvation Army Barracks. In 1920, it housed the Ancient Order of Hibernians, an Irish Catholic Fraternity; by 1932, it was an Independent Order of Odd Fellows gathering spot. In 1938, it finally became Gerrish Street Hall, a name that lasted through 1953. Though it seems to have been a music venue after this time, the *1954 Halifax–Dartmouth City Directories* lists 107 Gerrish as the Loyal Wilberforce Hall. And as late as April 25, 1974, Halifax City Council minutes refer to the building as the "Loyal Wilberforce Lodge, Independent Order of Oddfellows."

During the Second World War, Gerrish Street Hall was a community lodestone, rivalling the local church. And like the church, Gerrish Street Hall was where the music was: Duke Ellington played there; so did Lionel Hampton. It was where Nova Scotia music legend Bucky Adams first picked up the tenor saxophone. Gerrish Street Hall was where Black service members came for rest and respite, meals and entertainment—they weren't welcome at other canteens, so Gerrish Street Hall filled the void. Segregation in Nova Scotia, though not on the books, was real. So even as the hall served a great need, even as it provided food and fancy, music and mirth, it was left uncovered by the media at the time and unheralded by those who paid what little mind they did to voluntary work in Halifax. The Province-produced booklet "Nova Scotia Helps the Fighting Man," a compendium of wartime voluntary activities from the large to the very— very—small (consider: the Good Will Club of Salmon River, the Thumbs Up Club, the Fortnightly Club), fails entirely to mention Gerrish Street Hall in either its 1942 version, or in the almost twice as long, thirty-five-page 1945 edition. It's almost as if Gerrish Street Hall didn't exist.

Without the ephemera and castaway notes that the WVS's Edith Girouard had stuffed away before her move to Montreal, Haligonians today would know little about the day-to-day work of the Halifax branch of the Women's Voluntary Services. And without the photo of Halifax Civil Emergency Corps Platoon 7E, would we know anything at all about this home guard? Or about the volunteer work at Gerrish Street Hall?

〜ᴧᴧ〜

Margaret David got her best outfits in the 1940s at the Metropolitan, a discount department store known as "the Met," on the Gottingen Street main drag. She'd go for dresses, sometimes, or a blouse and a skirt. "They had nice things," she remembers. "We often thought it was nice." She gives me a knowing look, just like my grandmother Marie used to, as if to say, *you* know what I mean: "The best we could have. Oh my heavens." Margaret's mother, Ella Jane, would help with her hair. She wore short heels, which were a challenge, given her size-eleven feet, and a dash of lipstick. Her four brothers and sisters pinballed around her while she perfected her look. They were under strict instructions not to mess with Margaret, the youngest, while she was getting ready to perform. "You can look," Ella Jane told them, "but don't touch." Soon, Margaret would leave for Gerrish Street Hall, a three-minute nip from her Creighton Street house. If the weather was stormy, someone would come in a car to pick her up, along with the others in her trio: May Chandler Sheppard and Margaret Thomas. They were known as the 3Ms.

At Gerrish Street, the 3Ms would be backed by a band—sometimes an Army ensemble, sometimes players from the community, such as Charles Adams, Bucky's father. Margaret can't remember the songs they sang, but she remembers looking out from the elevated stage onto the standing-room–only crowd, who were smiling and clapping and whooping for more. "They made us feel good," she says. Margaret talks about music as a salve, as a wonder, as a comfort. It's something that both transported her out of her community and held her close to it. "The way that music is? Well, I guess you'd call it harmony. You all get together, different voices…everything feels nice, you know? Everything is going okay."

And it is. On this day, Margaret is one hundred. Hair pulled back, perfectly manicured burgundy-painted nails. She is warm. And she is damn funny. "You can stay," she jokingly tells her daughter, Wanda Lewis, when Margaret and I sit down to talk about Gerrish Street Hall and her volunteer work during the war, "as long as you stay quiet." Margaret's home is in the uptown Gottingen Street community where she was raised, went to Joseph Howe School, and brought up her own children—nine of them in all. She is a member of the same church she attended as a child—where she was married, and where she honed her singing skills with choir director Portia White, the internationally celebrated contralto.

Margaret was born in Hammonds Plains, "a country place," she calls it, and moved to Halifax when she was seven or eight. The city, as so many other women in this book have described it, was a materially quieter place then than now. "You had one thing. That was it, you know?" For her, that one thing was singing. And that one thing became much bigger when the war started and the wartime work at Gerrish Street Hall took off. The hall hosted day-long events with music and picnics and games. Community members and visiting servicemen would spend the whole day. Other times, there would be supper dances, just like at the North End Services Canteen. Men would purchase tickets and come to sit at long communal tables for their meals. They'd be served through a small pass-through window. No menus exist in the public records. No tickets that tell us how much it cost to get in. The archival record of the North End Services Canteen is scant—bulletins and photos and a few newspaper stories. But it's a wealth compared to Gerrish Street Hall.

Margaret didn't only entertain. She volunteered as a dishwasher and with setup some days, making tissue paper flowers out of old paper. Someone would show the volunteers how to do it, and they would string them around the hall. Two different colours. "Beautiful," she recalls. Other women would wash the wood floors before events. Margaret saw the hall through teen eyes, widened by the excitement of Halifax's deluge of visitors. "We thought it was fancy." The best part? The excitement of the new. Singers would come—men waiting to be deployed, who would arrive at Gerrish Street Hall to dance or perform or play instruments. Servicemen—ones from other provinces, from other countries—would show up to dance. Her future husband was one. Arthur Gordon was in his Army uniform at the hall when Margaret first saw him. She would never—could never—walk up and talk to him, but that's where May Chandler Sheppard, her 3Ms sister-friend, came in handy. While Margaret stood and stared and "just wondered," May walked right up to Arthur, who was from Fredericton, New Brunswick, and introduced herself. "She could go right up to a person," Margaret says, "and talk to them in their face. 'Who are you?' or whatever."

I ask Margaret what she was doing while May was off schmoozing with Arthur.

"I was trying to dance." Deadpan.

What she wasn't doing was questioning why Gerrish Street Hall's patrons were almost exclusively Black. Nor why Black servicemen like Arthur, in uniform, serving their country just like any others, weren't allowed to go anywhere else. Because she knew, in that place, at that time, that was just the way it was.

⌒∧∧⌒

On the other side of town, Charlotte Guy slunk quietly up the wooden back staircase at the Waegwoltic Club, careful not to wake her father and stepmother. This was no easy task in a crinoline ball gown and dyed-to-match heels while carrying a twenty-five–pound piano accordion. Once in her bedroom, she plopped down the instrument and squeezed out of her shoes. She had worked all day until six at Mills Brothers, the large, high-end downtown department store that carried Halifax's only selection of imported fashions, including tonight's gown. After work, she managed a quick bite, a stop to gussy herself up, and then she caught a lift out to Herring Cove in one of the two station wagons serving performers with the Halifax Concert Party Guild. She performed all evening for service members at Sandwich Point Battery. Finally? Home. It was eleven o'clock. She removed her makeup and got ready for bed, steeling herself. She would get up the next morning and do it all again.

Charlotte lived at the Waegwoltic, a members-only tennis and sailing club in Halifax's deep south end, on the Northwest Arm, with her family. Generations of Waeg managers and their families have enjoyed living quarters in the clubhouse, which was once the summer home of Alfred Gilpin Jones, a Nova Scotia lieutenant-governor. Charlotte's father, George Guy, left his post as assistant manager at the Royal Bank to run the Waeg in 1941, and moved in his family. Charlotte had graduated four years earlier from the Halifax Ladies' College, the sprawling Barrington Street private school that had been taken over at the start of the war as a YMCA hostel. She, like Margaret, was eighteen when the war began and lived in the soup of the changing city, thrilled at the influx of men and the rising buzz. Pre-war Halifax was a ghost town, where, Charlotte says, if you saw anyone, it was someone you knew. In 1939, "the whole atmosphere changed."

Charlotte characterizes the shift in familiar references. The central feature? "All the men running around." Back then, there wasn't a restaurant on every corner. There was the Green Lantern on Barrington and there was Norman's on Morris. They overflowed into the streets. Jay White, in *Conscripted City*, cites an anonymous source who says the congestion in Halifax produced territorial discrimination in cafés and restaurants. "Establishments were unofficially declared 'Navy-only' or 'Air Force–only' and service men unfamiliar with turf rules were unceremoniously evicted by military police." Like everyone else, Charlotte's family had service-men in for meals. Every Sunday, her father would go up the street and come home with a couple of sailors. It's worth remembering here that the Waegwoltic, as a private club, welcomed all officers as automatic club members. It was one of the many leisure and sport facilities at the disposal of those with the right rank. For a naval rating to gain admittance? That would have required George Guy's say-so.

After graduating from the Ladies' College, Charlotte had begun working at Mills Brothers. She was sixteen and it was unspeakably glamorous. Mills Brothers was a big deal in Halifax, and Charlotte worked in every role she was handed: selling, merchandising, creating window displays, and, later, travelling to Europe annually as a buyer. As a shop girl, her teen eyes were keenly attuned to Halifax's abrupt maturing, and she was fortunate to have a front-row seat for the action through the large Mills Brothers' display windows that dominated half the block of busy Spring Garden Road between Queen and Birmingham Streets. Mills Brothers was Charlotte's in to working life. It would be the only job she ever had. It was also her entrée to becoming one of Halifax's biggest and most in-demand wartime performers, as a member of the Halifax Concert Party Guild.

———— \~⋏⋏\~ ————

The Halifax Concert Party Guild was started by Hugh Mills in January 1940. Mills was familiar to Haligonians as "Uncle Mel," the name he used as a presenter on CHNS Radio. Uncle Mel hosted a thirty-minute daily children's show called "Reading the Funnies," as well as a Saturday afternoon talent show, on which Charlotte was a frequent guest. Like the Concert Party Guild, CHNS was an entertainment and community powerhouse during the war. The station had launched in 1925—small-scale, inside Argyle Street's Carleton Hotel. It moved in 1928 to the Lord Nelson Hotel, taking over the entire eighth floor for its 500-watt transmissions, and soon, the seventh floor, too. And CHNS kept growing. In 1938, the station constructed a three-storey purpose-built station on Tobin Street. The move, which allowed for a significant upgrade to its studios, couldn't have been better timed. With the war, CHNS ramped up its community presence, catering to the city's burgeoning population, and to service members eager for entertainment. Its new studio was large enough to accommodate a twenty-four-person regimental band and a large audience. Another happy accident was its proximity to the waterfront and the Nova Scotian Hotel. It was on the same street as the Ajax Club. "Uncle Mel" used his Saturday amateur talent show as a recruiting ground for the Concert Party Guild, which was in perennial need of performers to fill its requested shows. Mills, of course, was the eponymous owner of Mills Brothers and, so, Charlotte's boss. He had helped launch the Theatre Arts Guild in 1931; the clubbable actor and community leader was embedded in the Halifax stage scene. So it was a cinch that when the war started up, Mills and his wife, Jean Mills, would make space in a small rear office of the department store for the organization of a concert party.

Concert parties existed anywhere troops were stationed or passing through. Former Mount Saint Vincent University professor Patrick O'Neill traced the history of these essential voluntary organizations in his essay "The Halifax Concert Party in World War II." These common entertainment troops had catered to service members during the First World War; during the Second World War, the Victory Entertainers of Hamilton, Ontario, were the first to perform at Stanley Barracks in Toronto in September 1939. As had happened two decades earlier, other groups—musicians, singers, actors, and female impersonators—

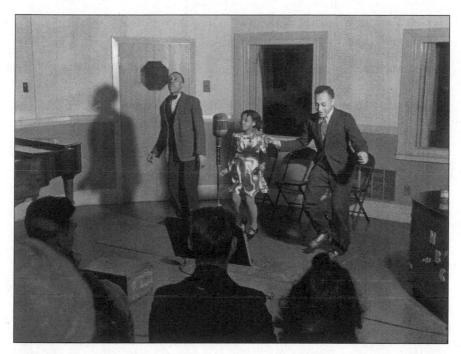

Tap dancers performing for Uncle Mel's Talent Club at CHNS, 1941.
(NS ARCHIVES)

soon formed across the country. Of all the elements of volunteer work that were organized, in Halifax or anywhere else, entertainment was perhaps best recognized by the federal government. Ernest MacMillian, from the Toronto Conservatory of Music, wrote to War Services Deputy Minister T. C. Davis in the fall of 1942 that the United Nations had recognized "the importance of music in stimulating morale among the forces." Though a little late to the, um, party, in September 1942, Auxiliary Services Director E. A. Deacon requested that one small concert party be organized in each Canadian military district to supply outposts.

Like the Women's Voluntary Service, the Halifax Concert Party Guild was a volunteer clearinghouse. It combined a number of smaller entertainment groups under its umbrella: the *Halifax Herald* Harmonica

Band, the Orpheus Male Choir, and the Marsh Family among them. Mills also had a solid stable of individual friends (and employees) to draw from in pulling together his concert party. One was a musician he worked with at the Theatre Arts Guild who, like Charlotte, played the piano accordion: Lila Tredwell.

Lila and Charlotte formed a duo, and soon, a trio, with Julius Silverman, a violist and later concertmaster with the Halifax Symphony Orchestra. Charlotte was a McGill Conservatory-trained classical pianist from the age of six, who had taken up the piano accordion in her spare time one summer at a friend's cottage. It served her well in the war, when she was never sure whether any venue she would be shuttled to nightly would have a piano—or one that was in tune, at least. The instrument allowed Charlotte to entertain on trains, in tight ships' quarters, and in hospitals. What was new for Charlotte was popular music, which she had never played, but quickly learned—"everything from hoedown music to tango and dance music. Everything. Everything," she says. The trio became the Concert Party's most in-demand talent, not only because of their adaptability and indispensability—they were called on to accompany other dancers and singers—but for the lure of their own hour-long per-formances. "We were twice as busy as anybody else," Charlotte says. They held their audiences rapt, whether in a proper hall with a stage, lighting, sets, and seating; at a downtown hostel; performing for Babe Ruth at No. 1 "Y" Depot during his visit to Halifax in 1942; or at an outpost the three had to get to over craggy rocks on foot, Charlotte and Lila lugging their instruments, wearing their dyed satin heels. One night at an anti-aircraft base in the woods somewhere Charlotte can't pinpoint, she was accompa-nying a performer who was set up on top of two pushed-together tables when the lights went out for what turned out to be an emergency drill. The men in the audience rushed to their guns while Charlotte and the performer waited in the pitch black for a nerve-wracking ten minutes. At other times, she, Lila, and Julius could be found playing at the Sir Sandford

Fleming Park bandstand, where service members would watch from small watercraft or sitting on the grassy slope. "We played every night. I don't know how we did it."

Charlotte, quite by accident, became a musical star. This was no small achievement in the world of the Concert Party Guild, which was the heavyweight champion of Halifax wartime entertainment, and which had a heft of support to match. Mills's collection of volunteer talent comprised some seven hundred individuals, none of them paid: musicians, singers, and dancers, as well as actors, yodellers, comedians, and magicians. Jean Mills, and Hugh's sister, Gertrude, from their small office at the back of Mills Brothers, organized ten to fifteen shows per week for the duration of the war, often wrangling twenty performers for each one. The Halifax Concert Party Guild was registered with the War Charities Act and welcomed donations from individuals across the country, just like the North End Services Canteen and the Ajax Club. (Are you noticing a pattern here? It's Dolly McEuen, who was listed for part of the war as an authorized collector for the Concert Party Guild. No one can accuse these organizations of slacking off, but neither could anyone say that the pool of executives from which they pulled their members was deep.) In-kind contributions poured in as well. If the two donated station wagons couldn't hold the ensemble and gear for a given night's show, the Army or Navy would send out vehicles to help with transportation. The American Theatre Wing, a broad war relief organization run mostly by actors, donated costumes and set pieces. If they weren't in character attire, Charlotte and Lila wore ball gowns. Charlotte had several. These were not blouse-and-skirt combos from the Met on Gottingen Street. They were imported satin-and-crinoline jobs from New York, by way of Mills Brothers. One afternoon in Charlotte's living room, she showed me her remaining ones, in great shape, except where her Siamese cat had eaten some of the tulle. They looked like they might still fit her.

Charlotte, born on May 13, 1921, was only a few weeks older than Margaret. (And both, coincidentally, were only a few months ahead of my grandmother, Marie.) Both were performers, steeped in music from the time they were in diapers, and both saw their lives change, particularly through the lens of music, when war came to Halifax. Giving consideration to their dual wartime experiences as performers is a good way to understand Halifax's pernicious racial divide. But the city's stratification and division went well beyond Black and white.

The whole of this book shows the split in value between the war work of women and that of men. But there were layers of value placed on all kinds of identities. Merchant mariners' work was seen as less important than those on naval ships. Officers had far more privileges baked into their lives in Halifax than non-officers. This particular imbalance, though unfair— and problematic, as evidenced by the saga of the Ajax Club, which served to mete out some recreation equity to ratings—was at least grounded in a hierarchy the could be pointed to, in the form of actual rank. Other groups' discrimination had far less rooting in the obvious. Take, for example, the way service wives were looked down upon. I find this phenomenon one of the war's oddest. It also ranks as perhaps one of the least-documented episodes of wartime caste discrimination, save for the fantastic research of Katherine Anne Ling, who focused two post-graduate theses on these women and their plight.

Ling points out in *Servicewives in Wartime Halifax* that, with their husbands' enlistment, these spouses were drafted into a form of active service. They became, effectively, single parents, household managers, and "the propagandized symbols of home and stability for which Canadians were told they were fighting." In Halifax that symbolism was dramatically two-sided. On the one hand, these women represented a national cultural lionization. On the other, they became sneered-at emblems for the overcrowding that was decimating city resources. The men who overtook Halifax were at least fighting or working in war industries. And fighting and working were considered necessary. The women who followed them to Halifax, meanwhile, were personae non gratae—ostracized for being in the city, even as they dealt with the loneliness and lack of support that automatically accompanied being in an unfamiliar place. The municipal government did nothing special to support them, nor did the province. The federal government, meanwhile, had launched that poster campaign warning civilians without business in Halifax to keep away, implicitly targeting war wives. (A quirky disambiguation: service wives who were permanent Halifax residents, like my grandmother, were, for the purposes of this discussion, *not* service wives. They were just Haligonians who happened to be married to service members, and decidedly outside the scope of people's shade-throwing.) In this pseudo-hostile climate, service wives naturally found comfort among one another, in volunteer and social groups. Ling cites numerous examples of service wives contributing voluntary labour, including at dances, canteens, hospitals, and recreation and reading centres. This evidence is entirely contrary to the prevailing opinion, which saw service wives almost exclusively as a burden on the city who were failing to put in the volunteer effort required to win the war. It's with a cringe that I note this opinion seems to have been held, at least in private, by Edith Girouard.

On June 25, 1944, the Women's Voluntary Services head made a routine availability status call to a Mrs. Kirk. And Mrs. Kirk, for her part, apparently gave Edith an earful. She took the opportunity to unload on Edith about the way she and her daughter, Miss Kirk, had been made to feel unwelcome and unneeded by the WVS, a place, Mrs. Kirk told Edith, "strangers were not wanted," and matching "other organizations (that) have this attitude of excluding strangers." Edith was so unsettled by the call she wrote a follow-up letter. It's a half-defence of the WVS's actions—and a compelling one, too, given that the office's note-taking was supreme and

Edith was able to call on precise details and dates to explain the mis-understanding—and a half beg-pardon. "We are only too eager of your assistance, and that of all visitors!" she writes, though she obviously can't help tacking on a little dig: "Indeed, Halifax women have been working so hard for so long, that we are coming to depend on visitors more and more!" How Mrs. Kirk and her daughter were "strangers" is a question left unanswered by this correspondence, but it's likely Mrs. Kirk was a service wife. At least, she was a visitor to the city, and likely accompanying her husband, who may have been engaged in war work, if not in the war effort—and seen in a similar light.

Edith's letter's tone is hyper-cordial; she's clearly looking for a solu-tion. But it must be cast in context. Ling provides it amply—the city wanted nothing to do with service wives except to avoid their perceived drain on municipal resources. And Edith herself had written, in private correspondence in 1943, that service wives were "not really doing anything yet," and in a letter to Halifax Mayor John Lloyd that Halifax women were doing "more than their fair share." The bias against service wives was abiding, and it defied fact.

Here's something else: Edith's animosity toward service wives is par-ticularly odd, no? I mean, Edith was married to Army Second Lieutenant René de la Bruère Girouard. She was, herself, a *service wife*. But this is where another sheath of discrimination layers on—or, more accurately, another layer of indemnity. Edith was not only a born Haligonian and therefore immune from the service wife tinge, she was also the wife of an officer, which was a stand-in for a higher social class and another prophy-lactic against scorn.

None of this, of course, was spoken. Neither, mostly, were the other norms of social, racial, and religious hierarchies in Halifax. (*Mostly*, anyway: during the war, the Canadian Red Cross, though desperate for blood, refused donations from Black men and only allowed it in limited cases from women.) The largely unvoiced nature of these biases is, in part, why they were so deep and difficult to shake. And it's, in part, how Canadians remain generally smug about the country's systemic racism, for example, compared to that in the US. The myth that Canada "never had slavery" because it appeared in a mildly different legislative form here than in the US informs the way many Canadians today see, acknowledge, and respond to anti-Black racism.

The IODE, the women's charitable organization, did a great deal of volunteer work during the war, but it was also steeped in tacit racism— its work was always in service of the promotion of British, a.k.a. Anglo, values and norms. Whiteness and Protestantism were firmly the baseline during the war. Neutral. Any other markers of identity or race equated difference; worth noting, if not disparaging. This is the same rationale that normalized the inclusion of unnecessary information on WVS registration cards—those notations about where people were born or their religion. One woman whose card can be found in the WVS files is Ethel Pelley, who aimed to help out with knitting. Her registration card notes, uselessly, "dropped out in grade ten." The same normalization of pointing out difference or fetishizing sameness among "others" was sometimes part of John Fisher's *East Coast Reporter*. In a profile of the volunteer work of the Allied Merchant Seamen's Club, Fisher interviewed club manager Clifford Taylor, who generalized, and felt it was worth reporting, that Black seamen liked Monopoly and Chinese nationals liked mah-jong. Taylor pointed out that there was "practically no friction between different nationalities," the baked-in conceit being that it would be natural for there to be conflict.

All these ideas provided the invisible scaffolding for implicit (and explicit) segregation. And so it was that those who fell outside the cultural, racial, and religious "norms" of WASPishness formed their own clubs and service organizations—the Greek community, the Jewish community, the Black community. These groups primarily served their own members, but they welcomed others, too. So, while a Black naval rating might not have been welcome at the YMCA for a steam bath, if a white rating showed up at Gerrish Street Hall for a supper-dance, he wasn't turned away.

The element of exclusion that perhaps most affected volunteer work? Not religion, race, ethnicity, temporary residence, or, strictly, class, but instead, socio-economic status. Women with money had more time on their hands. They weren't required to hold paid employment to shore up household income, and they were more likely to have help in the home, in terms of housework and childcare, that would also make their days freer. This was no small matter. Several articles in *Chatelaine* magazine addressed the crisis of domestic workers leaving service for war work. An April 1942 feature, "My Maid's Gone Into Munitions," advised women how to cope. It was strictly a "news you can use" feature, recommending using a tea wagon to help with the burden of serving meals. A meatier feature in June 1944 considered a more long-term problem: "Will Maids Come Back?" The piece doesn't advocate for universal childcare or suggest that women could lay off on the Olympic-level competitive entertaining that helped—and still helps—define social worth. Instead, it's a series of proposals for elevating domestic work to make it more palatable to women who will have to return to service when the men come back and take all their wartime jobs. "When war ends," the un-bylined story reads, "there will be four-and-a-half-million Canadians seeking jobs. Our returned men will naturally have priority." Women would then inevitably go back to being maids, and "unless drastic changes are made, they will be most unhappy."

The intersectionality here can't be ignored. Women with social and financial privilege were more likely to be white and Protestant. That these women volunteered relentlessly in Halifax (and elsewhere) wasn't a function of commitment, but time. That they rose up to become organizers was likewise no marker of dedication, skill, or intelligence, but of expectation and the willingness of practically everyone involved in volunteer work to recreate existing social structures within volunteer organizations—white wealthy women at the top; those without that share of the privilege carrying the water. The Old 400s on deck; everyone else below. This structure was replicated at the Ajax, the North End Services Canteen, the Women's Voluntary Services, and other facilities. It reverberates through history, too. The first challenge to capturing the stories in this book is a gendered one: volunteer women's roles during the war were seen as less valuable than men's military contributions, so those contributions weren't recognized then and aren't recognized now. The second challenge deals with race, socio-economic status, and culture. The stories of Black women? Of working-class women? They were even less likely to be seen, and for their stories to be catalogued. This in no way reflects poorly on the commitment or work of Dolly McEuen, or Edith, or Charlotte, or any others. It's a recognition that other women may have worked just as hard, yet today, we don't know their names.

⌒᰿⌒

"I looked in the pocket," says Charlotte, thrusting a business card–sized pink stub toward me, "and guess what?" The stiff paper had softened over time, but the ink was unfaded: "Cunard White Star Limited. Forw'rd Dining Room. Second Sitting." The table number was marked in blue pencil: "17." She had found it, where it had been abandoned in the pocket of her dress uniform jacket some seventy years earlier. The meal ticket was from her trip home from Europe, after the Halifax Concert Party Guild 1945 tour. Hugh and Jean Mills were asked by the Canadian Army to bring over a small contingent of the Concert Party Guild's best performers. As always, performers wouldn't be paid, but there were costs to the trip, so Mills sought donations to fund the logistics. The *Halifax Herald* stepped up, as the paper's owners had done so many times in the past, to support the Concert Party Guild.

This bigger donation, floating a thirteen-person European tour, meant recasting as the Halifax *Herald* Concert Party Guild. Lila and Julius and Charlotte went with Hugh and Jean Mills and eight other performers, travelling July 19, 1945, aboard the SS *Île de France*. (They left Mills's sister, Gertrude, back in the small Mills Brothers office with her phone and her Rolodex to continue on with bookings; with so many service members still in Halifax, the shows literally had to go on.) After the tour, Charlotte travelled home on the RMS *Aquitania*, almost a year later than the others, arriving in Halifax on July 29, 1946, after staying on in England for a series of surgeries on a facial hemangioma—also known as a port wine stain—she had been born with. Luckily, she had one pair of pumps and one ball gown with her, which I could guess, looking at the exploding cotton candy of crinolines and tulle on the gowns tossed over her living room sofa, must have taken up serious real estate in her allowed baggage for the tour: two duffel bags. The fancy dress came in handy: "I remember I was invited to the captain's table one night." If she kept that meal ticket as a souvenir, it's gone now.

Volunteer entertainment was a ticket itself, for Charlotte. A golden one. The war's arrival in Halifax had opened her eyes to a bigger world—a world that had landed on her small city's doorstep. It was the same with any teen in town. But joining the Concert Party Guild and giving her every-waking–non-working hour over to entertaining service members had given Charlotte more access to that foreign world than most. She met French servicemen at Victoria Road's Maison Surcouf, Norwegians at the rebranded Ajax Club and once on a whaling ship docked in Halifax Harbour. She boarded the hospital trains with her piano accordion and played through the aisles of sick and injured. She played every canteen in a city full of canteens. Charlotte performed more than a thousand times during the war.

Her volunteering would then, on the Concert Party Guild tour, give her a chance to see Europe at the end of a bloody war—a Europe that really only existed for a short window, before rebuilding began. They travelled some six thousand miles over Germany, Belgium, Holland, and England in the summer and fall of 1945, to any place Canadian servicemen were awaiting repatriation. The modified battle dress they wore—the same as the Canadian Women's Army Corps, but with leather buttons instead of brass and a left-arm patch that screamed "CIVILIAN CONCERT PARTY CANADA"—gave them a level of confidence and clout, but it wasn't going to protect them in what was still a dodgy environment. "Everything was bombed," Charlotte remembers, "and you didn't know whether you were going to step on something." Their sole remuneration was nine hundred cigarettes a month, in long cartons. Charlotte didn't smoke, so she gave hers away. It made her very popular everywhere she went.

Charlotte kept entertaining. When she returned to Halifax after her hospital stay, she moved back into the Waegwoltic Club with her father and stepmother, and returned to her old job. She only moved into an apartment of her own, above Mills Brothers, in 1960. She left that apartment, and the job, two years later when she married Donald Jeffries and moved to Boulderwood, off the Halifax peninsula, on the Northwest Arm. After the war, Charlotte and Lila, for the first time, were paid to perform. "We played for every convention and every hotel. We played here, there, and everywhere. All over. I remember once they flew us to New Brunswick for the curling championship and we had to walk around on the ice with the accordions." In her kitchen, Charlotte kept a hanging rug; safety-pinned to it were newspaper clippings and photos of her time performing. Dead in the middle, the largest, is a black-and-white of Hugh Mills, bowtie and moustache, fedora in his right hand. It's a candid shot, clearly captured as Mills was mid-stride toward the passenger side of a station wagon. He wears a surprised smile. Written in ink across his body: *To a Grand Trooper and a dear Friend, our Charlotte, from Your Uncle Mel.* "I keep saying I am going to take this down, for years," Charlotte tells me, standing in front of the display. Even with this time capsule of her wartime achievements, photos with famous people, her gowns and unique dress uniform jacket, Charlotte performed the familiar refrain of so many women wartime volunteers: "Everybody did it. It needed to be done and nobody thought about it; we just did it. I still don't feel like I did anything special. It's just the way life was."

This was the last time we spoke. Charlotte died in 2019, at ninety-eight.

Volunteer entertaining was a ticket for Margaret, too, but a different one. She watched the city land on Halifax's front step, just like Charlotte, but at a remove. She didn't work at Mills, or live at the Waegwoltic Club. She stuck to a smaller patch of the city: encircled by her warm family home on Creighton Street, Cornwallis Street Baptist Church, Gottingen Street, and Gerrish Street Hall. She sang on CBC Radio, she recalls, but while her immense vocal talent might have found her a solid footing as part of the Concert Party Guild, she didn't join. She never sang at a canteen, or a foreign seamen's home, or aboard a whaling ship docked in the harbour. She didn't tour Europe at the end of the conflict and trade cigarettes for souvenirs. The 3Ms sang any time they were asked to be on the program, and Margaret and Margaret and May carried on their trio after the war, too. Margaret also sang at the church, which in modern day became New Horizons Baptist, to shed the name of Halifax's atrocity-ridden colonial "founder." She married Arthur in 1944 when he returned from his Army service. They settled in Halifax, where he worked construction, and had nine children. She still lives on Gottingen Street.

Singing was Margaret's salve and her great joy, and it was her entrée, at Gerrish Street Hall, to the new. "Anybody coming in—strangers talking to you, or whatever—they would *show* you something. I liked to know what it was, or see what it was," she says. She might have loved to climb aboard a whaling ship, to twirl in imported ball gowns with dyed-to-match shoes, to sing, even, at the North End Services Canteen, just down Gottingen Street from Gerrish. But it wasn't going to happen in wartime Halifax, and Margaret didn't ever wonder about the possibility. Gerrish Street Hall? "That's all we had."

Every year in January, the Nova Scotia Mass Choir presents its annual "Dr. Martin Luther King Jr., The Dream Continues" tribute concert. In 2015, the renowned Halifax-based gospel choir chose the Halifax Civil Emergency Corps Platoon 7E as its honouree. This was the first time most Haligonians had ever heard about the efforts of these volunteers, and the first time many outside the Black community in the uptown area surrounding Creighton, Maynard, Gottingen, and Agricola Streets had ever heard of Gerrish Street Hall. (I lived on Creighton Street for a decade and my kids attended the very same school Margaret had in the 1920s and 1930s. Though I walked within a few metres of the former site of the hall every day on my way to the kids' school, and made the acquaintance of grandparents in the neighbourhood who would have visited the hall, I didn't know of it until I started researching this book.) In the years since the Nova Scotia Mass Choir's tribute, several crowdsourced attempts have been made to identify the volunteers in the photo—the only "official" copy that came close included last names and first initials. Joining Pearl Adams, Arthur Sampson, and Walter "Duck" Johnson are a collection of Jacksons, a Smith, a Berry, and a Kellum, among others. Also identified? Miss J. Brooks and Miss A. Bundy. All of them, finally, one small step closer to their stories being told.

Chapter Nine

YOU'LL NEVER KNOW

May Feetham and Elsie Moorhouse were laughing, Elsie with her right arm raised in mock-serious point-making, May with her head turned to gaze at Elsie, her best friend and the Red Cross Voluntary Aid Detachment (VAD) captain. This inseparable pair were often laughing or smiling together. Today's particular joke took hold as each sat on a folding deck chair, likely on the *Lady Rodney*, a passenger liner-turned-wartime hospital ship. The two weren't in their Red Cross nursing auxiliary uniforms, but instead were gussied up in skirts and blouses and heels—Elsie with a broad fur-collared coat; May in personality-fitting simpler attire: a gathered-sleeve below-the-knee coat and tulle-covered calot hat. This is a different May from her official Red Cross VAD portrait—white long-back nurse's cap, white Red Cross pinafore apron, big teeth, apple cheeks.

The Red Cross Voluntary Aid Detachment corps was launched in 1940 to provide women the opportunity to volunteer in transport, administration, and auxiliary nursing aid. The Department of National Defence, when the program launched in 1940 in conjunction with the Red Cross and St. John Ambulance Brigade, hoped to recruit six thousand women to volunteer. Some fifteen thousand lined up to take on the work, including May, who was by then forty. This wasn't first aid. It was nursing aid, which required serious training and a significant time obligation. The women received no pay. This commitment was different from that of women who helped knit comforts and served at canteens; different, even, from that of someone like Charlotte Guy, who was called upon daily. Red Cross Voluntary Aid Detachment nurses gave themselves over in quasi-military long-term roles, often involving danger. And that was certainly true for May Feetham, who crossed the ocean from Halifax during the Battle of the Atlantic a staggering seventeen times.

Her other volunteer nursing aid duties took May to the Halifax Infirmary Merchant Marine ward, the Halifax Children's Hospital, and the Halifax Infants' Home. She ran blood collection. She even spent the summers of 1942 and 1943 as a Girl Guides camp leader when there was a shortage of volunteers for that role. While her VAD work spanned five-plus years from October 1941 through February 1947 (when the Red Cross Corps stood down and May went on reserve duty), all of her ocean-going trips were wedged into a brief span at the war's end: from 1944 through early 1947. Her ninety-something niece, June O'Brien, is the holder of May's photos and citations. The keeper of the story. "When I gathered all these things together," she told me, "it dawned on me what she was doing."

May was born in 1899 or 1900; both years are in the record. She arrived as Mary Deborah, but they always called her May. She was single all her life; after the premature death of her mother she had been tasked with raising her two brothers, Edward and Luke. Luckily for May, she genuinely loved children and loved, June says, caring for others. Her work as an escort officer, then, would have been a good fit. May travelled from Halifax to England and Holland to bring back the war brides of Canadian service members and their children. During the crossing, she occupied the children to give their mothers a break, and cared for any in the family who were ill. Once landed in Halifax, she saw them through to the Port Nursery, and fed and cared for the children while their mothers filled out customs and immigration paperwork. She then continued the journey, accompanying the women and children by train as far as Montreal, familiarizing them with Canadian money and norms along the way.

Marjorie Langin also volunteered at the Port Nursery, welcoming women with coffee and doughnuts and giving them the scoop about their often long journeys ahead. "They would say to you, 'Is it really a long distance to Alberta?'" Marjorie recalls. "'Well,' I would say, 'well, darling… you couldn't walk it.'"

The last war brides' escort ship left England on January 17, 1947, with 691 brides. Based on her service record, there's a good chance that marked May's seventeenth trip across the Atlantic.

⌒ᴧᴧ⌒

It's impossible to imagine that May Feetham would not have known Sadie Fineberg.

Fineberg in a word? Vivid. In fact, that's precisely the word her son Elliot Fineberg uses to describe his mother. His evidence is solid: serious updos—I'm talking intricate buns, sprayed and set—flamboyant scarves, corsages. Sadie's style was stellar. She was gregarious and loving, and everywhere all at once, it seemed. Sadie volunteered at the Port Nursery during the war, where she held the babies and fed them their milk, played with children, and chased toddlers. The war brides disembarking from their ships with May would have undoubtedly encountered Sadie, who, it's said, kept in her pocket a giant wad of Kleenex for wiping kids' noses. She always had bread and honey cake to give the new arrivals, too, but it seems unlikely the next part of the legend is true: that she baked them herself.

"She wasn't much for the kitchen," says her daughter-in-law Betty Fineberg. Elliot concurs. "She didn't enjoy housework." Nonetheless, she took on the role of making refreshments for Halifax Concert Party Guild events:

Elliot remembers sandwiches upon sandwiches. (He also remembers she got the bread a block over at Ben's Bakery on Quinpool, further putting to rest the home-baked bread myth.) She also organized and hosted a coterie of women on Shirley Street—where she lived with her husband, Morris, a grocer, whom everyone called MB—to knit for refugees. But the port was her ken, and the war, the match-strike on her lifelong volunteer efforts. When the war started, Sadie felt a twinge that she could be of need as immigrants, refugees, war brides, and others were arriving. The thirty-nine-year-old headed down and offered her services. She was multilingual—French, English, Polish, some Yiddish, and a bit of Russian from MB, who came to Cape Breton from Russia in 1909. There were another two languages in the mix as well, but Elliot can't remember which.

"Her work really started when the war ended," Elliot says. He's referring to her marathon of volunteering at organizations that included the Canadian Mental Health Association and the women's branch of B'nai B'rith, and many other organizations. But her heart was at the port. In 1948, the city awarded her a badge—it looked like a detective's badge, Elliot says, though it's been lost—to commemorate her work and formidable volunteer presence. If they were trying to encourage her to retire, it definitely backfired. Sadie just carried on heading down to Pier 21 every day. She met every single ship that docked with newcomers for eighteen straight years and stayed on for more than forty years in total, until her death in 1982.

For some women, like May Feetham, wartime volunteering was a burst of activity, followed by a return to so-called normal life. For others, like Sadie, voluntary war work represented a continuum, just as it did for Dolly McEuen. She had enough money left over in the Interallied Hospitality Fund after the war's end to create a scholarship for naval veterans to study at McGill University in Montreal. On top of the scholarship, Dolly sponsored a ski cottage in the Laurentian Mountains for the pleasure and benefit of recipients. In 1973, Dolly and her niece, Mhairi, who had been the Ajax

Club's volunteer librarian, founded the McEuen Scholarship, a full-ride award supporting Canadian students for four years of study at Scotland's University of St. Andrews. Marjorie started giving of her time as a Langin, and kept on giving as a Lindsay, after she married her sweetheart, John, in 1948. She spent decades as a dedicated volunteer and philanthropist, supporting ventures small and large across Halifax. For her, 1939 Halifax was a catalyst: "The outbreak of the war was the beginning," she tells me. But it was also a different kind of giving. "When I volunteer now," she says, "I give something of me. But (during the war) I was given something."

Historian Jay White, in *Conscripted City*, notes with regret that the bulk of the network of women's war service organizations was "quietly dismantled when women volunteers returned to raising families on a full-time basis." White concedes that, as individuals, many volunteers became more politically or socially conscious. "As a community, however, Halifax derived little of lasting value from the remarkable record of civic altruism achieved during the war."

—∿∿—

Did the war *really* not change Halifax as a community? Did the war only impact the lives of individual women? If I could ask Edith Girouard, who tried everything she could to have some—any—service organization take over what she built with the Women's Voluntary Services, and failed, she might agree that women's wartime structures were for naught. Me? I'm not so sure. The experience of Halifax women volunteers has been portrayed, when it's been portrayed at all, simplistically. But the truth of those experiences? Complex.

The primary fuzziness centres around time. That the Red Cross, the St. John Ambulance Brigade, the IODE, the Salvation Army, and other large service organizations carried on work after the war is no shocker.

It's their business. But for individual women, the idea of taking on "war work" implies a hard stop at war's end. For Halifax women, that means VE day. May 8, 1945. Alas, no one snapped their fingers and drained the city of service members, war workers, or from-away families on VE day. The mood may have lightened slightly, but where the rubber hits the road, in the need for accommodations, entertainment, leisure, and food, the city was no different May 8 than it was on May 7 or May 9. There remained oppressive levels of need. William D. Naftel reminds readers in *Halifax at War* that food rationing was not only slow to disappear in Canada, but in late 1945, rationing of meat and sugar actually intensified because of overseas need.

Those servicemen, as they left Europe and Britain, headed to one city: Halifax. Beginning in June 1945, the half-million–odd men who had left for war through the city over the past six years were now returning, and at a rapidly accelerated pace. A hurricane of war brides came in tandem. By June 1945, the Canadian Press reported, the stream of returned veterans was so steady Halifax was rolling them out—sometimes at a rate of almost two trains an hour. Mrs. A. O. Saunderson and Mrs. W. S. Robertson of the Halifax City Committee reported that, through all of 1945, volunteer need carried on unabated. And their volunteer organization responded. On one day alone, a group of thirty-one volunteers spent two hours feeding hundreds of repatriated service members and war families. Four volunteers made sandwiches and coffee to be served from a mobile canteen set up at the Halifax Armoury. "From improvised tables, tomato juice and biscuits were given out. At another table there were unlimited quantities of milk, and several people were busy keeping the queue in order for there was no let up to the steady stream of men, women, and children of all classes."

A material proportion of the returned men could not leave Halifax at once. These were the injured, who came in on hospital ships. The first hospital ship arrived in Halifax in 1942, after the raid on Dieppe. It was met at the port by women volunteers from the St. John Ambulance Brigade and the Red Cross Voluntary Aid Detachment—women like May Feetham. In fact, members were on hand to meet every hospital ship through 1943, and then every single ship that arrived—hospital, troop, war bride escort alike—through the end. Those who needed immediate care were seen to by nursing aid volunteers like May. A mobile canteen was set up, as well, so those disembarking could have snacks and hot coffee. Marjorie Langin was one of the uniformed volunteers working the mobile canteen, serving coffee and doughnuts. And as she told it, one day, unexpectedly, there appeared her Uncle Jack. There were two versions of this story, at least, that Marjorie told. In one, Jack, her mother's youngest brother, was *leaving* on convoy duty. In the better version—which is, conveniently, more likely, given the circumstances of her volunteering—Jack was arriving home, one of the first down the gangplank. Marjorie darted from her canteen post and ran to Jack. She leapt at him, hugging and kissing him, saying, "Oh, Uncle Jack! This is so wonderful!" A chorus rose around them, servicemen shouting, "I'm your Uncle Jack! I'm your Uncle Jack!" Marjorie called it her one moment of utter fame. "I was never so popular in all my life." Women volunteers carried on with their sandwich-making and tomato juice–serving and warm-welcoming long past VE day. The daily deluge of repatriated service members didn't peter out until 1946, the last war brides' escort not until 1947.

The collection of money, clothing, and goods for overseas relief was another volunteer movement that ramped up as hostilities ceased, rather than winding down. Understanding the volume of that relief is a little like capturing sand in your palms. The total is inevitably lost in the counting, and the numbers mean little anyway—what does twelve million pounds of clothing look like? How many people does that clothe? How long does it take to collect? To ship? To distribute? Twelve million pounds, by one account, represents only one month's collection for Canada. There were thousands of quilts, thousands of knitted items: sweaters, mittens, blankets. Gazillions of socks. Over three years, Nova Scotia women prepared, packaged, and sent to England one hundred and sixty thousand pounds of apple jelly for war nurseries and schools. Overseas relief coordinators were off-handedly referred to in the media as "middlemen of mercy" which, while a catchy alliteration, was wrong on two counts. First: these were women. Second, they weren't an army of mere shippers. They were the ones doing the sewing and knitting and pickling and preserving. The collection and distribution wasn't their defining work. They were only steps in the process.

The need was monumental. Europe was decimated, its physical infrastructure totalled in many cases, its work forces downed, and its stockpiles of all number of essentials emptied through a calculated campaign of depletion by way of invasion and pillaging, or through the disruption of shipping and merchant services. Each side of the war had worked to crumble their foes' manufacturing sectors. To destroy the means of distribution. Each side worked to starve the humans on the other. And, so, the need for relief both came into clear view and became more achievable once the bombing and Bren-gunning stopped. Relief was needed in Britain and all over the European continent. Name a country and it was probably on the list of Canadian relief-recipient nations: Lithuania and other Soviet states, Greece, Hungary, Poland, and on and on and on. In January 1947, Colonel P. L. Browne, the National War Services department's new director of voluntary war relief, wrote a letter indicating that from September 1939 to December 31, 1946, Canadian overseas relief totalled $60 million in goods and cash. That's the equivalent today of roughly $930 million.

In its 1945 annual report, the Nova Scotia Red Cross took pains to say that "for Nova Scotia, and especially Halifax—the true Atlantic gateway to Canada—the hostilities alone ceased, while much of the work incident to the war is still going on and will continue." A December 1945 editorial in the *Globe and Mail* noted that even seven months after VE day, the transformation of the city from its wartime frenzy was "imperceptible." The housing situation was still desperate; there were still queues for movie theatres. There were, the piece said, "still more uniformed men than civilians on the streets." Women's volunteer work continued.

The end of it, though, wouldn't be when the last troop ship landed, or the date its passenger manifest cleared the city, or the day the last war bride was escorted by train westward. It's dissatisfying, but it's impossible, really, to point to the end of Halifax women's wartime work. That's because it was a subtle shift, for so many, from doing the work for war and doing the work for peace. I'm not suggesting that most, or any, women volunteers were making sandwiches for hundreds of people on a routine basis postwar; obviously May Feetham wasn't crossing the North Atlantic into the 1950s. But the work of women volunteers was materially different from the work of service members, who were specially trained, away from home, and on a well-defined mission. Sanctioned and formal. So much of the work of Halifax women volunteers was the opposite: informal, social, carried out in the home, nipped in here and there between other duties, and requiring either no special skills, or skills that were already baked into their everyday lives. The men's work had a box around it. The women's work bled around the edges. Sharon MacDonald says the work they did wasn't conveniently siloed. "It wasn't just that they were doing relief for overseas," she says. "They were still making quilts for the Red Cross that would be used if a local family had a fire." Broadly, then, it's that idea of volunteering on a continuum: the war was acute and extreme for Halifax women, but it fits into a pattern of women's work. As MacDonald wrote in *Hidden Costs, Hidden Labours*, "With their long history of charitable, community-based groups, [women] have developed strategies for getting much practical work done with few resources beyond their own time, labour, and ingenuity."

And there's this: I can sit here and tell you that twelve million pounds of used clothing was gathered, that $60 million in goods and money was collected, but the truth is that we don't *know* the truth. We just don't know how much was really collected. We don't know how much was really done. We don't know the cost and we don't know the hours. I don't just mean the counting was shoddy, or incomplete. I mean that women's unpaid labour, in the home and in the community, remains uncounted by the traditional markers of economic progress. In planning circles, it's said that if something matters, it's a budget line item, not merely a talking point. Well, women's volunteer labour has never been on the balance sheet. The United Nations, in 2021, valued women's unpaid care and domestic work at 10–39 percent of most nations' GDP, noting in a policy document, "It can contribute more to the economy than the manufacturing, commerce or transportation sectors." If it's not counted now, it certainly wasn't counted during the Second World War. The war represented a moment, perhaps, when women could have turned the tide—keeping intricate tallies of their time and energy expenditures. We'll forgive them for not doing so in the fog of it. Many groups didn't keep records at all. Others did so haphazardly. I've noticed it's not uncommon to see a statement or annual report mentioning "many" contributions of a given item, or hours of time, or "a great deal" of something. When counting was done, accounting was not. We might get the number of pairs of mittens knit, but no sense of the value of labour or raw materials. MacDonald writes that, "during the Great War, no attempts were made to provide a monetary value to women's volunteer labour. In the Second World War, this situation hardly changed. Occasional reports give a monetary value to supplies made. However, it remains a mystery how the value was calculated."

On top of all this is the nature of this work being, at a certain level, untrackable. When MacDonald was researching *Hidden Costs, Hidden Labours*, she sent out a survey questionnaire through the Women's Institutes of Nova Scotia and other volunteer organizations, large and small. A quarter of her respondents, all of them wartime volunteers, chose not to circle their estimated number of hours worked. Perhaps they didn't recall the work, five-plus decades on. Perhaps they just honestly didn't know. I've asked myself this question—how many volunteer hours?—and

I understand the potential reticence. There was a time in my own life when I was raising two kids, with my husband often away (and when he was home, he was working long hours), while I worked two different jobs equalling full-time, about half of that in my home office. I volunteered on an as-needed basis at my kids' school, co-launched a large community event, and chaired two non-profit boards. The commitment varied wildly week to week; the only consistency was that it could happen from early morning to late at night and that it was peppered in amidst the rest of my paid work and domestic duties. How many hours a week did I volunteer? No. Sweet. Clue.

So, how to count? "Perhaps the sheer enormity of the relief work," MacDonald writes, "can only be grasped by quantifying it and yet, endless lists of numbers of bandages and quilts and knitted socks have a difficult time competing with lists of battles and dead soldiers."

All this wobbliness around quantifying and valuing women's unpaid volunteer labour feels like it's baked into the work. Just the way it is. But there was also, during the war, a significant amount of energy put into framing this industriousness to benefit the government in its extraction of labour resources. Women were a means to an end—the end being winning the war. This was founded on the notion that women—both volunteers and those in paid employment—would rise up at the war's start and silently recede at its end, reinstating the status quo by evanescing into their earned place in the kitchen.

For working women who were paid, this groundwork was laid by way of a tightrope of communications. Women were sold on the idea that working was emancipation, but, crucially, emancipation by emergency. Once the emergency was done, they would be as well. The persistent myth—

that the war emancipated women from the kitchen and the home—alive more than seven decades later, just isn't borne out by the facts. In 1941, women made up 19.8 percent of the Canadian labour force. At the height of women's wartime work participation, in October 1944, they made up 27.1 percent. But the "tremendous increase in the number of women workers during the latter half of the war," writes Roslyn Louise Cluett in her 1984 thesis *Soldiers of Industry: Women in the Canadian Labour Force, 1939–1951*, "seemed to have almost vanished overnight." Indeed, women were urged in both certain and subtle terms, with the winding down of hostilities, to get themselves back where they belonged. Out of uniform, out of coveralls, into aprons. By 1951, women made up just 22.3 percent of the labour force, barely a titch above the level a decade earlier.

While women in the paid labour force were expected, for the supposed good of the country, to go back to their domestic duties, women volunteers were in a different position. Conveniently, for the powers that needed to entice them to re-right the pre-war family-structure–ship, women volunteers had really never left the domestic sphere. Their work might have been extreme in volume and time commitment, and obviously that was the case nowhere more than in Halifax. It might have seen women taking on roles they hadn't before, such as home nursing, first aid, or acting as volunteer fire wardens, like the women in the Home Guard. But the work was rooted in the home. This made the need for these women to "recede" to the postwar status quo, with men as the breadwinners and women as domestic managers, all that much easier to achieve. What else helped? That inimical lack of counting and accounting. The sense was: you made bologna sandwiches in your kitchen before the war. You made *more* sandwiches, and maybe in some other kitchen, during the war. Now it's time to go back to making those bologna sandwiches in your kitchen. It was always basically the same work, only temporarily amplified and recast. The propagandist cherry on top? Aren't you glad the war's over and you don't have to make so many sandwiches now?

Lucky girl. And, hey, check this out: if you play your cards right, maybe you can get a new dishwasher!

There can't have been many Canadians who proved more keen to spread this message of domestic duty than Byrne Hope Sanders, the wartime editor of *Chatelaine* magazine. Her monthly editorials ran under the header: "As an Editor Sees It." How, exactly, did this editor see it? In a nutshell: Do your housework and volunteer and know that you are on the side of all that is right and good. "Whenever I hear a woman say, 'what can I do? I feel so helpless,'" Sanders wrote in September 1940.

> *I know that she has romantic visions of racing madly over broken roads, driving an ambulance; for performing deeds of dramatic heroism under fire. As she would, should the need arise. But I want to say to her, the easiest thing—at least what seems like the easiest thing—is always the hardest to do. Remember France's command to her sol-diers*—defend the two feet of France on which you stand. *That's really the command to Canadian women, don't you think? Defend the infinitesimal part of Canadian life which is your home.*

Sanders's editorial consistency, over years and years, is enviable, if nothing else. The home front was the war front. Categorically. In August 1941, she actually recommended literal conscription for women into volunteer work. She was unrelenting. Also? Unforgiving. She urged women: "Reject your moods." Her summer editorials reminded readers not to lapse in their duties these lazier months. (This was a real problem—the files of the Halifax Women's Voluntary Services show clearly that women's commitment and giving of time waned during the summer months, while the need for volunteer help during July and August did not dip.) For me, it's just that Sanders's was so damn relentless. She never once dropped the veil, never conceded that women volunteers might be tired and needing a break, or might need a morale boost of their own. It was 100 percent service 100 percent of the time. Duplicates of Sanders's messaging, or vice versa, can be found in advertisements throughout *Chatelaine*. A February 1942 full-page Department of Munitions and Supply ad shows a woman, lost in thought, her chin resting on her left palm, a wedding ring visible. The reader sees a collage of images of men at work in war industries and fighting, and the headline takeaway: "Brave men shall not die because I faltered." The rest of the text is a lecture in behaviour, including the need to keep one's husband fit and happy, to be thankful of him, and not nagging for his attention. "Be sympathetic, patient and understanding.... Give him a happy smile when problems you may not be able to share cast their shadow across his face."

The idea of housework as patriotism was so entrenched, and the postwar analysis of women's voluntary labour so scant, argues Sharon MacDonald, that it's been a given that women stepped up to help out of patriotic compulsion alone. The truth, she wrote in *Hidden Costs, Hidden Labours*, is more tangled. "Between the extremes of vocal patriotic women and vocal war resistors lay the vast majority of women who neither spoke out for, nor against, but did what they had to do to help themselves, their families, neighbours, and even strangers survive the crises of war." In other words, most women weren't overtly protesting the war, or overtly in the Byrne Hope Sanders camp. They were just...getting by. It strikes me that this must have been patently so in Halifax. Haligonian women watched their city begin to weaken and soon crack under the strain of wartime activity. They stepped up for myriad reasons, central among them, surely: the city, and its population, were hurting badly and needed help. That their extraordinary contributions were ignored after the war reinforces a point MacDonald makes: "Apparently, for women, work was its own reward; praise was an added bonus."

～⋁⋀⌣

Charlotte Guy Jeffries is first up, walking well. She is bundled in a warm coat and colourful scarf, which is good, because it's an unseasonably cold November day, under 10°C, and, in Halifax, it always feels chilliest on the waterfront. Charlotte is here today, near Pier 21, where Sadie Fineberg greeted immigrants and May Feetham wound her war bride charges through customs, to unveil the first of three statues created by Marlene Hilton Moore erected in Halifax to honour the city's women volunteers. One figure is an African Nova Scotian canteen worker and another a girl beside a wagon piled high with salvage materials. The third is a seated woman, the knitting in her lap contained by a Mi'kmaw basket. Charlotte walks up to the knitter as a crowd of hundreds, locals and local dignitaries alike, smile and look on. The full-sized bronze figure is draped in a broad iris-purple cloth, and there's a moment's pause as it's untied from behind for the reveal.

"A moment of high drama!" Charlotte quips, holding both her arms wide. She might not be wearing a ball gown today, but she still knows how to work a crowd. Off comes the cloth, and Charlotte snuggles into the crook of the seated knitter's neck as cameras click. The resulting photo went far and wide. The accompanying story heralded the first-ever full-sized Halifax monument to honour women: The Volunteers/Les Bénévoles. Margaret Gordon unveiled the canteen worker. Joyce Purchase, the girl with a wagonload of salvage materials. The Volunteers/Les Bénévoles came to fruition on that cold November day in 2017 because of the work of the Halifax Women's History Society, who planned the monument to raise the profile of Second World War Halifax women volunteers, and to start to correct an error in the city's representation, which sees the historic port awash in full-size statues of white men. The society raised half a million dollars, and, en route, peoples awareness of these women's momentous feats.

In fact, recognition of volunteers was on the radar of the provincial government by mid-war. The 1942 edition of the pamphlet "Nova Scotia Helps the Fighting Man," is a stab at telling the story of volunteer organizations that "have neither the time nor the facilities to tell the story of their achievements." Premier A. S. MacMillan, in his foreword to the postwar follow-up 1945 edition, goes one better, calling the pamphlet an attempt at "a comprehensive picture of the fine work done by volunteers citizens, *largely women*." Those are my italics; it's important because the earlier 1942 edition doesn't credit the bulk of the work to women. Comprehensive, "Nova Scotia Helps the Fighting Man," was decidedly not, failing to mention the Home Guard and Gerrish Street Hall. One has to wonder if MacMillan or his wife, Martha, had any influence on the content: Dolly's Ajax Hospitality Headquarters gets a section, while the Ajax Club on Tobin Street is missing entirely. Despite the obvious omissions, MacMillan rightly calls women volunteers' work "a record of achievement that tops everything of its kind on this continent."

And then? Poof. Forgotten.

This disappearance of this history is in part at the feet of women, and even women volunteers themselves, who were complicit in their own vanishing. They were told their work was patriotism. And patriotism was a baseline, not an achievement. They were reminded, and saw in the city around them, that everyone was doing their part. A singular act is extraordinary, a community effort, though made up of individual acts, is somehow less so. Plus, the women didn't tell their stories, which paled in comparison to those of battles, violence, and deprivation overseas. While these women failed to recognize the value of their own contributions, the next generation, the Baby Boomers, purposely avoided recognition of these deeds. Second-wave feminists worked diligently to break out of any notion that biology held them to the home as it had their mothers. As MacDonald writes in *Hidden Costs, Hidden Labours*, "For those who have had to struggle to create a place for themselves in the workplace, there has been the need to distance themselves from the domesticity of their mothers and the traditional nurturing work most of them did during the war."

And as MacDonald says today, sitting in her bright condo living room in Dartmouth, Nova Scotia, "I think women, in general, don't take a lot of credit for what they do. You are not supposed to brag; you are not supposed to think that your contribution is all that important." Third generation feminists, like me, sopped up the myth that the war made space for women in the workplace. Neither from our humble grandmothers, nor from our own well-meaningly blind mothers, did we ever hear the stories. We were never told. So we never knew to ask. We assumed all along that we understood who won the Second World War.

What we didn't realize was that it was actually Halifax women volunteers.

Chapter Ten

THE NEARNESS OF YOU

Marjorie Lindsay stood up to the podium at the private reception inside Pier 20, following the unveiling of The Volunteers/Les Bénévoles. She took a brief moment, and smiled out at the crowd, turning her head left and right. She had a story to tell. It was the one about Uncle Jack and his arrival (or perhaps departure) seventy years earlier, just one pier over from where she spoke on this day, where the young victory roll–adorned Marjorie was working the Red Cross mobile canteen. She regaled the crowd with the kissing and the hugging, and the shouts of "I'm your Uncle Jack! I'm your Uncle Jack!" and how she felt like a movie star. "It was a part of my life that was so very special," she told the crowd, who were indisputably pleased to be sheltered from the out-of-character November chill. "I am so thankful…to be here today and to be honoured by all of this." Then Marjorie pulled out her favourite wartime one-liner, encapsulating her school-girl impression of Halifax: "It's a terrible thing to say, but, for a young girl, I had a wonderful war!"

Marjorie could rise to the moment, and she did on this day. But months later, as we were sitting to have tea, she admitted that she wasn't all-in on the fuss. It was a shared sentiment. The three unveilers, too—Joyce, Margaret, and Charlotte—all possessed a mild sense of bewilderment that their unsung wartime contributions deserved any applause. "I didn't feel that I deserved anything," Charlotte told me later, "though I thought it was nice of them."

—◦◦◦—

By early 1945, the writing was on the wall for the war. Over a few short months, German troops had been surrendering in the order of hundreds of thousands. In April 1945 alone, the Western Allies captured some 1.5 million prisoners. Through Allied liberation or panicked German withdrawal, occupied nations were, bit by bit, reclaimed; the scale and scope of Nazi concentration camps revealed. On April 30, Hitler died by suicide; hastening the pace of territorial and individual capitulation. On May 7, Germany signed its unconditional surrender, to take effect May 8. It was all over but the crying.

And the volunteering.

The battles, discoveries, and negotiations that ended the conflict didn't change the trajectory of women's voluntary work in Halifax. Even though it's clear reading federal government memos that by early 1945 the recreation for service members was being viewed with an eye to winding down, getting there would take another year-plus. Postwar, the need for magazines continued. A memo from October 1945, months after VE day and even two months after the surrender of Japan on August 14, 1945 (the war as a whole wasn't technically over until September 2, 1945, when American General Douglas MacArthur accepted the Japanese surrender), the National War Services department circulated a memo stressing that distribution of magazines and reading materials shouldn't be reduced by more than 10 percent for the balance of the year. It wasn't until January 1946 that magazine exchanges started to wind down their work. But, truly, the government's approach to entertainment, accommodation, food, and recreation didn't needed much in the way of a drawdown of power and resources. The feds had spent six years focussed firmly on battle. Remember that Canadian Navy boss Rear-Admiral Leonard Murray, by Stephen Kimber's assessment, had no interest in keeping men happy. He didn't have time for concerns about well-being. He just needed men fit and committed. I suppose the great fear was that paying attention to what was not strictly battle and battle-readiness might cost the war. And who knows, it may have. But that approach also cost Halifax. Dearly. The city was bruised and battered by May 1945. And, finally, it broke.

Halifax's VE day riots lasted from late on May 7, overnight through May 8. Glass washed over the sidewalks like water from a heavy rain after more than twenty-five hundred commercial plate glass windows were shattered and the store contents looted. The cost of the melee was estimated at more than $5 million—the equivalent of $78 million today. The conditions that led to the riots were long—long—simmering: the pent-up rage and disappointment of service members and merchant seamen who felt unsupported in and by Halifax, and the explosive frustration of sneering Haligonians who just wanted their city back.

"Crowded lodgings, exorbitant rent, overburdened laundries, and scant supplies, all had a part in this ill feeling," wrote Thomas H. Raddall in *Halifax: Warden of the North.* "So did the growing indifference of shop girls, café waitresses, and others overworked in the incessant rush. Another cause of irritation was the scarcity of taxi cabs, due partly to the absence of many peacetime cabbies in the services and the preoccupation of the rest with the more lucrative forms of hire." While Halifax blamed service members for upsetting their lives and city, service members blamed Halifax for not providing—or not providing enough of—what they needed. The real blame goes to the federal government, who forgot the forces unless they were at battle or near to it, and who used Halifax as a means to an end with no regard for how it might leave the city damaged in the end.

All this antagonism might have added up to mere long-term rancour—with Haligonians complaining for decades about the war, and with service members, war workers, and service wives leaving Halifax with a bad taste in their mouths and a vow never to return—but for a spate of bad decision-making on May 7 and 8. First, Rear-Admiral Murray, oblivious to the six years of teeth-gnashing in his midst, allowed nine thousand naval members to go ashore around suppertime on May 7. There were no legal bars, few canteens, and soon, restaurants were closed. By nightfall, a mob, comprising merchant seamen, service members, and civilians, set tramcars ablaze and broke into the Nova Scotia Liquor Commission, which lost eight thousand cases of beer, fifteen hundred cases of wine, and sixty-five thousand quarts of hard liquor. As police struggled to regain calm, civic leaders wound themselves into pretzels to encourage proper—or at least non-vandalistic—celebrations, such as the planned entertainment by Uncle Mel's Halifax Concert Party Guild at the Garrison Grounds. (Halifax Council meeting minutes for April 30, 1945, a week earlier, include an itemized list of events for "V Day," whenever it might arrive. Notably incorrect in retrospect is the notion that many families who had lost loved ones wouldn't be in the mood to celebrate. And notable for keeping in tune with Halifax is this eye-roll of a line: "We are encouraging all people to go to church and worship." Council was not reading the room!) Even after the disastrous evening of May 7, Rear-Admiral Murray remained oblivious, or unbound by reason and hoping for the best, when he allowed another ninety-five hundred men go ashore on May 8. Sensing a repeat of the previous day's events, still-operating restaurants and movie theatres closed early. But by that point, it was too late. The arse was out of 'er.

The Second World War was Halifax's chance to shine, or at least mature a little. Alas, no. In fairness, the deluge dumped in its lap by the federal government was more than a town with 68,000 souls and no traffic light could handle without significant help, and that help simply never showed up. But it was also Halifax's fault for not stepping out of its provincialism, for fearing the new ideas of come-from-aways like Dolly McEuen, for cleaving to reverence for the Old 400s and to prohibitionist thinking. A particularly blistering (and for my money, fair) opinion piece ran in the May 22, 1945, *Globe and Mail*. Naval Volunteer Reserve Lieutenant-Commander B. M. Tate split the blame in half, noting that service members had spent six years blaming every disadvantage they experienced on the greed and closed-mindedness of Haligonians. Meanwhile, "this resentment, more childish than reasonable, has been reciprocated by Halifax, which has blamed wartime overcrowding for anything that anybody didn't like." The tension, never earnestly addressed by the feds or any other level of government, was allowed to fester. Many in Halifax blamed the riots on the lack of access to booze, either on VE day itself, or by drawing a straight line from the province's treatment of the Ajax Club, and by extension, all naval ratings in port, to the riots. "It is relatively unimportant that the liquor stores were shut (on VE day)," Tate argued. "To have kept them open would probably have changed nothing."

The malignancy was deep and cancerous.

As much as the Second World War revealed Halifax's intractable conservatism and gripping one-horse-ishness, the war also changed the city. It did make it a bigger place, once the postwar population settled. Many civilians who came for war work stayed on, and many returning veterans did so with wives and children they hadn't left with. The population, by 1946, was 115,136, counting both sides of the harbour. But don't imagine too great a social leap. Even with the wartime influx of international merchant mariners, and the generally positive experience of mingling with men of different cultures and races, Halifax did not become a multicultural haven. The informal racial segregation of institutions and neighbourhoods continued, as did the formal segregation of the province's school system, which was on the books until 1954 and which lingered through the 1980s. The province's residential institution for Indigenous youth, Shubenacadie Residential School, didn't close until 1967.

The majority-Black Africville community never received the municipal services the rest of the city enjoyed, even though homeowners there continued to pay their taxes to support the absent infrastructure. In 1962, Halifax City Council voted to remove the community and began expropriating property, which it had been doing over decades anyway, whenever it needed bits and pieces of land for industrial purposes. Seaview United Baptist Church, the centre of the community, was torn down in 1967. The city sent in the demolition equipment in the middle of the night.

Prime Minister Mackenzie King shepherded Canada through repatriation and retired in 1948. Allan MacDougall Butler became the fourth in Halifax's cascading series of not-particularly-noteworthy wartime mayors, winning by acclamation less than two weeks before VE day. A good party man, Alexander Stirling MacMillan retired as premier of Nova Scotia on September 8, 1945, so his predecessor, Angus L. Macdonald, could slide back into his old job leading the province. In 1952, the city began construction on a Halifax Harbour span named after their beloved Angus L. But Macdonald died suddenly in office in April 1954—before the bridge's opening the following year. Today, people call it "the Macdonald," but more often it's simply "the old bridge." What is it, though, if you think about it, is a defining visual marker in the city, like the Golden Gate Bridge is to San Francisco. Where's the bridge named after the thousands of women?

⌣⌣⌣

My grandfather Ted returned from the war for a well-deserved break. Over six years of convoy duty, he spent a year and a half on the perilous Murmansk Run, sailing into the Arctic Ocean to deliver war materials to the Soviets. His remaining time saw him crossing the North Atlantic, patrolling the Mediterranean and taking part in the D-Day landings.

Finally, he and Marie could settle down. Sort of. Ted was career Navy and there was no certainty in that job. In fact, the trajectory of his service is dizzying to a civilian like me. He was posted to Ottawa for two years, then back to Stadacona for three, where he became President of the Chiefs' and Petty Officers' Mess. Off to Victoria for nine months and Cornwallis, Nova Scotia, for two years. Then, back to war—serving on HMCS *Haida* in Korea. He sent postcards back to Marie and my mom, Joan, from Oahu, Hawaii, and other locales. In January 1954, he was posted again to Stadacona, so he and Marie moved into their first bed that wasn't either in his parents' home in Ottawa, in married quarters at Cornwallis, or in Marie's childhood bedroom on Stairs Street. They landed on Bayers Road. I have sweet photos of my mother—gap-toothed in a snowsuit— in front of their building. Their greatest adventure as a family would be the next move, to Bangor, Northern Ireland, while Ted oversaw the refit of HMCS *Bonaventure*. And on and on it went. Cornwallis. Stadacona. HMCS *Provider*. HMCS *Cormorant*, the patrol vessel he commanded from November 1958 through August 1960. He retired on January 31, 1968, a gesture of protest against the unification of the services' three separate branches—Army, Navy, Air Force—into a single command. Day one of the new scheme was February 1, 1968, and Ted wasn't going to have anything to do with it. He helped found Royal Canadian Legion Branch 160 and pivoted to the job he would have for the rest of his life, working as the live-in superintendent at a large apartment building in north Dartmouth. You'd better believe that lobby terrazzo shone. When I was small enough, I perched on the front of the upright industrial vacuum he used in the hallways, like a tiny, happy bird.

Marie moved with Ted when he was posted for long periods— Ottawa, where my mother was born, Cornwallis, Northern Ireland. But her postwar existence looked much the same as that of wartime, minus the strain of fretting about Ted's convoy duties. She continued to live at home with Nettie and Arthur. She spent time with her sister Dot, went to dances whenever she could, resplendent. Her costume jewellery got a lot of play, and she benefitted from working in the field of women's clothing, which she never stopped doing, and where she could access discounted gowns. This perhaps sounds posh, but Marie was more Margaret David than Charlotte Guy. She shopped at the Met. Not at Mills Brothers. I bought her a pair of leather gloves from Mills Brothers in the early 2000s. I remember the way she raised her eyebrows when she pulled back the Christmas wrapping paper and discovered where the gift was from. I had arrived in Dartmouth in 1977, living half with my grandparents and half with my mom, in the same shiny-floored apartment building. On nights when my mom and Marie attended their weekly bowling league, Ted and I made Jell-O and watched TV. He would put me to sleep in his and Marie's bed, but lingered to chat. I would ask him to tell me a story about the war. And he would. Simplistic accounts—we did this, we did that—but not entirely sanitized. I knew what a torpedo was, and, vaguely, the gravity of being hit by one. I remember I understood the term "depth charge" when my grade two and three friends did not.

I never asked Marie to tell me a story about the war.

～ᐱᐱ～

Planning for war commemoration began at the instant of the conflict's end in 1945, even as Halifax continued to struggle against the raging currents of repatriation and the leagues of men streaming back through the gates. Almost an entire box at Library and Archives Canada contains memos about plans for dedications, and the trend toward memorial parks and gardens rather than cenotaph-type edifices. As part of its memorialization, the provincial government updated "Nova Scotia Helps the Fighting Man," to recognize volunteer efforts. With the riots in mind, though, it also feels as if the update was a rearguard action to undo the bad memories of May 7 and 8. The focus on women in the new edition was appropriate.

But, now, let's not lose ourselves in thinking this was something it wasn't. "Nova Scotia Helps the Fighting Man" was a stapled-together pamphlet. Eighteen folded pieces of paper. It's not a war monument. It's not a cenotaph, a park, or a garden. By the time authorities had gathered to decide how to honour the dead and remember the battle, they had already forgotten about women volunteers. This pattern wasn't Halifax's. The pattern was all over. *The London Times* published a meaty treatise on the war in May 1945, its headline screaming comprehensiveness: *THE LONG ROAD TO VICTORY: A Historical Narrative and a Chronological Register of the Events of the War in Europe and Africa 1939 to 1945*. It is dense. Twenty illustration- and photo-free pages. There are precisely two—*two*—mentions of women, the first noting that women died in the Blitz, and the second that men *and* women "gave their property and lives to the cause." And so they did.

Women weren't told they did nothing. But in the building of memorials—whether parks, gardens, plaques, or whatever else for men and for battles, and in the recounting of the war in magazines and newspapers, in feature films and documentaries—women's volunteer work and sacrifices simply were not reflected. So, no, women weren't *told* they did nothing. But their lack of commemoration is another form of the same. In Halifax, memorials for the war proliferated. There's a statue of a naval rating on the waterfront at Sackville Landing and a large granite cross at Point Pleasant Park. A ten-foot Winston Churchill stalks the former site of the main branch of the Halifax Public Library (itself a war memorial opened in 1951). The Churchill statue commemorates the British prime minister's secret visit to Halifax in 1943. There are some seventy-four cenotaphs and war monuments across Nova Scotia. One is the Dartmouth Cenotaph, which Ted attended annually on Remembrance Day.

The year he told me he wasn't going I knew something was wrong.

RIGBY, Edward Albert "Ted"—83, Dartmouth, died June 30, 2003, in the New Halifax Infirmary. Born in Ottawa, he was a son of the late Joseph and Sophie (Gamble) Rigby. He was a veteran, and served overseas in the Second World War and also the Korean Conflict as a member of the Royal Canadian Navy from where he retired as Chief Petty Officer...

It goes on, as obituaries do. It names his sisters and brothers, and Marie, who had spent, she often joked, "sixty-three years with the wrong man." It did not mention that Ted died of heart failure, and that I lay my head gently on his rattly chest as he breathed his last.

Marie, the "recycled teenager," as she called herself, held out to ninety-two, the last of her siblings. As she had been from my childhood, she was the one continuing and central maternal part of my life. And, I am so glad to say, of my own daughters', who loved her as fiercely as she loved them. I wrote her obituary.

RIGBY, Marie Jeanette—92, of Dartmouth, died Sunday, Jan. 12, 2014. Marie was born in Halifax to the late Arthur and Jeanette (Ferguson) Crompton, Oct. 22, 1921. She was a long-time salesperson in women's clothing, working at Heinish's, New York Dress Shop, and the House of Bridal Fashions. Marie was passionate about dancing, especially with her late husband, Ted Rigby, and never said no to a night of bingo. In later years, Marie enjoyed attending karaoke at Lake Loon Golf Centre and outings on the #53 bus. Marie always had a smile and loved a party. She will be profoundly missed by so many.

There was a book in what I wanted to say about Marie, and in what I wanted to say *to* Marie, and so much more I wish I had asked her about when I had the chance.

BIBLIOGRAPHY

Bruce, Jean. *Back the Attack! Canadian Women During the Second World War—at Home and Abroad*. Toronto: MacMillan of Canada, 1985.

Grant, Dorothy Annette. *Turn the Other Cheek: A Story of Courage and Perseverance*. Victoria: Friesen Press, 2016.

Hansen, Randall. *Fire and Fury: The Allied Bombing of Germany, 1942–1945*. Toronto: Anchor Canada, 2009.

Kimber, Stephen. *Sailors, Slackers and Blind Pigs: Halifax at War*. Toronto: Doubleday Canada, 2002.

Ling, Katherine Anne. *Servicewives in Wartime Halifax, 1939–1945*. Dalhousie University, 1994.

MacDonald, Sharon M. H. *Hidden Costs, Hidden Labours: Women in Nova Scotia During Two World Wars*. MA thesis: Saint Mary's University, 1999.

MacLennan, Hugh. *Barometer Rising*. New York City: Duell, Sloan & Pearce, 1941.

Metson, Graham. *An East Coast Port...: Halifax at War 1939–1945*. Whitby, Ontario: McGraw-Hill Ryerson, 1981.

Naftel, William D. *Halifax at War: Searchlights, Squadrons and Submarines 1939–1945*. Halifax: Formac Publishing, 2008.

Naftel, William D. *The Photo History of a Canadian City at War 1939–1945*. Halifax: Formac Publishing, 2009.

Nova Scotia Helps the Fighting Man. Halifax: The King's Printer, 1945.

O'Neill, Patrick B. "The Halifax Concert Party in World War II." Theatre Research in Canada, 20:2 (Fall 1999). https://journals.lib.unb.ca/index. php/tric/article/view/7086/8145.

Pierson, Ruth Roach. *Canadian Women and the Second World War*. Ottawa: Canadian Historical Association, 1983.

Pierson, Ruth Roach. *They're Still Women After All: The Second World War and Canadian Womanhood*. Toronto: McClelland and Stewart, 1986.

Raddall, Thomas H., and Kimber, Stephen. *Halifax: Warden of the North (Updated Edition)*. Toronto: McClelland and Stewart, 2010.

Taylor, Dianne J. *There's No Wife Like It*. Victoria: Braemar Books, 1985.

White, James (Jay). *The Ajax Affair: Citizens and Sailors in Wartime Halifax, 1939–1945*. MA thesis, Dalhousie University, 1984.

White, James (Jay). *Conscripted City: Halifax and the Second World War*. PhD diss., McMaster University, 1994.

ACKNOWLEDGEMENTS

The eighteen folders that comprise the Halifax Women's Voluntary Services records at the Halifax Municipal Archives were loaded with valuable information, and the kind I love—everyday minutiae from which to pull a narrative. Thanks to Leslie Pezzack for donating these documents and to the late Zilpha Linkletter for understanding their worth and squirrelling them away. I generally hold archivists in high esteem for their seemingly bottomless well-spring of interest in other people's projects. I specifically admire the Halifax Municipal Archives's Susan McClure, who guided my research, and Elena Cremonese, for working on the mystery of the location of Maison Surcouf. Thanks, too, to the on-duty archivists at Nova Scotia Archives and Records Management, to Chara Kingston from Army Museum Halifax Citadel, and to Catherine Butler and Sandra Bell at Library and Archives Canada, my visit to which was supported by an Access Copyright Foundation Marian Hebb Research Grant.

Shelley Fashan, Angela Johnson, and Sherri Borden Colley helped network sources. Sharon MacDonald lent me boxes of material from her own research projects to flesh out my own. Twitter coughed up a material number of helpers for some of this book's more nuanced details, such as the clarification of Halifax neighbourhood names. Twitter also connected me with Sharon Murray, who put her knowledge and expertise to work locating many erstwhile downtown Halifax buildings wiped off the map in the name of urban renewal, and Michael McCluskey, who helped me match up maps of wartime jetties with current-day Halifax streets, and who figured out, from latitude and longitude coordinates, where my grandfather dove into the Pacific Ocean on February 17, 1938.

Nasha Nijhawan is probably too busy to remember that she took time out to help me untangle some historic legal wording. Megan Jones enthusiastically identified animals in every archival photo I sent her. Kharim Schliewinsky offered naval-term disambiguation. Lyndsay Armstrong transcribed interviews and became appropriately enthralled by the women's stories she spent so many hours listening to. Neve McCormack assisted with archival research. Christina Pasquet was my dedicated sartorial expert; I called on her frequently and at early hours to identify hats and shoes and coats in old photos. Anja Pearre let me, practically a complete stranger, into her home on Young Avenue and took me through every single room, so I could have enough detail to write the scenes inside the house. This encounter happened by virtue of the ever-thoughtful Judy Wells, who made several calls on my behalf to her universe of friends, most of the "do you know so-and-so who used to live in such-and-such neighbourhood and who was friends with another so-and-so and whose mother did this-and-that?" sort. I wish she could have read this acknowledgement before her passing.

Frances Gregor and Kim Pittaway nudged this project into my lap. Without their trust, this book would never have come into being. Thanks to Whitney Moran at Nimbus for getting on board and to Angela Mombourquette for editing that makes me sound like a much better writer than I know I am. Lynne Patterson was the first reader of this manuscript; I thank her for her friendship, her military expertise, and her writer's eye.

Going to the gym every morning is my mental and physical salvation, and it's made not only restorative but incredibly fun by the 6:30 A.M. Onside crew. Thanks, too, to my walking partner, and de facto story consultant, Simon Thibault, and to Katherine Woolhouse for distracting me with bar trivia.

I'm thankful for the steadfast support of my mother-in-law, Joanne Ritchie, and of my dad, Richard Lowe, whose tendency toward silence fails to give a true impression of just how much he thinks about those he loves. I am indebted to my chosen family: Dave Hayden, Andrea Dorfman, Christine Oreskovich, and especially Kyle Shaw, whose tech support recovered 8,500 words of this manuscript, and, therein, preserved my will to go on.

The Volunteers was supposed to take a summer to write. I won't tell you how long it actually took; suffice it to say that I am filled with gratitude for my husband, Kevin Lewis, who helped me get the job done, and for my ~~children~~ noise-cancelling headphones, which kept my chatty, lovely teens, Lily Lowe and Georgia Lewis, at bay.